1960

A slice of
bread and jam

TOMMY RHATTIGAN

Mirror Books

Published by Mirror Books,
an imprint of Trinity Mirror plc,
1 Canada Square,
London E14 5AP, England

www.mirrorbooks.co.uk
twitter.com/themirrorbooks

Executive Editor: Jo Sollis
Editor: Aileen O'Brien
Art Director: Julie Adams

ISBN 9781907324604

First paperback edition

Printed and bound in Great Britain
by CPI Group (UK) Ltd, Croydon, CR0 4YY

Every effort has been made to fulfil requirements with regard to
reproducing copyright material. The author and publisher will be
glad to rectify any omissions at the earliest opportunity.

For the sake of ease, some events in Tommy's life have been condensed into a
12-month period, however, all events happened in or around 1963.

All names and identifying details have been changed to protect the
privacy of individuals.

Cover picture: Mirrorpix library image, not associated with the author
or his story in any way. Posed by models.

A slice of bread and jam

Contents

This book is dedicated to the memory of
my youngest brother, Michael.

Also, to my children, who found it hard to envisage
the idea that I had lived in a Victorian slum on a
cobbled street, lit up by gas-lamps!

Prologue

I was on the swings in the park, waiting for my brothers Martin and Nabby to show up and totally oblivious to the evil lurking right beside me. Standing just a short distance away, her head leaning slightly to one side, a young blonde woman gave me a coy look and the briefest of smiles. Behind her stood a man, his hand in his overcoat pocket as he dragged on his cigarette and stared over in my direction. I'd first noticed the two figures walking past the park near Ducie Street when they had stopped and I'd seen the flare of a light as the man lit his cigarette. Then the pair headed through the park and towards the play area. Little did I know, these strangers were sadistic killers who had marked me out as their next young victim.

The man and woman stopped about fifteen yards away from me and had a brief conversation before she turned suddenly and headed over to the swings, while the man stayed put, looking about him as he dragged on his fag. When she was about five or six feet away, she stopped and I let the swing slow under its own momentum. I could smell her heavy perfume and hairspray, a mixture that reminded me of my two eldest sisters, Mary and Rose, who would smother the stuff all over themselves.

Standing face-on to me, her hands dug deep into her coat pockets, the woman looked me up and down. My senses told me she was about to say something, but as I had waited expectantly for her to speak to me, she said nothing and instead threw me a quick smile which I returned, letting her know I felt comfortable in her presence and was approachable. She then stepped a little closer with a bright wide smile spread across her face.

To all intents and purposes she had not seemed any different from the people I met while out begging on the streets with my brothers and sisters. Some of those people would kindly take us into their homes and feed us before sending us on our way with the odd copper or two. So when the woman invited me to follow her back to her grandmother's house in Gorton for a slice of bread and jam, it was nothing out of the ordinary. And so I agreed to go with her, following her through the ever-darkening streets on the edge of Longsight, with the man a short distance behind us. We were heading back into Gorton to a house that I had believed offered a place of safety and a bite to eat. In reality, I was, in fact, walking between two evil child killers who had other ideas for me.

PROLOGUE

Before I take you on that particular journey and share with you the intense emotional atmosphere that wrapped itself around me as I sat inside the old terraced house in Bannock Street, let me first take you to the beginning of 1963. Walk with me through that one particular year in my childhood, a year that led up to my encounter with two of the most reviled killers this country has ever known. There is no set plot to this book, just vivid memories from my childhood and of a bygone time when the streets of Manchester were the playgrounds of its children.

CHAPTER 1

The Three Stooges

I am seven years old. I have three older brothers, Paddy, Shamie and Martin. And I also have four older sisters, Mary, Rose, Helen and Maggie. I have three younger brothers, Michael, Nabby and Gosson, as well as two younger sisters, Bernie and Kathleen. With me, Tommy, that makes thirteen Rhattigan kids in all - unlucky for some!

Most of them, save for Michael, Gosson and Kathleen, were born in the Republic of Ireland. Over there, Daddy was known as a tinker, a tinsmith, or a "dirty feckin' auld gypsy", depending on who he was dealing with at the time. He mended or made pots and pans and sharpened people's knives for a living as we travelled along the roads between Athlone and Dublin. Despite having enlisted in the British Military Police during World War 2, serving out in India, he had not been able to hold down a proper job since leaving the Army. And so, with no prospects in southern Ireland, he decided to uproot and better himself over here in England, taking the whole family off across the Irish Sea to a new life in Hulme, Manchester, where he signed up at the Labour Exchange.

Closest in age, Martin, Bernadette and me usually spent all our time together and would occasionally be joined by our younger brother Nabby (real name Francis). I was a year younger than Martin, while Bernie was a year younger than me, though she looked older than her age on account of her height. She was a good few inches taller than Martin and me. Daddy called us the Three Stooges because we were always getting up to all sorts of mischief. Sometimes he would have to stagger out of the pub to fetch us from the police station. And while there, he'd pretend he was so pleased to see us just as any concerned and decent parent would be, only to beat the living daylights out of us with his leather belt once he'd got us home.

I was the fastest runner, so I would be the one to grab a purse or any loose money left lying around. Even the odd unmanned cash till wasn't safe and if ever the opportunity arose, my grubby little fingers would be in it. On one occasion, in Marks & Spencer, Martin had run past a till and banged hard down on the keys to cause the drawer to shoot open. I followed a split second behind him, snatching up a handful of paper money and stuffing it down the back of my jumper while making a quick dash towards the main exit.

We got caught before we'd managed to get out of the doors and were taken back to a sort of custody room by two of the women cashiers. On the way, I noticed in one of the mirrors that I had this weird looking hump on my back. So I rounded my shoulders and stooped down a bit, trying to look slightly deformed in the hope that no one would cotton on to the fact that the money was hidden there.

"Just hand back whatever money you took and we'll say no more," promised Dave, one of the two uniformed security guards.

"We didn't take any money. Look!" Keeping myself slightly bent over, I turned out my pockets to show him they were empty. Martin did the same.

"You were seen running away from the till."

"Only because we were looking for someone to tell! Honest!" said Martin, pretending to cry, before going on to tell the security guards some cock-and-bull story about us seeing a young lad stealing money from the till.

"Can you describe this young lad?"

"If yah take us around the store, we could point him out ta yah if he's still in here?" suggested Martin and, to our amazement, the security guards agreed with the idea.

Walking down the first aisle, we spotted a young kid of around eight, with his mother, walking up in our direction. "That's the kid!" cried Martin, pointing an accusing finger down the aisle.

"Are you positive?" asked Dave.

"That's him!" I backed up my brother. "I'd be able ta spot him a mile off with that pink patch on them glasses he's wearin! An' his mammy saw him an' never said a word!" I added for good measure.

"Right, wait there with these two, Roy, while I go and have a word with them."

"How dare you!" Jaysus!" The woman had gone mad and began beating the burly security guard over the head, with her handbag at first and then anything else she could lay her hands on!

"Help me Roy!"

"You two wait here."

Yeah, right! We were on our way before Roy had got halfway down the aisle to help his set-upon mate.

Martin was the best actor in Manchester and brilliant at performing an epileptic fit. If there'd been anyone showing any interest in us, or there'd been a time when we needed a distraction, Martin would suddenly go into a fit. Like a child possessed by the Devil himself, he'd writhe on the ground, his eyes rolled back to show the whites of them, as well as frothing bubbles of spit from his mouth.

Bernie, on the other hand, was very special to us. And a different kettle of fish altogether. Daddy said the doctor said our Bernie had two people living inside her: one is Bernie herself and the other, though to all intents and purposes is still Bernie, is a different Bernie altogether, though he didn't have a clue who the other Bernie was. It didn't make much sense to any of us, how Bernie could be living inside herself, especially when we could see her every day, though I had wondered if the reason why she ate a lot was on account she was eating for two!

Daddy also said the doctor said the other Bernie, living inside Bernie, was a very angry person, which was the reason why she could be the nicest person in the world one minute, and the wildest of banshees the next! But we saw the wild side of our young sister only when she was hitting someone with a lump of wood, or throwing missiles at them, to protect us, or herself. Up to a point and besides eating for two, she could do almost all the things Martin and I could do, though not as well as us. But if there was one thing we were all equally good at, then that would have to be lying. We were so good at lying, we often convinced ourselves that the lies we told were the truth!

Once, the police had caught us driving Danny McCarthy's horse and cart through the streets. Danny McCarthy was the local rag-and-bone man - though we had never seen any bones in his cart, only old rags and scrap metal, along with other odds and sods that no one had any use for. McCarthy would always leave Goliath, a giant amongst the carthorses of Manchester, tethered to the lamppost outside the Red Rose pub, which was just around the corner from Stamford Street, where we lived. He'd go to the pub every Friday afternoon without fail and wouldn't show his face again until closing time, when he'd be carried out by his friends, drunk and unsteady on his feet, to be thrown onto the back of his cart before Goliath would be given a smack on the arse and shooed on his way, obediently taking his master all the way back to his yard.

Bernie had this notion that she knew how to ride the big beast. "It's just like riding a donkey," she said, inviting Martin and me along for the ride. Without questioning her ability to do this, we hopped up onto the cart and sat back, waiting for the ride of our lives.

"Only up to the other end of the road and back again," she said. "No one will ever know."

Grabbing hold of the leather reins, our sister giddy-upped the horse, but Goliath just gave her a sideways glance, before sticking his head back into the maize bag hung round his neck and continuing to munch away. She tried shooing him a few times, but the stubborn black stallion still refused to budge an inch no matter how loudly we shooed it. Picking up the horsewhip, Bernie gave him a few taps, gently at first and then more vigorously, until the other Bernie inside Bernie suddenly made an appearance. Standing up in the cart she whipped the horse, screaming at him to, "Feckin' move yah poxty thing! Or y'er for the knacker's yard!"

Any other horse being flogged in such a manner would probably have been on their way by now, but not Goliath. He wasn't budging for love nor money and certainly not for the Devil child whipping his behind. He held his ground and turned his huge head to glare back at Bernie with his big dark bulging eyes, before snorting snot out of his wide nostrils as if to say, "You can beat the shite out of me all day long, little girlie! But I'm not moving from this spot!" At least not until the moment Martin had taken it upon himself to jab the pointed end of McCarthy's umbrella right up Goliath's bum, causing the stubborn beast to give out a loud long whinny before rearing up on his hind legs and bolting off down the street at great speed!

It didn't matter how much the three of us swore our apologies to the giant horse or how hard we pulled on his long leather reins. The beast wouldn't stop and turned into Dale Street at breakneck speed. All Martin, me and Bernie could do was to hold tightly onto each other and pray to the Divine Virgin Mary, Saint Martin de Porres (that was our Mammy's favourite saint, he's a black man) and every other saint Father Murphy had brainwashed us with, to save our sorry souls. Or at the very least, send us all to heaven instead of languishing in purgatory if this should happen to be our last day on the earth.

By all accounts, purgatory is a place where dead people had to wait until they were purified from all their mortal sins, before being allowed to join all the other purified dead people in heaven. And if there was any truth in Father Murphy's account, then it looked likely, with the amount of sins we'd committed, we would be floating around in the dark for a long while to come.

The police joined us along the Stretford Road just as we passed the Town Hall. In the leading car, a fat policeman leaned out of the window and screamed at us, "Pull over!" But we didn't know how to pull over. Martin screamed back, advising the copper he'd have to shoot the horse dead!

For at least ten minutes, traffic and people dodged frantically out of the way as Goliath hurtled towards them. Only after he'd done two circuits around Piccadilly Circus did he finally come to a standstill, before lifting his long hairy tail and doing his business.

With no time for us to thank the Divine Virgin Mary, Saint Martin, or any other saints for saving our wretched souls, we quickly jumped from the cart as an army of policemen headed in our direction. I led the way as we dodged down a couple of side streets before dashing across the busy high street into Woolworth's and heading straight up the escalator to the toy department. A new range of cowboy and Indian outfits were on display so we stripped off our grubby clothes and pulled them on. Then we ambled boldly past the posse of policemen scouring the place for three filthy urchins.

We were almost at the main entrance doors and freedom when we were stopped in our tracks by the loud shout of the keen-eyed store-detective.

"Stop the cowboy and Indians!"

We may have been surrounded, but we were not going down without a fight. The three of us stood facing the long line of red-faced coppers in a standoff. Dressed as Big Chief Sitting Bull, complete with the head of feathers, I raised my plastic tomahawk high above my head and threatened to scalp the first copper who came near us, even though the nearest copper to us was already as bald as a coot. Martin, dressed as the Lone Ranger, drew his two silver revolvers and was threatening to shoot the bollocks of anyone who dared to come near him. And Bernie, dressed as the Lone Ranger's sidekick, Tonto, already had an arrow in her bow and was taking careful aim.

Of course, we were outnumbered and easily overpowered. But not before Bernie had managed to get an arrow off. A spectacular shot, caught the snitching store-detective a glancing blow by his right eye, causing him to howl like a baby.

Stripped of our weapons but still dressed in our stolen outfits, we were frogmarched out of the store and carted off to the police station where we stubbornly insisted on giving our names as the Lone Ranger, Tonto and Big Chief Sitting Bull, much to the annoyance of the overweight desk sergeant. He gave all three of us a clip round the ear before threatening to throw us in a cell and chuck away the key.

We retaliated with our own threats, warning him of the dire consequences of what he'd done and swearing, "As there's a Jaysus in heaven, our Mammy and Daddy, along with all our uncles and aunties and our cousins and nephews, will come down ta the police station and beat the living daylights out of yea before settin' the station ablaze!"

We agreed to call a truce on the offer of sausages, eggs

and chips and steaming hot cups of sweet tea, which we eagerly tucked into. But once our bellies were full, we continued with our intimidation tactics right up until the early hours of the morning, when we fell in an exhausted sleep.

It wasn't until the following afternoon that we were reunited with Mammy and Daddy after they suddenly realised we were not at home. Woolworth's allowed us to keep the stolen outfits on account that they'd slung our stinking clothes in the bin. Daddy's attempt to have the store charged with the theft of our clothing which, he said, were only bought for us a few weeks earlier, fell on deaf ears. The store detective dropped the complaint of assault against Bernie, who insisted she hadn't deliberately fired the arrow at him and was in fact aiming it at one of the policemen. As for Goliath, though he was none the worse for his adventure, I swear he always raised his trotting pace whenever he caught a glimpse of us walking along the streets.

CHAPTER 2

On the Rob

Hulme, with its blighted wastelands, Victorian terraces, dark streets, derelict houses and factories, was probably one of the largest slum-cum-demolition sites in the whole of Manchester. Every day, we would watch the heavy bulldozers hard at work, finishing off what the Blitz of the 1940s had done to the rest of the city. There seemed to be a sense of urgency about eradicating all evidence of the Victorian era and its innumerable smoking chimneys, which blocked out the sun and poisoned the air and our lungs. And so the blighted landscape around us changed steadily as the mills, the factories and the slums were flattened, leaving areas of wasteland referred to locally as "crofts". Nearly a decade later, these empty spaces would be filled by an even bigger blight on the landscape, the curved tower blocks of the Hulme Crescents, an ugly concrete jungle that was part of a regeneration scheme for the area. The massive new housing development was a design disaster that quickly became just another kind of ghetto, but without the neighbourliness and sense of community that we shared in our Victorian slums.

We watched those old terraced houses come tumbling down. In every street, we'd be met by rows of empty houses standing in solemn silence as they waited for the huge ball and chain to come knocking on their walls and put them out of their misery. And every day, we watched people piling their furniture and rugs and other personal belongings into the big removal trucks, before they'd drive off, never to be seen again.

Some people would stand for a while, looking back silently on their home and perhaps reflecting on the decades of memories they were about to leave behind. These were the people who closed their front doors behind them, as if locking the echoes of their past away. While others just hurried off without bothering to close their doors or even take one last glance backwards, only too pleased to be given a second chance in life. Where were they going? We hadn't a clue. Nor did we really care. By the time a removal truck had got halfway along the street, a rush of grubby-faced children would suddenly appear out from their shadowy hiding places and descend upon the empty property. And there, like scavenging rats searching out a meal, we took anything and everything that wasn't bolted down, because anything and everything had its value.

I was always the first one down into the dark coal cellar. Martin, Bernie and I would stand guard over the wrought-iron manhole cover leading down into the dark cellar at the front of the house. To the unsuspecting eye, we looked just like any ordinary, run-of-the-mill scallywags with a bogey (a hand-made go-cart made of old wood and pram wheels), watching the progress of the removal men as they went about their business of emptying a house. We'd always ask if we could lend a hand, knowing full well the owners of the property would decline our kind offer, too busy keeping an eye on the removal men to have to worry about us stealing from them as well! But it all added to our ploy to stop any of the other children hiding somewhere in the shadows, ready to make their move and getting down into the cellar before us.

I was small for my age and, with a little push from Martin, I could just about squeeze my skinny body head-first through the small hole, before sliding down the concrete chute into the cellar below. Martin would then throw a small hessian bag down after me and I'd scavenge around with my bare hands for any remnants of coal, hurriedly filling the bag, as my brother and sister peered down through the small hole above my head, offering words of encouragement.

With most people not bothering to take their coal with them, at times there'd be enough to keep the fire going for a few days or so. Once I'd filled the small bag, I'd offer this back up to Martin, who'd tip it into one of the two larger hessian coal sacks we always brought with us in our bogey to carry the coal home. We'd repeat the process until we had either filled the two larger sacks or emptied the cellar of whatever coal there was.

Next, I'd use the small crowbar Bernie passed down to me to force off the small lock on the gas meter, if it hadn't already been broken into by the leaving occupants or, as often happened, the removal men. Sometimes, I'd find the odd shilling. Though never as much as the change I'd find in the gas meters of an occupied house. Daddy made me break into those boxes after pushing me down the coal chute. But he always checked the house first to make sure there was no one at home, or that the occupants were either too old or too infirm to give chase if they caught me in the act.

My Daddy was an expert at robbing people's houses. He had a knack of being able to weigh up people's vulnerabilities. Just one knock on any door and he could tell by how long it took for someone to answer whether the job had any potential or not. If the door wasn't answered after a few good loud knocks, then either no-one was at home or the occupants were totally deaf! If anyone came quickly to the door, Daddy would look them up and down, always able to spot any potential weaknesses. If it was a no-go, he'd just make up some cock-and-bull story or invent the name of a person he was trying to trace.

Early one evening he knocked on a front door, which had been answered by an old woman, probably in her eighties. She'd took one look at Daddy and thrown her arms wide open.

"Is that you, Jim?" she asked excitedly, peering out through a pair of thick bifocal spectacles.

Daddy was stunned into taking a backward step, almost falling over me in the process, when she'd suddenly called him by his actual first name.

"Oh! And look at you, little David!" The old woman smiled down on me with her stained dentures. "My, aren't you growing into a handsome young man! Come in! Come in and make yourselves at home!"

Glancing over my shoulder, I'd half expected to see Jim and little David standing behind me, but there wasn't another living soul around, barring myself, Daddy and the old woman herself. I was just on the point of telling her, "My name isn't David", when Daddy suddenly stood on my left foot, before pushing me in through the open doorway, ahead of him.

There were a number of birthday cards on the mantelpiece above the lit coal fire and Daddy quickly read a couple, discovering the woman's son was called Jim, and her grandson David. I then had to endure the next ten minutes or so sitting next to the auld girl on the small sofa by the coal fire, with her fussing over me and asking me all the usual sorts of questions a granny would ask of her grandson. How was I getting on at school? Was I keeping out of trouble? Why hadn't my sister Theresa, accompanied us? It was a wonder she was still alive with the amount of illnesses she told me she'd suffered with. And, I suspected, if she'd known what

Daddy was up to it probably would have killed her off altogether. It was no wonder she'd hardly seen much of her real family, with the way she'd gone on and on.

I'd hardly been to school in my whole life but I couldn't tell her this. And so I used my imagination and told her I was top in my class at spelling, history and maths. In fact, I was tops at every subject in the school, including one they didn't have - lying!

She must have thought I was a feckin' genius! Though I was grateful she didn't ask me a question on any of those subjects, otherwise I probably would have had to have one of Martin's sudden fits!

"So, have you had a nice birthday Mammy?" Daddy reappeared in the lounge where he plundered the woman's handbag and purse.

"All the better for seeing you son," she smiled over blindly at the empty chair by the table.

"I'll just go and make sure you've plenty of coal in the cellar, then," he said, winking at me. "If not, I'll have the coal man bring you a few bags around in the morning."

When we were finally leaving, the auld woman began to cry. Daddy, his pockets laden with the contents of her jewellery box, the gas meter and her purse, promised he'd come back to see her soon. She'd fumbled in her handbag for her purse so she could give me a few shillings to buy myself some sweets, but Daddy was having none of it and told her, "He gets enough sweets as it is." He insisted on giving his new mammy a ten-shilling note for her birthday.

CHAPTER 3

My Dad the Hero

We lived in one of Hulme's older Victorian slums, at 24 Stamford Street. The house was a cold, damp dump. The only pattern left on the peeling wallpaper was damp stains and green mould. The floors were bare and there was no bathroom. The toilet was outside in the backyard and our toilet paper was small squares of old newspapers hanging from a piece of string on an old rusty nail (the shiny magazines were the worst!). Our large tin bath was chained to the outside wall underneath the backroom window, so an eye could be kept on it in case any thieving scumbags tried to steal it for scrap.

Mammy would fill the tin bath once every second Sunday, scrubbing all of us younger ones clean to the bone, one by one. In the winter months she would bring the bath inside the house and scrub us in front of the open fire in order of age, the eldest going first. Paddy, Shamie, Mary, Rose, Helen and Maggie all went to the bathhouse up on Leaf Street, so I got to go second after Martin. And although the water would just be hovering on lukewarm at the start, by the time it came to scrubbing little Michael, the youngest of the family, the water would be filthy and cold.

While Paddy and Shamie shared their own bedroom, we five younger boys squeezed into a tiny box bedroom, which was just big enough to fit a small bed but nothing else. We slept like a tin of sardines, Martin and me at one end of the bed, with Nabby, Michael and Gosson down the other end. My six sisters shared the front upstairs bedroom, which had a double bed and a small single, plus a small sideboard and a wardrobe. Mary had the small single bed to herself and the others all slept in the big bed.

I liked their bedroom because the light from the gas lamp outside lit up their room with a soft yellowy-orange glow. Sometimes, when our two eldest sisters stayed away from home, which became more often than not, Martin and me would sneak into the girls' room and sleep in the big bed with our other sisters, while Helen slept in the single bed. Mammy and Daddy had their own bedroom downstairs at the front of the house.

Stamford Street was a long street of Victorian terraces lit up at night by gas lamps. Unlike some of the streets in Hulme, most houses were occupied, but the few that were not had already been vandalised and stripped bare, with all of their windowpanes broken by local children taking pot shots at them. Daddy used our backyard to breed chickens. He'd built a small run and roosting box along the side wall next to the outside toilet. My favourite chicken was a big grey cock, about the size of an Alsatian, which Mammy named King Dick and who spent most of his days chasing chickens amorously around the yard.

Unlike Mammy and Daddy, we rarely got to eat chicken, though we did have a roast dinner on St Patrick's Day and Christmas Day. And if Daddy, when one of his regular customers called to the house, was not minded to kill a chicken himself, he'd send me or Martin out to do the job. I loved cutting off their heads on the chopping block and letting them run around the yard, scaring the others chickens half to death until, suddenly realising they had no head, they keeled over and died with the shock of it all.

Sometimes we found dead chickens that had died overnight for one reason or another. Daddy would sell these chickens to the yellow-skinned men who wore the turbans around their heads, in the belief they'd be none the wiser if they'd got the scutters after eating them, as they always had the scutters with the kind of food they were used to eating!

Now and again we'd see a colony of cat-sized rats scurrying out into the back alley from the empty houses in nearby Dunham Street. A flock of around eighty pigeons had also set up home in one of the empty houses. People had complained to the local council about the stench and the bird droppings everywhere, especially on all the clothes hanging out on the washing lines. The man from the council said they were far too busy to be dealing with the likes of pigeon shit and rats, with all the demolition and rebuilding works going on in the area. He also said it wasn't going to be long now before the whole of Stamford Street and Dunham Street were demolished along with the rest of Hulme and we'd all be moving into new houses.

One weekend, someone took it upon themselves to get rid of the problem once and for all, and tried to smoke out the vermin living in the empty house on Dunham Street. Unfortunately, they set Mrs Whitmore's house alight in the process. Thick smoke was belching out from her roof, but luckily my Daddy was in the alley at the time and barged his way through her back door to save her.

Ten heart-stopping minutes later, he reappeared through the front door, carrying the unconscious old woman over his shoulder in one of those fireman's lifts, to the loud applause of the neighbours gathered outside. Just at that moment, two fire engines came screeching around the corner, followed closely by an ambulance and a police car.

"Come away from there, Tommy!" My hero Daddy was suddenly, and for the first time in his life, showing concern for my safety. Picking me up off the ground in one swift movement, he carried me back along the street and around the corner into Stamford Street without saying a word. I could smell petrol and smoke on his clothes and hands as he plonked me down near the entrance to our back alley.

"Get to the house straight away! Here! Give these to your Mammy, and be quick about it!" He snuck out a purse and pieces of jewellery from his inside coat pocket and stuffed them inside my jumper, before walking off back around the corner in the direction of Dunham Street.

When Mrs Whitmore was discharged from the hospital a few days later, she came around to our house in the middle of the afternoon to see Daddy. She brought a large box of Dairy Milk chocolates with her as a token of her gratitude for him having risked his own safety to save "a helpless old woman who'd not long on this earth and who didn't deserve to be saved". She told him she would have rewarded him with something much more substantial, only someone had stolen her purse, robbed her gas meter and taken her priceless jewellery while she'd been laid up dying in the hospital. She believed the culprit might have been one of the firemen (who'd risked life and limb to save her house from burning down to the ground!) She said she'd written a formal complaint to the Chief Officer of the Fire Brigade, as well as a letter to Her Majesty the Queen, giving Daddy a mention.

"Good on yah missus," said Mammy, shaking her head with dismay. "Sure they're all thieving heathens! The feckin' whole lot of them!"

She offered Mrs Whitmore a cup of brewed tea, which the auld lady had been on the point of accepting before suddenly having second thoughts and declining Mammy's kind offer. She'd probably remembered the last time she'd had a cup of Mammy's tea and how, when she'd taken a swig, she'd almost choked to death on the mountain of tea leaves resting at the bottom of the cup.

Daddy was keen to know how much the stolen items of jewellery were worth, as he had sold the lot to someone he knew for four pounds and ten shillings though he'd haggled for a fiver. When Mrs Whitmore told him they were worth at least one hundred and fifty pounds, it brought on a severe coughing fit from Daddy, which he blamed on the tea dregs.

Not long after Mrs Whitmore had left the house, two detectives called around. Daddy told Bernie to answer the door. "If it's the milkman, the rent collector, or anyone else wanting money tell them I'm not at home," he instructed.

We heard Bernie relaying this to the two detectives standing in the open doorway, but they invited themselves in anyhow, so Daddy had to come out from hiding under his bed.

They told Daddy they'd not been wholly convinced by the reason he'd given for his clothes smelling strongly of petrol when they'd first spoken to him at the scene. He'd explained that the small tube of petrol he usually carried in his pocket to refill his lighter had split when he was carrying Mrs Whitmore out of the smoking building.

They also informed Daddy that Mrs McKinney, who lived further down in Dunham Street, said that just before the house went up in flames, she'd been out in the alley putting out the bin when she'd seen someone hurrying up it with what appeared to be a large petrol can. She believed the person she saw was Daddy.

As well as telling the two detectives he didn't possess a petrol can (he'd left it down in the cellar), he told them Mrs McKinney was a blind auld bat, a mischief maker and last but not least, "a lying feckin' heathen of a Protestant who hated all the Irish Catholics". He added for good measure: "We are a family of God-fearing people!" To prove the point, he went to the cupboard in the backroom and took out the large family Bible with all the family names and dates of birth written inside it. Kneeling before the two bemused detectives, he swore on the Holy Bible and on the lives of all the names written in the book that he was telling the truth. "Otherwise, God strike the lot of us down dead!" It was a wonder any of us were still alive.

The coppers had had enough and had left us in peace, but not before warning Daddy they'd be keeping a close eye on him in the future. He threw them a smile, telling them they could keep an eye on him for the rest of eternity and they'll not catch him putting one foot wrong as it wasn't in his nature! After seeing the detectives out of the front door, he returned to the back room, fuming.

"Quick, boys!" he said to me and Martin. "I want yah ta nip out the back way down ta Mrs McKinney's an' break every feckin window of the auld whore's house!

Hurry now! An' watch out for them coppers!"

CHAPTER 4

Unholy Terrors

It was Martin's birthday. And better still, it was Saint Patrick's Day. The day when all the Irish Catholics joined together to celebrate their patron saint. Daddy wasn't in a celebratory mood. In the morning he had been cussing about a dozen chicken eggs that had disappeared overnight from the backyard, until Mammy told him she'd given them to Bernie for the school's food stall.

"But them eggs have probably been lyin' around for months upon months," protested Daddy. "I found them underneath the roosting box!"

That year, St Wilfrid's School were putting on a fete in celebration of the big day. And we didn't have far to walk from Mass to the school to get at the free buffet as St Wilfrid's Church was right opposite the school. The only downside to all this was we had to go to church and listen to the boring priest drone on about glorious St Patrick and how he'd commanded all the snakes to get out of Ireland and how they'd just upped and left. We all had to wear large fist-sized clumps of shamrock, which our Uncle Oliver, one of Daddy's younger brothers, had fetched over from Ireland a few days earlier.

Paddy and Shamie came down the stairs, looking half-dead and telling Mammy they were not feeling too good and probably wouldn't be able to make it to the church, though there was every chance they might be able to make it to the fete. Mammy told them, "Ye'd better be at the feckin' church by the time the rest of us get there, or else the auld man's belt will be at yer arses!" As the sulking pair headed out the back door, she warned them not to be showing her up like they'd done the previous Sunday, when they'd been competing against each other to see who could fart the loudest during Father Murphy's sermon.

It was teeming down with rain and Mammy said she hadn't the time to be lighting a coal fire or bringing water to the boil, so we were to make do with standing out in the backyard to wash ourselves. It was brilliant! I loved the heavy rain. Especially standing naked in the open air as the heavy droplets pricked every part of my body into life. When I closed my eyes I could have been anywhere but Stamford Street. And the water was clean.

The previous day, Mammy had taken Maggie, Martin, Bernie, Nabby, Michael, Gosson, Kathleen and me on our three-monthly trip to the Welfare clothing store to have us kitted out with second-hand clothes. The two women on duty stood peering down their snooty noses at us from behind the safety of the tall counter, as one of them marked off our names and dates of birth on her forms. I don't think Mammy liked them very much and she kept referring to them under her breath as "lesheens".

After sizing us all up, the women set about plucking items of clothing off the rails and, along with an assortment of clean underwear, put them on the counter for us to fight over. Nabby bagged a Victorian-style navy sailor's outfit, complete with the large white square collar that hung down at the back. Martin and I bagged ourselves matching grey corduroy outfits, consisting of a white shirt, a grey jacket and matching pair of short grey trousers. The two women turned their noses up to the ceiling as we undressed hurriedly in front of them. They threw our dirty rags in a big heap on top of the counter, followed by our smelly socks and skid-marked underwear, which they swiftly picked up with their large wooden laundry tongs before throwing them into the waste sack.

They put some black slip-on plimsolls and girls' sandals on the counter, but no proper boys' shoes. And as none of the pumps would fit Martin and me, we each had to make do with a pair of girls' brown sandals. Not that we minded, they were more comfortable than the Wellington boots we'd been given the last time, which had left large red welts around our legs because we'd worn them for so long.

One of the women remarked to Mammy how smart we all looked. She said Martin and me reminded her of TweedleDum and TweedleDee in our identical matching outfits. We scowled up at her, but she had ignored us and said to Mammy, "If you are minded to, you might like to make a donation in the Poor Box, there at the other end of the counter?" But Mammy wasn't minded to and had declined the kind offer on a technical point.

"As I'm one of the poor people that collection is intended for, then there's no need ta be putting me own money in the box, seeing I'd only be getting back the money I'd given ta meself when I already had it in the first place. Which is a feckin' waste of time, if yah ask me!"

Making our way through the busy waiting area towards the main exit, there was a loud clattering noise, just like the sound of a collection box being dropped on the ground, as Nabby dropped the collection box he had been hiding under his new duffel coat. "Jaysus, Mary an' Joseph!" Mammy gave out, hitting me around the head because I was nearest to her, as an army of accusing eyes stared at the box before fixing back on us. "Y'er going to get us all corrupt!" she scolded, before bending down and quickly scooping up the full collection box in one movement and slipping it into her large bag. Then she hurried out through the main swing doors, with the rest of us not far behind her.

For the St Patrick's Day celebrations, Mammy spent a while pinning the big clumps of shamrock to the lapels of the new outfits we'd got from the Welfare the previous day. She asked Daddy if he was coming along to the church service, but Daddy said it was too much for him, with his bad back-an-all and he'd feel better just sitting in the pub celebrating in the warm.

She said nothing, knowing he'd only start another blazing row with her if she'd tried to push the point of him being an Irishman and so should be at the church respecting his Patron Saint. She tried to get to the church on most Sundays, or any other special day. It gave her the opportunity to meet with family and friends and to catch up with any gossip she might have missed out on. Though it seemed to me that, even without the gossip, she always knew everything that had been going on around Hulme.

The rain had slowed to a drizzle by the time we set off for the church. But it hadn't dampened our spirits, or stopped us from singing "Hail Glorious Saint Patrick, Dear Saint of our Isle" which was the only hymn we knew that mentioned the auld saint's name.

We followed Mammy as her high-heeled shoes clippety-clopped along the pavements, in the direction of St Wilfrid's Church. She had her work cut out trying to stop her broken umbrella from turning inside-out and trying to stop us splashing in the puddles. She hollered in vain and by the time we reached the church, the lumps of shamrock had already withered through lack of water, while our new sandals and socks were soaked through.

"Good morning ta yah, Mrs Rhattigan." The scowling face of Sister Mary greeted us at the doors of the church. Her evil-looking, lop-sided eyes behind large bifocal glasses gave us the once-over, while her lips stayed permanently pursed like a dog's arse.

"Mornin, Holy Sister." Mammy bowed her head to the auld dragon.

"Ah, will ya get a look at those fine children of yers," she scowled at us. "All washed and dressed like little angels. They're a credit ta yah so they are, Mrs Rhattigan!" The patronising auld hen suddenly shoved the wooden collection box right up under Mammy's nose.

Slightly turning her back away from the nun's beady eyes, Mammy carefully fumbled inside her purse, so as not to let the loose change rattle. "I've only the ten shillings to me name," she said, pulling out the ten-shilling note and showing it to Sister Mary, while tipping her purse over to show she had no change. "I'll put a few extra coins in the plate on Sunday," she lied.

"Ah sure, that'll be fine." said Sister Mary, suddenly snatching the ten shilling note out of Mammy's grasp. "You're a saintly woman an' yah don't even know it so yah don't. An' with all those mouths ta feed as well!" The thieving hen had quickly slipped the ten shilling note into the side pocket of her starched black habit before Mammy could snatch it back.

We all waited with bated breath for Mammy to give the thieving auld hen a box on her warty hooter, but to our shocked surprise Mammy just gave the smiling nun another bow of the head. Then, smacking Martin angrily around the ear, she ushered us into the packed church where we joined our older sisters, alongside Paddy and Shamie, in the pew which they'd saved for us.

Cathy McCarthy was sitting in the pew in front of us. She glanced over her shoulder at me and threw me a big smile, and I smiled and winked back at her. But Mrs McCarthy had to go and spoil the moment, telling her daughter to turn round the other way, before giving me one of her evil glares. Mr McCarthy was staring over his shoulder at Bernie. It was difficult to see most of his facial features on account of his large bristly grey beard and long sideburns, which covered most of his face, so all you could see were his wide, dark unblinking eyes peering from his bushy eyebrows, and his big, purple-veined hooter. He'd not forgiven my sister for terrorising his horse. And he even had the cheek to call at our house with a vet's bill not long afterwards, demanding Daddy should pay for Goliath's sore backside. But Daddy had told him, "That feckin' horse should have been for the knacker's yard years ago and if yah don't feck off pronto, I'll be shoving that bill up yer hole!"

The wooden collection plate was passed from one row of pews to another, with Sister Mary standing at one end of the pew, keeping her beady eyes on the offertory plate, while the keen-eyed Sister Gertrude stood at the other end. Paddy and Shamie were in fits of giggles, desperately trying to suppress their laughter as they stared at Sister Gertrude. She was a strange-looking nun, with a hump on her back, furrowed eyebrows and one leg shorter than the other. The sole of her left shoe was at least a foot thicker than the sole of the right shoe, stopping her from toppling over altogether. It seemed all the nuns we came into contact with had some sort of physical affliction or other.

As the plate reached Mammy, the natural instincts of the whole family flanking her suddenly kicked in and we all contracted a serious bout of whooping cough, causing us to move backward and forward, blocking the plate from Sister Gertrude's view for the briefest of seconds. But those brief seconds were all the time Mammy needed to screw up a couple of ten shilling notes into the palm of her hand before blessing herself and passing the plate along!

I thought, with the look on Sister Gertrude's face, she must have cottoned on to Mammy, especially when she stood staring down into the collection plate with her lips silently moving, as if she'd been mentally adding up the notes still left there. Then she had taken a sudden backward step, probably from the shock of seeing there were a few notes missing. She stared suspiciously into Mammy's eyes, searching for the slightest sign of guilt. But Mammy never felt guilty about anything and just threw the afflicted nun a smile back, blessing herself again with the sign of the cross as the auld hunchback hobbled off to the next row of pews.

After mass, Mammy spent a few minutes talking with Father Murphy and telling him what a beautiful service it had been. She told him she was looking forward to hearing him again this coming Sunday and asked him if he would give the family the honour of a blessing. He obliged in an instant, cutting a swift sign of the cross into the air with his podgy hand, while muttering some strange Latin words. And we were all purified!

CHAPTER 5

High Nun

With Mammy feeling a lot holier and richer, we took the few minutes' walk to St Wilfrid's School playground and the fete, where the distinct sound of Irish music could be heard. The whole of the school playground was packed with all sorts of stalls selling second-hand clothes, toys and other bits and bobs, as well as homemade jam and cakes. Martin and I made a beeline for the free buffet stall, but when we got there, the vultures had already eaten most of the food, save for the one large plateful of smelly egg sandwiches. I found myself cursing Mammy for wasting precious time asking Father Murphy to bless us. Though it hadn't stopped us from polishing off all the sandwiches!

Sister Joseph, our form teacher, was running the church stall with Sister Rosemary. They were selling religious paraphernalia: rosary beads, medallions and pictures of Jesus and St Patrick. Sister Joseph glared at Martin and me as we loitered around her stall, picking up the odd picture or medallion, hoping she'd be distracted for a few seconds so we could steal them. But she wouldn't be distracted and her hawkish eye stayed fixed firmly on us as she whispered into Sister Rosemary's ear, loud enough for us to hear, "Keep a good eye on those two thieving heathens!"

Like most of the other children in our class, I didn't like Sister Joseph. She was a miserable, tallish, fat Irish nun with a big hairy chin, who used her size and nasty gob to frighten us to death. She had a big wart on the left-hand side of her nose and a strange look in her half-closed left eye, as if she was forever studying the hairs growing out of the wart, while her other eye looked in the opposite direction. I'd wondered if God had given her that face to punish her for all her wrongdoings.

"If ye've no money ta be buyin' anythin' then there's no point in hanging around here now, is there, boys? So get away with yah before yah feel the back of me hand!" She shooed us away to the strains of "Oh Danny Boy!", which was emitting from the gramophone's loudspeaker.

Paddy and Shamie seemed to have put their arguments aside, at least for St Patrick's Day. They were standing over by the far wall of the playground talking to a couple of girls, when Shamie gestured for us to come over.

He asked us if the sour-faced Sister Joseph was still giving us grief.

"That she is," said Martin.

"Wouldn't it be a grand miracle if for once in her miserable life, she'd liven herself up a little?" smiled Shamie.

"It would for sure," I agreed.

"Well, we've somethin' that can make miracles work."
Shamie emptied some small, lemon tablets, six in all,
into the palm of his hand. "These'll put a smile back on
her miserable auld puss!" he said, as the two girls and
Paddy giggled. "Do yah want ta see the biggest miracle
St Wilfrid's has ever seen?"

"We would that!'

Handing the tablets to Martin, Shamie told us to slip
them into Sister Joseph's tea when she wasn't looking.

"What if she's not drinkin' tea?" I asked.

"Well slip them in ta whatever she's drinkin."

"But what if she isn't drinkin' anythin'?" said Martin.

"Then get the feckin' auld hen a poxty drink of
somethin! Just stop asking me feckin' questions will yah!"
said Shamie.

Looking forward to the biggest miracle St Wilfrid's
School had ever witnessed, Martin and I made off in the
direction of Sister Gertrude's tea-and-biscuit stall. "And
what can I do for yea boys?" Sister Gertrude greeted us
with her usual suspicious, furrowed eyes as she slurped
her cup of tea.

"Sister Joseph sent us over to fetch her back a cup of
tea,' said Martin.

"Did she now!' said the nun with the hump and the
one leg shorter, or longer, than the other, depending on
which way you looked at it. "Sister Joseph has never
touched a drop of tea in her whole life!" she said, before
going on to suggest we must have misheard her with all

the excitement of this beautiful St Patrick's Day festival! "It was probably a cup of coffee she wanted."

"Yeh! That's it!" said Martin.

"Yah might as well take along a cup of coffee for Sister Rosemary as well. Oh and some biscuits."

While she had her back turned to us, Martin slipped two of the yellow tablets into Sister Gertrude's tea, thinking two miracles would be better than the one. Perhaps they'd make her hump disappear and her shorter leg grow to the same length as her longer leg, or vice-versa.

Sister Gertrude placed the two matching china tea cups and saucers on the tray, along with a small plate of creamed biscuits, which she handed to Martin to carry, as he was the eldest. We paused for a moment, watching her take a big slurp of her tea and gulping it down, not knowing what we were supposed to expect to happen. We'd only ever heard about the miracles Jesus had done and had never seen one happen in real life.

"Well go on then! Before the coffee gets cold." The nun shooed us off on our way. Heading in the direction of Sister Joseph's stall, Martin slipped two of the tablets into each cup and we scoffed down the plate of biscuits.

"Sister Gertrude told us to fetch these over ta yah." said Martin, plonking down the tray on top of the stall.

"An' I suppose she sent yah over with the plate of biscuit crumbs for me as well, did she?" snarled Sister Joseph.

As none of her eyes were looking directly at me, I wasn't sure whether she was talking to me or Martin, so I opted to say nothing. Martin also opted to say nothing and we let her gibber on. I'd known by the look on my brother's reddening face what he was about to do. And seconds later, when he'd let a silent one off, Sister Joseph had suddenly stopped gibbering as she and Sister Rosemary, all red-faced themselves, attempted to break the world record for holding their breath the longest.

Hurrying across the playground, we took up a good vantage point on the corner of Mrs McCormack's homemade cake stand, where we could keep an eye out for their faces cracking into a miraculous smile - once they'd gotten over the pong.

We came across Mammy, talking to Mrs Reilly, Bridget Reilly's mammy, at her stall. Mrs Reilly taught Irish dancing once a week and she sold second-hand dancing shoes and kilts to those who couldn't afford to buy new ones. Martin and I had always fancied ourselves as Irish dancers. Sure, we'd learnt to jig just by watching our Mammy and Daddy, along with Uncle Paddy and Uncle Oliver and the rest of our aunties and uncles, dancing many an Irish jig in the streets after staggering out from the pubs at closing times.

Mrs Reilly was only too happy to snatch our sixpenny pieces out of our hands when we'd turned up for one of her lessons. We were wearing Scottish tartan kilts, which our Granny Liz - Mammy's mammy - had thrown together from a dress she said she hadn't worn since the beginning of the war, and we'd given the class an impromptu exhibition of our jigging skills. To our surprise, the class had seemed well impressed with us and we'd never had a lesson in our lives!

We jigged and spun around and around, but we got the biggest applause from the other children when we lifted our kilts to show we were "real fellas", which Uncle Oliver had told us we had to do to be the finest of Irish dancers.

It seemed the appalled-looking Mrs Reilly hadn't been that impressed. She said she was having none of it and had ranted and raved at us about how disgusting the pair of us were and of how we both should be ashamed of ourselves, banning us from dancing lessons before the first lesson had even begun!

"Yer not ta come here ever again, unless y'er scrubbed clean to the bone! And yea can hire - on second thoughts yea can buy - proper Irish kilts from me. I've a few nearly-new ones for sale. And yea can make sure y'er wearing underpants before daring to show yer faces in here again!"

Martin told her she could go and hump a donkey. He also said we wouldn't want to be coming to her dance lessons anyway, because she knew nothing about proper Irish dancing, not like our Mammy and Daddy and all the rest of our aunties and uncles knew. Before we rushed out of the church hall, we'd given her an encore and lifted the front of our kilts high up to our faces, causing her face to turn scarlet. She'd turned the air blue with her ranting while the kids screamed with delight – at least we thought it was delight!

As we strode up to Mammy, Mrs Reilly was in the middle of telling her about her fine troupe of Irish dancers. She'd turned out especially for St Patrick's Day and was going on about how the tears of joy always welled up in her proud red eyes whenever she'd watched her beautiful children dancing. She said it brought back memories of her own dancing career, which had been brought swiftly to an end when she had drunkenly staggered off the pavement just as a bus into Manchester came along and gave her a sideways glance. She'd somehow managed to escape with only the three broken ribs, two broken legs and a fractured hip.

"I could dance on a sixpence, so I could, Mrs Rhattigan, so I could."

"Well, yah had enough of them," I was tempted to remind her.

We spent a short while wandering around the fete, being shooed from pillar to post whenever we loitered at a stall for more than a few seconds at a time. I began to wonder if there had been a conspiracy against us and all the stallholders had mug-shots of our faces hidden under their stalls!

Martin said, "It must be our sour pusses that's drawing people's attention to us." He said we should smile more often. But I'm not the best of smilers. I hated smiling because of my gappy teeth. So the best anyone could expect from me was a tight-lipped grin. But I'm not too clever at keeping up a false grin either, which usually turns to a quivering grimace as my facial muscles and lips go into spasm.

When we approached Mrs Moses' toy stall, I gave her one of my best smiles. Mrs Moses was the head dinner lady at school. I didn't know whether she might have been a nun in the past because she also had an affliction. Hers was a permanent smile that just went up the one side of her face while the other side remained miserable, depending on which angle you looked at her. So I never really knew whether or not she was throwing a smile or an angry look at me.

"And what can I do for you two lads?" Mrs Moses asked politely. "Is there a toy that takes your fancy?"

Feck! What a question to ask two thieves! Sure, there were lots of toys on her stall that had taken our fancy, if only we could have stolen them. I felt my false smile slipping, though I had tried desperately to keep it going, and one side of my face began to twitch violently.

Mrs Moses - I hadn't been sure whether she was smiling or not - suddenly leaned right over her stall and asked me through gritted teeth, "Are you trying to make a fool out of me, Sonny!"

"Sure, I'm not!" I told her, but my attempt at throwing her a proper smile was doomed to failure as my twitching

44

mouth went into quivering spasms.

"Don't you be making a fool outta me you mother's curse, you!" she said, snatching up her walking stick and taking a swipe at me, just missing me by a cat's whisker.

Hurrying away from the mad woman, we decided to give up on the idea of looking around the rest of the stalls, for safety reasons. And with no miracle happening as yet, we headed over to the crowded dance area by the school's main entrance, where Mrs Reilly had already assembled her dance troupe and was giving them their final instructions before they took to the floor.

"Are yer dancers ready to begin, Mrs Reilly?" asked Mr Reilly, the fete organiser and father of Bridget Reilly.

"They are that, Mr Reilly," said Mrs Reilly.

"Then let the show begin!" said Mr Reilly, placing the needle of the gramophone down gently onto the spinning record. And that's when the miracle we'd been so eagerly awaiting actually happened!

As we watched the dance troupe get into full swing, it was impossible not to toe-tap to the rhythm of the Irish jig echoing out across the playground. Martin and me, along with a hundred other feet, had joined in the toe-tapping and clapping as we all got into the spirit of the Irish music. And that's when I first noticed, out of the corner of my eye, the dark shadowy figure appear.

It was Sister Joseph! But not the haughty, tight-lipped, miserable auld warty dragon that we knew. This Sister Joseph had a wild, glazed look in her big, bright, watery-blue crossed eyes, along with the widest of grins as the corners of her mouth almost touched both her ears. It was grotesque! Skipping like a teenager without a care in the world, she hopped into the dance area. With her habit hitched high above her knobbly knees and her woolly black long-johns on display, she danced a jig the likes of which I'd never seen before, nor, I'm sure, had anyone else in the watching crowd, judging by the looks on their faces!

Like a nun possessed, Sister Joseph's long legs jigged fast and free, sometimes she brought her knees up so high she almost whacked herself in the mouth.

Neither Mammy, Daddy, nor any of my aunties or uncles could have jigged the way Sister Joseph jigged in that moment. And if that wasn't enough of a miracle for one day, Sister Gertrude got in on the act, too. Suddenly lurching into view, yelling "Hallelujah!" at the top of her voice, she hopped around in a circle like a demented Red Indian doing a war dance, her club foot staying on the one spot as she flailed her arms in the air.

For a few minutes, we all toe-tapped and clapped louder as the nuns danced and howled and seemed to be having a high old time. Then Sister Gertrude accidentally kicked Sister Joseph right up her backside with her built-up shoe, which prompted the drug-crazed Joseph to turn on her heels and box the hobbling nun on the chin, causing Gertrude to stagger backwards into the gramophone player, before Joseph hurled herself on top of her.

"Sister Joseph! Sister Gertrude! Have yah no shame!'
Father Murphy suddenly appeared on the scene, all
red-faced and wide-eyed and bellowing at the top of his
voice as he pulled the warring nuns apart.

Having seen enough of a miracle for one day, we
hurried towards the exit and on our way out we saw
the normally timid Sister Rosemary stroking the long,
bristly, grey beard of Mr McCarthy. The unsmiling Mrs
McCarthy, standing with the love of my life, Cathy, was
rooted to the spot as the drug-tripping nun was telling
her, "What a fine-looking auld horse yah have here, Mrs
McCarthy."

CHAPTER 6

A Win on the Bingo

The city of Manchester survived on the success of its ethnic minorities and their diverse cultures. And it was those minorities who ran the dress shops, the corner shops, restaurants, coffee houses, strip joints and the whore houses. They were all owned by the Indians, the Chinese, the Pakistanis, the Jews and every other ethnic group, barring the Irish.

I once overheard my Auntie Mary asking Mammy, "Why is it the Irish fellas don't own any of the big businesses in Manchester?" Mammy replied, "The Irish fellas only know about religion, beer and humping. And that's why some of them have given their lives up to the church and the rest ta the pubs, ta get away from all the children they've bred."

Every Friday without fail, Martin, Bernie and me would beg in the city from nine at night right up until the early hours of Saturday morning. We'd start off with a penny, spending hours asking passers-by if they could change the penny for two ha`pennies. Most people gave us the two ha`pennies and took the penny, but there were the few people who'd tell us to keep the penny, too, so this was how we'd managed to accumulate ten shillings or more in coppers, which was the target Daddy had set for us. The alternative was usually a good hiding with his leather belt.

It was much harder to beg in the earlier parts of the evening, especially because of the higher number of policemen out on the beat at that time, in search of the drunks, prostitutes and homosexuals hanging around the public toilet blocks. They ignored the down-and-outs unless they were causing a big scene. They sent the whores on their way, but they always arrested the homos, giving them a good beating in the process.

If they ever managed to catch us begging, they'd just take all our hard-earned pennies, telling us to hop it and go home. Thankfully it was only on the rare occasion we got caught. But we still had to play a cat-and-mouse game until midnight, when the coppers would wind down their presence on the streets and car patrols would take over.

With the cafés and the nightclubs closed, most streets were empty save for the odd staggering drunk. Groups of alcoholic down-and-outs gathered close to the Central Plaza where they would lounge and sleep beneath the huge statue of Queen Victoria who sat on her throne and scowled down her nose at them.

One night, an old drunk staggered from a side street in front of us and asked Bernie, "How much for a gobble!" Bernie asked him to show us his money first. And we watched him like vultures as he fumbled around in his trousers, with me at the ready to snatch any money from his hand and run. But instead, he suddenly flashed his mickey at us and chased after us as we ran off down the street.

We ran into Market Street where the drunk, staggering in hot pursuit, tripped over his own feet and fell arse-over-tit in a heap. We cautiously made our way to him, with every intention of robbing every last penny he might have had, if he'd not already spent the lot on booze. But just as we got to within a foot of him, he suddenly rolled over onto his back and started crooning, "I'm singing in the rain!" as he pissed high into the air, sending a fountain of liquid cascading down all over himself. We ran off in fits of laughter and after counting out our takings - eleven shillings! - we hurried off home, happy in the knowledge that there would be no beatings for us.

The following afternoon me and Martin were peering in through the display window of the Hippodrome Bingo Hall, just as the odd-looking fella wearing tight trousers and a pink shirt carefully placed the huge chocolate easter egg on top of the display stand. We watched with drooling mouths, as he wrapped the wide purple ribbon around the middle of the egg, before tying a large neat bow to it.

On either side of the tall mahogany stand stood two smiling shop dummies, each wearing a flowery summer skirt. We watched with curiosity as the fella turned his attention to them and went about straightening down the hems of each skirt, before taking a backward step and, with his hands on his hips, paused to admire his handiwork. Satisfied, he walked off out of sight into the inner part of the Hippodrome.

Five minutes later, in the same display window of the Hippodrome Bingo Hall, a tall mahogany stand stood devoid of its huge chocolate Easter egg with the big purple bow neatly tied around the middle of it. On either side of the display plinth, the two shop dummies were still happily smiling, despite the fact that, from the waist down, they were now as naked as the day they'd came out of the mould.

"Quick, Tommy!" Martin's voice was urgent as he held open the main entrance doors of the Bingo Hall and I rushed out onto the damp street carrying the huge chocolate egg, which was wrapped inside the two summer skirts.

Outside, the usual drizzle of rain drifted across a miserable grey sky as Martin's skinny legs set off running down the long street in the direction of the bombed-out Radnor picture house. He stayed a safe distance ahead of me, keeping a sharp eye out for any coppers as I followed, struggling to see over the top of my heavy burden. It was always better if only one of us carried the ill-gotten gains. That way, in the unlikely event of getting caught, only the one carrying the stolen booty also carried the can while the lookout just walked on by without a second glance. And, since Martin had wheeled the large four-wheeled baker's trolley loaded with freshly made cakes and baked bread rolls away from the bakery the previous day, it was my turn to carry the goodies.

The Radnor picture house had stood derelict since before I was born. Some parts of the floors had fallen in on themselves, but underneath the debris the ground floor remained intact, though the auditorium had been completely stripped bare of all its fixtures and fittings. The middle section had caved into the basement causing it to slope in on itself so it resembled a huge bomb crater.

One of our favourite pastimes, and an escape route if the police did call, was to hurl ourselves out of a top window and onto a street lamp-post standing some three feet away, down which we would slide to the pavement below. Some older, and much braver, kids would launch themselves from the rooftop. And it wasn't just the lads that got up to this kind of thing. The girls were just as daring, especially a girl called Catherine, who would have been around ten or eleven years old and was probably tougher and more daring than most boys the same age. She would just step up onto the windowsill and launch herself out without pausing to see if the lamppost was still there!

When we reached the back of the picture house, Martin had pulled away a loose board across one of the exit doors, allowing me to crawl in through the gap with the huge chocolate egg. And it was only after he followed me in through the gap did he relieve me of my burden, before handing the two flowery skirts back to me and quickly scuttling off over the mounds of debris into the dimly lit auditorium.

"Where'd the feck did yah get that feckin' thing from!" Shamie asked Martin. For a twelve-year-old, Shamie was renowned for his toughness and could beat the crap out of almost anyone, even lads much older and twice his size. There were only two ways our brother knew how to fight and that was One Way or The Other: either beating the crap out of someone fair and square, or beating the crap out of someone with the first object that came to hand! We were proud of him and only too glad he was our big brother because nobody dared pick a fight with us while we were in his presence.

"Found it," I lied.

"Stole it," said Martin at the same time.

"Found yerself some skirts as well then did yah Tommy? They suit yah down to the ground they do!" scoffed Shamie, causing me to go all bright red, as a barrage of guffaws and wolf-whistles resounded from his friends standing around him.

"Yah big Nancy boy yah!" laughed my toothless cousin Paddy Ward.

"Don't call me little brother a feckin' Nancy boy!" Shamie had turned on his heels to eyeball Paddy. "Call him a Nancy boy and yah call it me, too. Is that right?"

"Ah. I was only joking with him, Shamie!"

"Then say sorry, before I knock those last few rotten teeth of yer's down yer long skinny neck!"

"What?"

"Tell Tommy y'er feckin' sorry!"

As quietness suddenly descended upon the auditorium, I looked directly into Paddy Ward's eyes and, for a brief moment, was sure that I detected a slight hint of defiance in them. Half expecting him to show his hand and put up a fight, I took a couple of backward steps to be sure I wasn't going to be in any harm's way if it were to all kick off.

Shamie, though, had already read the threat and his hands had turned into great big fists clenching tightly, until the knuckles had turned white, ready to pummel Cousin Paddy's broken nose into the ground if the need had arose. But unfortunately, Paddy got to keep his last remaining rotten teeth.

"I was only kidding yah Tommy," said Paddy, directing a gummy smile in my direction, though he'd deliberately not used the word sorry.

"That's all right Paddy." I accepted his apology with a sense of power over him, though I knew if he had wanted to, he could have kicked the living daylights out of me.

With the tense atmosphere gone, I made up a story about stealing the giant Easter egg and the two skirts from Woolworths. I got my version in before Martin could tell Shamie the truth, that we'd stolen it from the place where Mary and Rose worked! They'd only been in the job at the Bingo Hall a few weeks and if they'd found out we'd stolen from their place of work, our lives wouldn't have been worth living.

Taking the large Easter egg and the two skirts off us, Shamie slipped a hand into his pocket and gave us two shillings for them. Not that we had any choice in the matter. He banged the egg down hard against the ground, breaking a large hole in it, before snapping off a couple of good-sized lumps of chocolate, which he handed over to me. Reaching a hand inside the egg, he then pulled out a handful of assorted wrapped chocolates, which he handed to Martin. The rest he would sell on, along with the two skirts, making a few extra bob for himself.

We didn't mind how he did business, and in any case chocolate for Easter was better than the treat of boiled duck eggs Daddy had given us for the last few Easters. Tap the top and lift it off and the whole place would stink to high heaven! Of course, the stench didn't actually stop us from eating the eggs. As Mammy always said, "Yah have ta be grateful for whatever scraps of food yah get, cos yea'll never know when the next lot is coming."

CHAPTER 7

Ducking and Diving

One Monday morning the rain belted down in torrents and it felt slightly warmer than it had been for a long while, which Daddy said was a good sign that the big freeze was finally over. It had been a long and bitter winter that year, with the canals and even the sea freezing over. It was, said the older neighbours, the worst winter they'd witnessed in their whole lives.

It was Health Clinic day. Barring our two eldest sisters, Rose and Mary, the rest of us had to go into town to the school's clinic for our usual monthly bath, then the nurse painted our naked bodies with the purplish coloured liquid she had in a big red bucket. This, we were told, was supposed to stop us from catching the lurgy: scabies, nits and hundreds of other things lurking all over Hulme, just waiting to make a meal out of us. We were bathed in pairs before having the thick purple liquid applied all over our bodies with an eight-inch long-haired paintbrush.

The long bristles always tickled me and, when the nurse brushed around my bollocks, I loved it and couldn't help getting a stalk on. She'd smile, telling me I was a dirty little fellow, though it didn't stop her from tickling my goolies for a little longer. When she tried to tickle Martin's, he'd always come over all shy and held his hands over his mickey. So I would ask the nurse if I could have my brother's tickles instead.

On this particular day, after we'd bathed, I took a detour on the way out, creeping into the staff cloakroom while the others kept lookout in the hallway. Rummaging through the nearest handbag, I pulled out a large black leather purse and, with my heart pumping, I ran out of the cloakroom and through the main doors. The others followed me straight across the busy Stretford Road and down into the nearest alley, where we'd scrambled out of sight into one of the bombed houses to discover, when I'd opened the purse, that it was full of ten-shilling notes!

There was a mixture of excitement and panic from most of us as we stared wide-eyed at the amount of money we had. Bernie's expression, though, had remained calm. I'd often wished I could have been like her. She was so laid back, seemingly not afraid or too concerned about anything, unless the other Bernie showed herself. We were all streetwise and clever, inasmuch as we knew most of the streets of Manchester like the back of our hands. But Bernie, she seemed different. "Very intellectually clever," is what the education woman had told Mammy and Daddy when she'd come around to our house one morning, as we were all still lounging in bed, to enquire as to why none of us had been to school for the past three weeks.

Daddy had gone through his usual ritual of swearing
on the family Bible and our lives that he always walked
us to the main gates of St Wilfrid's every single morning
without fail. So we must be wagging off when his back
had been turned. In truth, education just wasn't one of
Daddy's favourite subjects, having no financial benefit to
him. And so, instead of school, he'd make us go begging
for money on the streets, or searching through empty
houses for scrap metal or wood for the fire. For us, this
was far more of an adventure than going off to school,
the dinners being the only good reason to go.

There was just over five quid in the purse, which
Martin slipped into his pocket for safe keeping. We
knew it was a lot of money, which was why we had been
shaking with fear and excitement. We'd never seen, let
alone touched, so much money all in one go.

Martin's first thoughts were, we shouldn't bother
with school today. Instead, he suggested we should buy
ourselves some broken biscuits and sweets, and take the
rest of the money straight home to Mammy and Daddy.
But Bernie had this notion that, if we did this, "It'll just
bring nothing but more trouble for us! They'll just spend
the whole lot on fags and more booze and then, when
the rowing starts, we'd be the ones for the blame and the
fists will come flying straight at us!"

She was right, of course, and none of us could, or
would, deny this. It was always our fault according to
Mammy and Daddy: "It's yer feckin' faults there's never

enough food on the table! It's yer feckin' faults we have ta live in a dump like this! If it wasn't for yea lot of feckin' bastards, we'd be livin' a better life than this! It's yer faults we've been driven to the drink an' sufferin' terrible with our nerves! It's yer faults we're a pair of uncaring feckers who only tink about ourselves!"

"I think we should take Michael, Gosson and Kathleen back home like we always do." said Bernie, "and then go off to Belle Vue Zoo to enjoy ourselves for a change."

And with none of us objecting to the idea, I threw the purse - which now only contained a small front door key and a couple of photographs - into the old fireplace to keep the dead pigeon company, and we took our two younger brothers and sister back home. We left them in the care of Helen, telling her we were off to school.

The walk to Belle Vue Zoo usually took us about an hour from Hulme, depending how much ducking and diving we'd usually have to do every time we saw a police car heading along the street, or if we became distracted by something else. The Zoo wasn't just a zoo in the ordinary sense of the word. It was also one of the biggest funfair attractions in the whole of Manchester, with amusement arcades, theatres and boating lakes, hotels and bars. And the Funhouse! One of my favourites!

The rain by now had stopped and the light breeze had begun to ease away the dull grey clouds, to reveal a blanket of blue sky high above us. And there were puddles galore, dotted all over the place, like liquid silver

glistening in the morning sun. How I loved my puddles!
Martin, Nabby and me were always competing with one
another to see who could make the biggest splash. Bernie
would always refuse to join in, telling us we were eejits!

One at a time, we'd take long run-ups to each puddle,
before launching ourselves into the air and landing with
an almighty splash in the middle of them. It was great
fun. And we were all just about equal with our splashes.
However, there was one large puddle we'd avoid at
all costs! It was originally a large garden pond, which
Martin found out to his detriment a few weeks back
when he'd taken a long run and jump before landing
right in the middle of it and suddenly disappearing
beneath five feet of filthy black water.

On the way to the Zoo we met up with our cousins
Paddy and Martin Ward, who were searching through
the debris at the side of the road. They, too, came from
a big Irish family like ours, but there were eighteen of
them, not including their mammy and daddy. Auntie
Helen - one of Mammy's sisters - was expecting another
baby any day. Daddy said her and Uncle Bernard, "were
like a pair of feckin' sex-starved rabbits, forever humpin'
each other!"

"Hi Bernie." Our eight-year-old cousin Paddy greeted
my sister with one of his charming smiles, which showed
off his dirty teeth. "Why aren't yah in school?"

"Why aren't yah in school yerself?" Bernie threw back
at him. She was good at throwing questions back at

people.

"Our school is closed for the day, isn't that right, Martin?" prompted Paddy.

"That's right." said cousin Martin, unconvincingly.

"And why is it closed?" asked Bernie.

"Ah, well…" Paddy gave it some thought before answering. "Our Headmaster suddenly dropped dead, for no reason at all. Isn't that right, Martin?"

"That's right, Paddy," his brother agreed, unconvincingly.

"That's funny!" said Bernie. "Our school's closed for the day as well, because our Headmaster suddenly dropped dead for no reason at all. It must be catchin'," she added, without the need for a prompt from any of us to back up her lie. "Isn't it a small world?"

"Liar! Liar! Knickers on fire!" goaded Paddy.

"They can't be on fire, cos I'm not wearing any - so there!"

"Prove it!" cried Paddy, swallowing hard.

"I've nothing ta prove ta the likes of yea, Paddy Ward."

"Come on! Let me see!" said Paddy, moving a step closer to my sister and attempting to lift the hem of her skirt to take a peek.

"I heard yer mammy's goin' ta have another rabbit soon!" said Nabby, coming to Bernie's aid, as well as saving Paddy from losing a tooth or two. We all fell about laughing, except Paddy.

"If it wasn't for Bernie here, I'd beat the shite out of

yah for that, so I would, Nabby," threatened Paddy.

"Are yah afraid of me sister then, are yah, Paddy?" smirked our Martin.

"Paddy's in love with Bernie." said cousin Martin, giving away his brother's big secret.

"No I'm not, yah liar yah!"

"Yea are! Every time yah see her, yah tell me, yea'd like to give her a big kiss and take a peek at her budgie!"

"Y'er a feckin' big liar, so ya are!" Paddy went as red as a tomato. "An' if yah don't want yer gob busted yea'd better shallup!" he warned his smirking brother. "Anyways," said red-faced Paddy, swiftly changing the subject, "where are yea going?"

"There and back to see how far it is," said our Martin, "An' if it's too far to go, then we won't be botherin'!"

"Can we come with yah?" asked Paddy.

"I'm not sharing our money with them two!" said Nabby.

"We've our own money," said Paddy, pulling out a handful of shilling pieces from his pockets. "We robbed our Granny's gas meter. Ah go on, Bernie, let's tag along, will yah? Please! We'll be no trouble ta yah?"

"Only if yah can make a bigger splash than our Martin can," said Bernie, throwing a wink in Martin's direction, before throwing a sly glance over in the direction of the pond!

"We'll go for that one over there," said Martin, pretending to ready himself to take a long run and jump.

"I'm older than yea, Martin," said Paddy, suddenly pushing himself in front of my brother, "So I'll go first."

Putting up no argument, my brother had stepped to one side, letting Paddy ready himself. And with a few words of encouragement from his own brother, we'd all watched on with bated breath as he rushed across the street and took one mighty leap into the air before disappearing out of sight beneath the smelly surface of the water! And with that, we went on our way, leaving cousin Martin to rescue his drowning brother as we headed off in the direction of Belle Vue Zoo.

CHAPTER 8

What Goes Around...

We hadn't been in Belle Vue fun park for all that long when we came across Billy the Kid, dressed as usual in his cowboy outfit with his holstered guns hanging down off his waist. He was with another group of losers and we started taking the mickey out of them, pulling ugly faces and trying to mimic them. But they just laughed and made ugly faces back at us, while Billy gave us a wave before doing a quick draw with both guns.

We were still pulling faces and making grunting noises at Billy's group as they climbed onto the rollercoaster. The man in charge of the ride suddenly turned to the three of us and shouted, "Hurry up you gormless gits, or you're going to miss your ride!" And so we hopped onto the rollercoaster without a second invitation, ending up tagging along with Billy and our new-found friends for most of the day, sharing our stolen money with them on hot dogs and candy floss and ice creams. What a day!

Once, when Grandad had finally returned home three weeks after running off with "that whore", our drunken Granny had moaned to Mammy, "Nothin' good ever lasts forever." And so it was that our fun in the Funhouse soon came to an abrupt halt because smoke had been spotted high above us.

There was a mad rush for the exit as panicking children and adults rushed around just like our chickens did when they were headless. We had not been aware of exactly what the problem was until we noticed the billowing black smoke descending quickly towards us from the roof space. We spent the next hour or so watching the fire crews working on the blaze, sadly to no avail. And our Funhouse, my favourite place, became a blackened shell, destroyed before my very eyes.

With five shillings to our name, which we agreed to give to Mammy and Daddy, we made a detour on our way back into Hulme. And it was just as we had approached the corner of Warwick Street, and the nearby Hippodrome Bingo Hall, when we heard a loud commotion going on outside.

It was hard to get a good look in because of the nosy crowd gathered outside the place. But when we did eventually find ourselves a small gap in the crowd, I was stunned to see my distraught sister Rose sitting in the back of a police car, crying hysterically. A few seconds later, a couple of uniformed coppers came out of the Bingo Hall. They were standing either side of our other sister Mary, who was wearing a patterned summer skirt just like the one Shamie had taken off our hands a few days earlier. The odd-looking fella we'd seen putting the giant Easter egg on display and straightening the hems of the skirts was standing off to one side talking with a third copper. And that's when it suddenly dawned on Martin and me. The skirt Mary was wearing, was in fact one of the two skirts we'd stolen from the Bingo Hall! Worse still, Rose was wearing the other one.

"When I get me poxty hands on you, Shamie! I'll feckin' swing for yah I swear it!" screamed Mary in the direction of our brother who was standing at the front of the crowd.

"Yah should have told Shamie the truth," said Martin, looking fearful.

"And let Mary and Rose kill the pair of us?" I said.

"What have yah done Martin?" asked Bernie who was wearing the frown that shows she knows we are in deep shit.

"Nothin," I assured her.

"We stole the skirts from the Bingo Hall," blurted Martin.

"Jasyus! The ones Shamie sold to Mary an' Rose!" cried Bernie.

"Aye! The same feckin' ones!"

"Looks like Shamie will probably be killing the pair of yah, I wouldn't wonder," said Nabby helpfully.

"Quick! Hide!" warned Bernie. "Shamie's heading this way!"

Getting a glimpse of our angry-looking brother hurrying away from the crowd and heading across the road in our direction, I just managed to duck down alongside Martin and follow him on all fours underneath the parked lorry.

"Have yah seen them pair of gormless gimpy-eyed fuckers?" growled Shamie.

"Yah mean our Martin and Tommy?" said Bernie.

"What other gormless gimpy-eyed, fuckers would yah know, besides yerself?"

"Saw them today in school," lied Bernie.

"Today in school me arse!" scoffed Shamie, "None of yah's have been ta school today, yah liar yah! The Truant Man was around at the house asking after all of yah - again! An' the auld man's going up the wall! So be warned!"

"What's happening with Mary and Rose then?"

"The pair got arrested for stealing the two skirts and the big fuckin' Easter egg them two humpy bastards said they'd stolen from Woolies, when they'd feckin' stolen them from the feckin' Bingo Hall! The poxty little bastards!" raged Shamie. "When yah do see them, tell them they'd better be gettin' to Confession because their Last Rites are comin' an' I'll be feckin' killing them after!"

We watched from under the lorry as Shamie's stocky legs hurried past and we waited until he was out of sight before we dared crawl out from our hiding place.

"It wasn't me that told Shamie we'd stolen the tings from Woollies!" protested Martin as he got to his feet. "It was Tommy."

"I had to tell him that! Otherwise Mary and Rose would have murdered us, for sure."

"Well, now they're going ta murder yah for sure," said Bernie.

"After Shamie kills yah first, I wouldn't wonder," said Nabby helpfully.

"Will yah shallup wondering before I box yah one in the gob!" I gave my little brother such an angry look, I thought he was going to burst into tears.

Instinctively putting a consoling arm around him, I assured him I would never have really boxed him in the gob. Even if he'd carried on wondering about the things he shouldn't have been wondering about in the first place. He accepted my apology with a bright smile before suddenly bursting into tears.

As it turned out, I had five beatings in twenty-four hours, which was a record even for me. I'd been expecting the three, but the fourth and fifth came as a complete surprise. I spent the first couple of days, after my sisters' arrests, avoiding the pair of them like the plague. And if they had happened to be around the house, I would make sure I had been in Mammy's sights all the while because they wouldn't have dared do a thing to me in front of her.

Mammy wondered why it was I'd not been able to keep still in the one spot for a minute, and she'd asked me if I had worms. I told her I'd not been feeling well. And when Mary had suddenly suggested I come over and cuddle up to her on the sofa and she'd make me feel better, I'd opted to run out the back way and off up the alley.

Besides both my sisters losing their jobs and having to pay for the two stolen skirts and the giant Easter egg out of their wages they'd had coming to them (which I'd overheard them complaining, didn't amount to much anyhow), they'd both agreed to the police caution and were warned they'd be sent to prison if there was to be a next time.

Daddy ignored their pleas of innocence, telling them, they were inconsiderate greedy feckin' pigs! He'd said they could have at least brought the Easter egg home to share with the family, instead of keeping it all to themselves. This had incensed my two sisters even more, with them promising me they were just biding their time to get a hold of me.

It hadn't taken too long for that time to come. They finally got me on the Thursday evening when I was offguard on the toilet outside. The unlocked toilet door suddenly swung outwards to reveal my two angry sisters, standing there like a couple of hungry lions who had cornered their prey and were now ready to devour it.

Steeling myself for the promised beating, I was stunned to feel a few feeble slaps around my head and the threat of having my bollocks cut off next time. My two sisters had avoided coming right into the toilet, probably on account of the stench. It had all been over and done with in a flash and I wondered why the feck had I gone through all that bother to hide from them in the first place.

The following evening, Martin, Bernie, Nabby and me were sitting playing snap at the dining table in the backroom when Shamie suddenly walked in from the back yard. Mammy and Daddy were on the small sofa near the fireside, having their usual few bottles of ale before going out to the pub for the rest of the evening. Mammy was already merry and giving us a rendition of her favourite song, "The Forty Shades of Green". Shamie had a wide grin on his face, which at the time seemed a little unusual, considering he had two black eyes and a swollen lip. We pretended to be oblivious to him and he made no eye contact with me at all. To my relief, he looked as though he was simply going to walk past us and I was wondering if the good hiding he'd got from our two sisters had made him lose his memory, when his fist made contact with my mouth, the momentum causing my chair to topple backwards, knocking over Mammy and Daddy's half empty bottles of ale. My third, fourth and fifth beatings of the week!

CHAPTER 9

Cabbage and Kisses

St Wilfrid's Catholic School wasn't too long a walk from Stamford Street. It would normally take us around ten minutes at a brisk pace, which was something we never felt minded to do unless we'd stolen something from a shop and the shopkeeper or the police were on our tails.

The journey to school had too many distractions for kids like us. And unless a mammy or a daddy took their kids to school, it was rare any of us made it on time for morning assembly. On those odd miraculous mornings when we did make it on time, this would have been a particular special day such as All Saints or St Patrick's Day or a day a group of pupils were making their first Holy Communion. These special days meant a party after the church service and you could be sure we would always endeavour to get there at the earliest opportunity for any party. Otherwise we'd amble through the streets of bombed-out houses with our keen eyes darting to and fro, sniffing out anything that might be of some value to us.

It was ten o'clock one morning and we still had not reached school, though we were only a few streets away. We found a huge discarded lorry tyre on one of the crofts. It was about a foot taller than us and as Martin was the eldest, he was the first to hop inside it, while Bernie and I rolled him along the street in the direction of the school. I let Bernie have her turn in the tyre before me, while Martin and me pushed her along. But after travelling only a few yards, she screamed for us to stop because it had made her feel dizzy. So I hopped in for my turn.

It was a strange sensation, rolling over and over at a gentle pace and seeing the world from different angles. And I was minded to thinking it was just as good a ride as some of those at Belle Vue. Round and round I'd gone without a care in the world, as the tyre had gradually begun to pick up speed, only realising something was not right when I'd heard Martin and Bernie, screaming, "Jump, Tommy! Jump!"

"This is the quickest yea'll ever get ta school yah little fucker yah!" I heard the demented laugh of my brother Shamie as he gave the tyre another push down Rutland Street. Whatever short life I had lived up to that moment, along with all the sins I'd ever committed, flashed before my very eyes. I couldn't jump out of the tyre because of the speed it was travelling. I was pinned inside and I couldn't even tell which way was up or which way was down, let alone how I could possibly survive unscathed, as the tyre flew off the pavement and onto the road, where it continued down the middle of the street, narrowly missing collision with several cars.

To my relief, the huge tyre eventually slowed enough for me to throw myself out of it just outside the main entrance gates to the school at the bottom of Rutland Street. I staggered to my feet, dizzy, shaken, but otherwise unhurt. I ignored the strange looks from parents standing around gossiping near the school's entrance, nonchalantly brushing myself down as if arriving to school inside a tyre had been nothing out of the ordinary.

Thankfully, Bernie and Martin arrived at my side a few moments later and I was able to throw an arm around my brother, pretending I'd not seen him in ages just so I could support my shaky legs. "Get me away from this lot will yah," I said. "I feel sick!"

"Are yah all right our Tommy?" asked Bernie, sweeping her tatty long blonde hair off her pale face. "Only yah look as if yea've seen a ghost!"

"It was feckin' great!" I assured her, my head still spinning and a false quivering grin etched across my face even as I puked my guts up.

"Jaysus! Yah could have been killed!" declared Martin, walking me through the gates into the playground. "A car just missed yah by that much!" Martin, smiling gleefully, demonstrated the distance with two fingers as the three of us had headed across the yard into the school.

Despite her miraculous jig on St Patrick's Day, I still didn't like Sister Joseph. None the wiser as to what had come over her that day, she blamed her unruly behaviour on stress. She seemed a little taken aback as Martin and me strolled into the classroom, much earlier than was usual for us. Calling us straight over to her desk, she glared suspiciously at us for a moment or two.

"Here yea are. Take these ta yer parents," she said, handing us each a small envelope with OXFAM written across the top in bold black lettering. Underneath this was a picture of a bald-headed black child of about two years of age, with a belly as big as hers. There were smaller words below the picture of the boy, which meant nothing to me because I couldn't read or write. Not that it had mattered, because she'd gone on to tell us that all the money we collected in the envelopes would be used to help the starving orphans of war-torn Africa. We hadn't a clue where Africa was and she hadn't bothered to tell us, so we were still none the wiser.

As I followed Martin to the classroom door, the auld hen stopped us in our tracks and hollered in her sternest voice, "Where on earth do yea two urchins think y'er goin'?"

"Yah just told us to take these envelopes home to our Mammy an' Daddy, Sister," Martin reminded her.

"Yah did say that Sister," I added.

For a big woman, she was very quick on her feet and she cuffed the pair of us around our heads, before ordering me back to my desk. She then grabbed Martin by his left ear and frogmarched him to his own desk. "I meant at home time, yah blitherin' eejit, yah!" she bellowed down my brother's ear while still holding on to it, making it go all red, much to the amusement of the rest of the class. "Sit there and don't speak until y'er spoken ta! And wipe that filthy green nose!"

Looking over at my brother, we didn't need to say anything to know what we were thinking. Smiling over at me, he wiped his nose with the dirty sleeve of his jumper. And in that moment, without having to say a word to each other, the two of us knew that Sister Joseph and the rest of the class were going to get their comeuppance, one way or the other.

Lunch times would see us marched off across Rutland Street, and around the corner to the annexe, near Cooke Street, where we'd have to stand in the long line moving forwards at a snail's pace towards the serving hatch and Mrs Moses, the head Dinner Lady with her permanent, lopsided smile. Even when she was telling us off, she always smiled about it, at least on one side of her face! Word around the school was, she'd been inflicted with a stroke from God. A stroke from the Headmaster Mr Coleman's strap, had never put a smile on my face. So I wasn't sure whether a stroke from God was a good thing or a bad thing for Mrs Moses. She didn't seem the sort of person to be committing big sins. And so I could only suppose, as it was a good thing to be smiling all the time, the chances were her stroke must have been a gift from the Almighty.

Mrs Moses splattered a couple of huge dollops of

overheated shepherd's pie onto my dinner tray and it smelled lovely. The peas I loved, the carrots not so much. And the cabbage - I hated the stuff! The mere thought of putting it into my mouth made me gag. Mammy cooked it for us when Daddy managed to steal it from the allotments. And if there wasn't the tiny worms or the slugs to contend with, there was always the grit crunching against my teeth. Mammy would go on at me to eat it, "as it's good for yah". But when her back was turned I'd slip it onto Bernie's plate, she loved the stuff.

Mrs Moses also told me I had to eat up all my greens because they would make me big and strong. And I told her I'd rather remain small and weak for the rest of my life, than eat that shite! But the smiling cook had still managed to slap a large dollop of stewed watery cabbage next to my shepherd's pie before I could move my tray away. I was tempted to pick up a handful of the disgusting stuff and throw it back at her, but she was saved by Bernie, who nudged me forwards along the dinner line, telling me she'd have it.

Outside in the playground, the new boy, Paul Morgan, hit another boy in the belly, leaving him doubled up on the ground in tears. Paul Morgan was a sly little bastard. He'd not been at the school all that long and had been putting himself about as a bit of a hard nut. Of course, he'd had the advantage over the rest of the boys because his right hand was false. The fingers were fused together like a plastic doll's hand and were turned slightly inwards into a half-clenched fist, which seemed pointless because the hand was just a solid lump of hard plastic and couldn't do anything. Not even wipe his bum. But I had seen him use the hand to good effect, only ever needing the one sly punch to win his fights.

As usual, Martin would go off to play football and I would sneak into the girls' playground to find Bernie. I sometimes ended up in a game of kiss 'n' chase, which I liked playing, especially when I got to chase after the rag-and-bone-man's daughter, Cathy McCarthy. She had the most beautiful Irish blue eyes imaginable and when Mammy was drunk and sung "When Irish eyes are smiling" I would always think of Cathy McCarthy. She was two years older than me, but the age gap didn't matter. We were in love and were going to get married when we got older.

I hadn't told her this at the time, but I knew she felt the same way about me because I didn't have to put much effort into catching her during kiss 'n' chase. When I did, she would instinctively close her eyes and purse her lips ready for mine. And when we kissed our lingering kisses, I always got this strange warm tingling feeling inside me, causing my mickey to go all funny, just like in the mornings when I'd first wake up. Or when the nurse down at the clinic tickled me with the bristles of the large paint brush.

Cathy's best friend was Bridget Reilly. They were always together and seemed inseparable. I wouldn't have called Bridget ugly, but I wouldn't have said she was pretty either. I suppose pretty-ugly would have been the fairest way of describing her, with her small, freckled pixie-looking face, her dainty little nose pointing skywards and her hazel eyes encircled by red rims. And all sitting on her unusually long, skinny neck and topped by red hair, reminding me of one of our chickens. She did not leave any of the boys alone and seemed to have taken a shine to me, always asking for a kiss, even when we were not playing kiss 'n' chase!

Just like me, Bridget was a fast runner and would chase me all over the school yard. The good thing was, she couldn't climb. So whenever she'd got to within a foot of me, I'd be up the drainpipe of the toilet block and there I'd stay, with the other lads, until she'd found someone else to chase or the bell rang for the end of playtime.

CHAPTER 10

Charity Begins at Home?

"A penny for the starving children of Africa!" cried Daddy, blowing a plume of smoke from his rollup. "An' here's me with not even two ha'pennies to rub together! An' she's given yah two envelopes! So it's more than a penny the greedy auld cow is after! More like a penny for her an' a penny for the darkies, if yah ask me." Daddy screwed up the two Oxfam charity envelopes before throwing them onto the coal fire. "There's more starving children in Manchester than the whole of the African tribes put together!" he went on. "Starving Africans me feckin' arse! It doesn't stop them breeding like feckin' rabbits in their straw huts, does it? They should cut off their feckin' bollocks so they wouldn't be having all those children to starve in the first place! Tell Sister Joseph, if she'd like to hand some envelopes out an' collect some money for the starving Rhattigans of Hulme, I'd very much appreciate it!"

"Sure, aren't most of the Africans over here anyways?" asked Mammy, standing with her back to the fire, skirt hitched up so she could warm her arse on the flames. It was a habit, Daddy kept warning her, that would give her chilblains or something worse. But she never listened.

"Jaysus! The whole of the feckin' African nations are over here, I've no doubt," said Daddy, blowing another plume of smoke into the air, "An' if it wasn't for me bad health stopping me from getting a job in the first place, sure I wouldn't be able to find a feckin' job anyhow, because the Zulus have taken all of them! Listen to me, the two of yah," he said, looking both of us straight in the eyes with his serious face on. "If yah happen to see any of them envelopes lying around the school, bring them home - I mean the feckin' full ones! D'ya hear!"

In the evening, Mammy sent me and Martin with a handwritten note to the corner shop for a packet of five Woodbines, a loaf of bread and a bag of sugar. The shopkeeper always let Mammy have things on the tick, which she had to pay back, once a week, when Daddy collected his money from the Labour Exchange.

Daddy had written the note with a pencil. He did all the writing because Mammy couldn't read or write to save her life. She wasn't able to even spell her own name and would have to draw a big X instead.

As she'd seen us out of the front door, Mammy suddenly remembered to tell us that old Ma Collins, who'd lived just around the corner from us at number thirty-six, had been taken into hospital the previous evening with a suspected heart attack and might not have come home yet. "So if the milkman has left her bottle of sterilised milk on the doorstep an' no thievin' bastards have stolen it yet, bring it home with yah. There's no point in lettin' it go ta waste. Get off on now!" she hollered after us as we hurried off down the street.

Making our way down and around the corner of Stamford Street, Martin stopped and asked me for the written note, which I'd handed over to him without question, watching in silence as he took the small pencil out of his trouser pocket, licked it, like Daddy always did, and began writing more letters under the words that Daddy had already written. When he'd finished writing, he handed the note back to me.

"You keep hold of the note," I offered.

"No! I mean that's okay," said Martin. "Anyhow, Daddy gave it to you to give to Ma Turner. She likes you better than me," he added. And so I slipped the note back into my pocket as we headed off to the corner shop.

Ma Turner was a small, plump, grey-haired old lady and though I didn't think she was as old as Sister Joseph, or Mrs Moses, I bet she wasn't too far off. You could just about see the top half of her grey curly head and bespectacled eyes peering out over the top of the shop counter and, for some odd reason we couldn't understand, she would always greet me and Martin, as "Laurel and Hardy".' It wasn't as if we'd had an ounce of fat on us, or even between the pair of us put together! We were always scratching our nit-infested heads, mind, so I could only assume that might have had something to do with it. Unless we came across as a pair of idiots.

When I placed the note down on the top of the counter, she picked it up and studied it for a few moments before reaching behind to the cigarette counter and getting down a packet of five Woodbines, which she handed straight over the counter to me. "Get them into your pocket before anyone sees them," she warned, before walking off to get the bread and sugar, tilling them up before packing them into a large brown paper bag. She spent the next few moments studying the note and shaking her head at the same time. I watched her lips moving as she tried to decipher the words Martin had written underneath Daddy's words and I noticed, too, how my brother had edged his way closer toward the shop doorway.

"What's the meaning of this?" asked Ma Turner suddenly, almost making me jump out of my skin and run out of the shop door, which Martin seemed to have been standing much closer to. Fixing her beady eyes on me, she asked. "What in heaven's name is derry?"

"I can't read!" I shrugged. "So I can't help yah there, missus. But me brother Martin can. He wro- I mean, he's able to read and write." I smiled over at Martin, who scowled across the shop at me.

"I think it's supposed ta say 'Dairy'," Martin was forced to answer. "An' I think the other word next ta it, says milk but I'm not sure as I can't read an' write properly meself."

"Milk?" muttered Ma Turner, squinting her little eyes

while staring at the note, "Ah yes! I understand now. So what milk does your mother want? Sterilised? Full?"

"A box of Dairy Milk Tray. It's our Daddy's birthday!" Martin suddenly blurted out, before taking another backward step onto the shop entrance doormat.

"A box of Dairy Milk Tray?" she studied the note and eyed Martin and me.

"Who wrote this?" she asked neither of us in particular.

"Me Mammy," I said.

"Me Daddy," Martin said, throwing yet another scowl in my direction.

"Daddy wrote the first bit!" I heard myself saying. "An' Mammy wrote the second bit. Daddy's teaching Mammy how to write!"

"Mammy can't write an' Daddy's teaching her," affirmed my brother.

"Ah!" smiled Ma Turner, "That would explain the difference in the style of writing and the bad spelling. Your Mammy didn't say how big a box she'd wanted?" She peered over the counter at the pair of us, but we were too shocked for words, thinking we'd actually got away with it. All we could do was shrug our shoulders.

"We'll start off with a small box and if it's the wrong one, then you can always bring it back and exchange it for the bigger one," she suggested.

We happily agreed and I cautiously took the small box of chocolates from her, while keeping a close watch on her eyes, which stared straight at me from behind her thick set glasses. I wasn't too sure whether or not the old woman had been codding us along all the while, just so as she could get close enough to box me one around the ear. But no! She gave me the box and the bag of shopping and had cheerfully waved us on our way, telling us to wish Daddy a Happy Birthday from her, as she jotted the items down in her IOU book.

Hurrying out of the shop and off down the street, we took the longest route home so we were able to greedily scoff down the whole box of chocolates before getting rid of the empty box over the wall of someone's backyard. When we reached old Mrs Collins' house we could see no "thievin' bastard" had stolen her bottle of sterilised milk, which was still standing on the top of the concrete steps leading up to her front door. And so I ran up the steps and stole it. When we reached the house we saw the lamp-man lighting the gas lamp directly outside the house. He greeted us with his usual "Hello you little rascals!" before suddenly asking us if we'd been stealing the milk again. We hadn't a clue how he could have known this, or if he'd just been joking with us, but we looked down our noses at him anyhow, before hurrying into the house.

Bernie suddenly appeared from the coal cellar, carrying a full load in the metal scuttle, which Martin took from her, tipping half onto the glowing embers of the fire. When Mammy came through from the kitchen, she angrily snatched the packet of fags out of my outstretched hand, immediately lighting one with her trembling hands while bemoaning the fact she'd almost died of her nerves at having to wait so long for them!

Bernie told us that Michael, Gosson, Nabby and Kathleen were all asleep in bed. Our elder sisters had gone out. Paddy and Shamie had had another row and Daddy had kicked the pair of them out of the house and told them not to show their faces in the house again until they could get on together. Which would have been a miracle! There had been no need to tell us that Daddy had gone off to the pub around the corner, because Daddy always went off to the Red Rose pub around the corner at the same time every evening.

Mammy came back out of the kitchen with a lit fag dangling from her mouth. "Here yeah are." She plonked the plate of three slices of bread covered in dripping down onto the table top, before dragging herself back off into the kitchen again.

We were all eyeing the thick crust, or "knocker", on top of the pile, but Bernie had been too quick for us and her hand had shot out and snatched the knocker up off the plate in the blink of an eye. We scolded her when she'd taken a huge bite out of it, telling her she should have let the eldest of us take the pick of the bread first.

"So, which slice would yah have taken first then, Martin?" she asked, chewing on the mouthful of bread and dripping.

"Well, I wouldn't have snatched the knocker, that's for

sure," lied Martin.

"What about our Tommy, then?"

"I would have taken one of the other slices and left the knocker for Martin as he's the eldest," I also lied.

"Well, as yah would have left the knocker for Martin, and Martin didn't want it in the first place, I'll keep it," she said as she sunk her teeth back into it.

Mammy reappeared a few moments later with three mugs of sweet hot tea. Daddy didn't think much of Mammy's tea and often said, "It looks like feckin' gum water!" because she would water the milk down so much, making it possible to see the dregs of tea leaves at the bottom of the cup. But we didn't care as long as it was sweet and hot and we swigged it down gratefully, sugary tea leaves and all, before she sent the three of us out to collect wood for the fire.

We left by the back way and up along the alley, bringing the larger of the two prams with us, taking it in turns to be pushed in it along the dimly lit streets, where the air was damp and heavy with the putrid smell of smoke from the coal fires spewing out from the chimney tops. The derelict houses nearest to Stamford Street had been completely stripped bare and so our searches took us further afield. But wherever we went, it never seemed to hold any fear for us. We felt comfortable in our surroundings, be it night or day. And were confident, as well as streetwise enough to know how to look after ourselves and each other. The fact we'd lived in Manchester for some time while roaming the streets until the early hours of the morning without any harm ever coming our way, might have filled us all with a misplaced confidence, bordering on total indifference to, the perils and dangers that we could possibly encounter. But for all our confidence, we did have the odd dangerous encounter...

CHAPTER 11

Meeting the Devil

As the empty streets grew ever darker, we walked further into the uninhabited areas of Hulme. And despite the odd gas lamp and the tiny glints of far-off lights guiding us on our way, we often found ourselves walking in relative darkness for the best part of our journey.

It was Martin's turn to ride in the pram and it hadn't taken long before he fell fast asleep. And as I looked down on his peaceful, dirty face, I wondered where he might have been in his dreams. Perhaps like me when I was fast off, he'd be in some distant land where the sun always shone and the air was always fresh and clean and there was no suffocating smog or filthy chimneys. Perhaps he dreamed of somewhere he didn't need to be going off late into the night on the scavenge for firewood or scrap metal, or begging on the streets for something to eat. A place where mammies and daddies danced and sang all their Irish songs without having to be drunk and violent towards each other and their children.

There were no sounds along these dark empty streets, save for the noise from a couple of loose spokes softly clattering on the front wheel of the pram. Me and

Bernie didn't usually have a lot to say to each other when we were out at those late hours of the night. It wasn't that we didn't speak to each other, we did. But as there wasn't much going on in our lives, our conversations were limited, and anyway we would be lost in our own thoughts, whatever they may be. As we walked, I kept my gaze fixed dead ahead. I always found it easier to take in my surroundings when looking straight ahead, as it somehow seemed to make me more conscious of those dark shadowy areas to the left and the right of me. It was just like when I stared up at any one particular star in the night sky and could see other stars further away out of the corner of my eye, stars I wouldn't be able to see if I looked directly at them. Daddy once told us that the bogeyman only lived in places where people lived and so we shouldn't worry about encountering him in these empty streets. But that didn't stop me from conjuring up those invisible threats that might possibly be lurking in the dark shadows of every derelict building, just waiting for us to pass by.

"Look! There's a fire further up!" said Bernie, bringing me back from my thoughts. Shaken awake, Martin jumped straight out of the pram like he hadn't been asleep at all and we quickened our pace in the direction of the fire. When we got to it, there wasn't a soul about, though there was a good amount of copper wiring, which had been burnt off from its layer of protective flex, lying next to another pile that had yet to be burnt off.

"They look like the dying embers of an old fire." said Martin. "Someone left in a hurry."

"Do yah think someone's tried to steal their stuff and frightened them off?" I asked, immediately wishing I'd kept my gob shut.

"Don't yah think the ones doing all the chasing off would have taken the copper with them? If they'd come ta steal it in the first place, that is?" said my brother, throwing me one of his, "yah eejit" looks.

I had been about to suggest, perhaps someone else could have come along to chase off the first lot of chasers. But I'd held back with that suggestion, just in case Martin had an answer for that as well to make me look an even bigger eejit than I already was. And in any case, he did have a good point.

With no owners around to claim the fire or the scrap copper, we instinctively set about picking up small pieces of wood lying about the croft and began feeding the fire back up. I could feel the warmth from the burning wood brushing against my bare legs as the tiny flames flickered back into life before rising up and licking around the pieces of damp wood we'd thrown on to feed it. Standing in silence around the fire, I was hypnotised by the flickering flames dancing to and fro, each one wrapped itself around another, like lovers or long-lost friends meeting again. I loved staring into the flames of a fire and I could happily have done so forever (so long as they weren't the flames of hell).

We eventually set about collecting up larger pieces of wood scattered around the outside of the derelict houses, which, as a rule, we would never enter at night because it would have been impossible to have spotted any potential danger in the darkness. I noticed a small wooden gate leaning up against the side wall of a house and I made my way to it as Martin was throwing the pile of unburnt flex onto the blazing fire. I caught a glimpse of Bernie loading an armful of wood into the pram and I had been on the point of calling her over to give me a hand with the gate, when I'd been suddenly gripped tightly and a big hand went around my mouth.

"Don't make a sound, or I'll squeeze the living daylights out of yah." I could smell the stench of stale tobacco and beer on the man's breath, as he grabbed me from behind and lifted me off my feet in one swift movement, before heading off with me into the derelict house behind us. I tried to scream a warning to my brother and sister, but no sound would come out. I tried kicking my legs in the hope the man might loosen his grip enough for me to wriggle free. But it seemed the more I kicked out, the tighter the grip around my mouth and my chest as I was carried off in the darkness.

Taken into the empty room at the front of the house, I could see the high flames of the fire outside dancing across the damp walls and ceiling as the man put me down, still with his hand tightly over my mouth.

"I'm not going to hurt yah," he spoke in a low

whispery voice into my ear. "I'm going to take my hand away from your gob and I don't want to hear a peep out of yah - or else. Just do something for me and then yah can go back to your friends," he promised. "But if I hear one peep, yah won't see them again."

He turned me round to face him. The flickering shadows distorted the man's face as he knelt in front of me and I felt the fear of God running through my whole body as he stared straight into my eyes. And though I couldn't make out all of the man's facial features, I could have sworn he was the Devil himself. Dumbstruck with fear, all I'd been able to do was nod my head and let my warm piss run down my legs.

"That's a good boy," he said, slowly taking his hand away from my mouth. "Not a peep." Then the Devil whispered, "Get down on your knees."
He pushed me down by my shoulders, forcing my bare knees to the hard gritty surface of the floorboards.

"Are we going to say a prayer to Jesus?" I asked.

"Yah can say a prayer to who yah want, as long as you say it in yer head."

I started with the Hail Mary, as the man turned me away from him so he was kneeling behind me. He pulled down my piss-soaked trousers before pushing me forwards and down onto my hands. Moments later I felt something hard pressing up against my hole, just as Bernie called out my name. I couldn't see her, but I had been able to see Martin through the window's broken panes as he stoked the fire with a long piece of wood and the flames suddenly rose up high into the air. For a moment, I thought my brother had made eye contact with me as he glanced briefly over in the direction of the window. And I had been on the point of calling out to him, when the man's big hand was back around my mouth, stifling my cry. All I could think at the time was, Daddy was completely wrong, when he'd said the bogeymen only lived where people lived.

The man was leaning right over me, shushing in my ear and telling me he wasn't going to hurt me, while trying to push his big mickey up me. And it had seemed my prayers to the Virgin Mary and the little Flower of Jesus were not going to help me out of this one. Not that I could recall them helping me out at any time. I'd never found myself in this sort of situation before and so nothing had automatically come to my mind as to how I could get myself out of it. It felt like having constipation and not wanting to squeeze because of the pain, but going in the opposite direction! I kept the cheeks of my arse closed tightly for as long as I was able to and hoped the Devil would realise he was trying to push a pencil into a needle hole. But this had only caused him to push even harder against me, until I'd no choice other than to give in and I relaxed.

The scream must have spilled out of every broken window pane and echoed across Hulme, if not further, as the Devil suddenly leapt up in the air and danced across the room. Martin had appeared behind him, carrying a long stick with the pile of burning electric flex and hot copper wiring hanging off it and dropped it straight onto the man's arse.

"Run Tommy!"

I pulled up my pissy kecks, rushing out of the empty house after Martin and past Bernie.

"Where did yah get ta!" There was a look of genuine despair and anger on Bernie's face. "An' who's doin' all that hollerin'?"

"Just run!" said Martin.

Managing to fasten the hook of my kecks as I hurried across the uneven ground, I reached the pram and began to push it along the street as Martin and Bernie hurried to catch up with me.

"What about all the copper wire!" Bernie asked Martin.

"Someone else has it!"

"He tried to shove his mickey up me hole!"

"Who? Martin!"

"The feckin man!"

"What man?"

"The man doin' all the hollering with his arse on fire!" said Martin. "Did yah see the way he leapt in the air, Tommy?"

Then Martin suddenly let off a long fart, which instantly brought the pair of us out in fits of laughter!

"Y'er a pair of feckin' eejits, yea two!" said Bernie,

shaking her head at us.

CHAPTER 12

Her Majesty's Soggy Shoes

One Saturday morning, Mammy told me to go off to Auntie Rosie's to see what was taking Daddy so long. "Sure, he's only taken half a dozen chicken eggs to her, not laying the feckin' things!" she snapped.

Auntie Rosie lived close by to us in Collins Street. She wasn't our real auntie as such. We just called her that because she was always nice to us. She was married to Uncle Mike, who also wasn't our real uncle. It seemed as if all the women neighbours got on well with Uncle Mike, but not with Auntie Rosie. We'd often hear them talking about her and saying things, such as, "He's too good for the likes of her!", or "She's as common as muck that one!" Once, when I was stealing from the corner shop, I'd heard Mrs Mosley from Philips Street saying to Mrs Kelly from Collins Street that "Mrs Tanner (Auntie Rosie) doesn't have enough time in the day to keep her drawers hitched up to her waist because of what she gets up to while her husband is out working all hours!". And I'd heard Mrs Kelly say, "She makes Mary Magdalene look like a saint!" There were lots of other things I'd heard the neighbours saying about Auntie Rosie, but I think they were all just jealous auld goats, because Auntie Rosie had a nice big pair of knockers. At least that's what I'd heard Paddy tell Shamie on one of those rare occasions when they were on speaking terms.

Paddy, the eldest of my brothers, was a Rocker and supported Manchester City Football Club. While Shamie, the second eldest, was a Mod and supported the greatest team that ever walked the earth, Manchester United. I could only suppose this was a good enough reason for the pair of them to have a mutual dislike for each other.

If I had to pick a favourite out of the two I would pick Shamie every time. Paddy was far too sullen and secretive and didn't pay much attention to any of us, unless he had wanted us to run an errand for him. Now fifteen, he worked as a labourer during the day and would be out most nights, often staying away from home all night. So we hardly ever came into contact with him. He was really handsome, with his swept-back jet-black greasy hair, tight drainpipe jeans and size nine winkle-picker shoes, topped off by his black leather-look plastic jacket with the large iron-on transfer of a tiger's head on the back. He was "a cross between Elvis Presley and James Dean" people told him - well, that's what he told us.

There were always girls hanging around the front of the house when Paddy was at home. Mammy was forever telling him, "Get them who-ers away from the house before the neighbours start thinkin' we're running a brothel!" When Paddy was going out and he'd not wanted the girls waiting out the front to see him, he would sneak out through the back way and zoom off on his bike at breakneck speed, up along the back alley, dodging dustbins as he went, while keeping the toe ends of his winkle pickers pointing skywards so as not to scuff them as he peddled like mad.

Shamie, on the other hand, was the complete opposite. He had lots of time for us and sometimes would even keep a lookout for us when he took me and Martin out to burgle a house for him. Unlike Paddy, Shamie didn't have a job on account of his bad back - just like Daddy's! The doctor said it must have been inherited, though Daddy's thoughts were, "Shamie is just a feckin' lazy bastard who should be out working to pay for his keep, instead of hanging around with gangs all the day and doin' nothin' but scratchin' his hole!" But Mammy would always defend Shamie on this point and she'd tell Daddy to leave Shamie alone as, "He's out all the hours of the day and night robbing to pay his keep. And so doesn't need to get a proper job."

Unlike Paddy, Shamie was outgoing, loud and forever fighting with anyone and everyone he didn't like, which was most people! And also unlike Paddy, he never turned his back on any of us in the street, always acknowledging us if and when we'd called out to him when he was with his gang. Sometimes he would let us tag along with him. I can only think of the one time when he hadn't acknowledged me. That was the day when he'd rushed out through the back gate of Auntie Rosie's house, with a wide grin spread right across his face, almost touching his ears, and his distant eyes glazed with a look of bewilderment. He hadn't said a word to me and had just nodded as he'd carried on walking past me in his trance-like state. At the time I had wondered whether he'd had an extreme shock of sorts. Perhaps Auntie Rosie had given him something special, like a big bag of sweets! Which in a way, I supposed, would cause extreme shock considering she was as tight as a duck's arse, in the sweet-giving sense of the word.

Sprinting across Stamford Street, I had made my way down the back alley leading to Auntie Rosie's house. I ran as fast as my legs carried me, hurdling over piles of discarded rubbish and dodging overflowing bins. And in those briefest of moments, I had been transformed into Hayes Jones the black American 110-yard hurdles champion. Mammy had once moaned about it always being "the darkies that won all the races" and Daddy said, "It's no wonder when they get plenty of practice running away from the starving lions chasing them all over Africa!"

Hurrying through into Auntie Rosie's back yard, I opened the back door leading in to her kitchen, where my keen sense of smell hit on the odour of greasy fried food, which had made my belly groan loudly with the hunger. "Daddy!" I called out before inviting myself in.

Just as in our own house, Auntie Rosie's kitchen was dark and damp and just small enough to swing a cat in it. On the stone draining board were two plates with scraps of fried egg and bacon fat on them. I helped myself to the leftovers before licking both plates spotlessly clean and dropping them into the sink of greasy lukewarm water. On hearing low murmuring noises coming from the front of the house, I called out to Daddy again as I made my way from the kitchen through into the back room, where I was met by the sight of four sets of Auntie Rosie's frilly underwear dangling over the clothes horse by the open coal fire. I was surprised by how tiny her frilly knickers were, in comparison to the size of her huge brassieres. I'd gone over to have a closer peek and a feel and was just on the point of imagining her huge knockers hanging inside the bra cups, when I suddenly heard Auntie Rosie angrily call out, "Take me, Jim, take me yah bastard!"

Where did she want Daddy to take her to? I hadn't a clue. She'd not mentioned the location but she did seem very determined to be taken to wherever it was she to wanted go! And I couldn't help thinking, if Mammy had been that impatient to go somewhere and had put out like that, Daddy would have probably told her she'd have to, "Feckin' wait til I'm ready! Or feck off and take yerself!"

"Oh fuck! Oh Jesus! Oh fuck-fuck! Oh fucking Jesus! Take me," hollered Auntie Rosie.

Dear Lord! If Father Murphy could have heard all that blasphemy, I'm sure he would have been shocked, especially by the use of the Lord's name in vain! I was on the point of calling out to Daddy once again, when he, too, had suddenly joined in all the blasphemy. "Ahh Jaysus! I'm coming! I'm feckin' coming!" he shouted. He didn't sound very happy and I wasn't sure whether it was because Auntie Rosie was putting out about going out somewhere, or because Mammy had sent one of us to fetch him home. Not wanting to be a punch bag for his anger, I hurried back out of the house, up the alley and home, telling Mammy, "Daddy said he's coming."

The sky was still full with large black clouds, though the heavy rain that had been with us for most of the morning had gone off to soak another part of Manchester. Not that it had bothered me. I loved walking in the rain, which not only cleansed my clothes and my skin from the day's grime, but also gave me a strange exhilarating feeling of freedom. I loved looking down into puddles and seeing the dim yellow glow of the gas lamps clearly reflected back, a pool of colour in those drab black and white surroundings.

In the evening, Martin, Nabby, Bernie and me made our way to the main car park just off the Stretford Road. There was once a row of shops there and the streets had buzzed with the everyday life of people out shopping, meeting friends and having a good gossip. Meanwhile, we would hide in the shadows as the delivery trucks parked up, waiting for our opportunity to steal something and run while the drivers' backs were turned.

With the shops now gone, the land was fenced off by the local council to provide more parking spaces. At the weekends these were packed with cars belonging to people who, as Father Murphy would say, "had enough money to waste on alcohol, bingo, drugs and whores". When it could have been better spent on his church. Strangely enough, he never did mention anything about his starving flock.

Whenever a car arrived, we would follow it to its parking spot and wait for the driver to park up and get out before we'd ask him or her if they would like us to keep an eye on it while they were off enjoying themselves. The small jagged pieces of metal we openly carried in our hands usually prompted the drivers to hand over a few coppers or the odd tanner. But, just as in all walks of life, we always got the odd fella (always the fellas) who would tell us to fuck off before they rammed the piece of metal where the sun doesn't shine.

We were plying our trade as usual when Bernie suddenly screamed, "Look! It's the Queen!"

We watched as the gleaming black car turned in through the wide entrance of the car park and glided silently past us. The woman in the back seat wore a glittering diamond tiara on her dark hair and turned her nose up at us, ignoring the best curtsey Bernie had ever done in her entire life, almost kneeling down on the wet gravelled surface. As we hurried after the car, following it to its parking spot, I asked Bernie if she'd ever met the Queen to know that the haughty woman sitting in the back of the car was actually the Queen. Only Martin and me thought she had looked more like Elsie Tanner from Coronation Street.

"Yah don't have to meet the Queen to know she's the Queen, Tommy!" said Bernie. "Yah only have ta look an' see what she's wearing to know she's the Queen. I mean, how would yah know a copper is a copper or a soldier is a soldier, if they're not been wearing uniforms?"

"Father Christmas isn't real, an' he wears a uniform," I said.

"He is real isn't he Martin?" said Nabby, with a pained expression all over his face.

"Course he's real Nabby!" Martin reassured our little brother. "Pay no mind ta Tommy."

"Then how come Father Christmas was a fat Pakistani, this year? And a skinny drunken Irish fella last year?" I asked. "And the woman does looks more like Elsie Tanner than the Queen!"

"What would Elsie Tanner be doing in a dump like this?" scoffed Bernie. And though that same point could have also counted for the Queen, I couldn't be bothered to argue with my sister. She'd only have an answer!

Skirting around the large puddle in the middle of the path, Martin disappeared for a moment or two before coming back dragging a large piece of old tarpaulin behind him. He had placed this across the puddle by the side of the car, so Her Majesty wouldn't get her feet wet when she got out of it. So there we stood. All four of us in a line, watching as the driver got out of the car first and standing on the tarpaulin while opening the back door for the Queen to step out.

"Can we look after your car, missus?" asked Martin, giving her a bow.

"And why would I want you to do that for me?" questioned the haughty Queen. She wore a stunning, figure-hugging blue silk dress with matching high-heeled shoes, along with a furry-white dead fox hanging around her shoulders. And she smelled beautiful, her perfume filling the air all around us and helping to disguise our smelly bodies.

"To stop anyone from scratching the paintwork," explained Martin.

"With something pointy," I added, letting Her Majesty get a good glimpse of my jagged piece of metal.

"Shall I give the little twats a slap?" enquired The Queen's driver, taking a step towards us.

"Leave them." The Queen's haughty attitude suddenly turned into a wide smile. "Cheeky little bleeders aren't you? Here." She searched inside her small silver purse before pulling out a crispy ten-shilling note, which she handed over to Bernie, who treated Her Majesty to another curtsey. Martin and me had bowed our heads to her, while Nabby had just looked on with a big scowl on his face.

When we noticed the heels of the Queen's shoes had gone straight through the tarpaulin and the dirty water had begun seeping up through the holes, we rushed off and hid behind another parked car as she turned the air the same colour as her sodden blue shoes.

Then an Austin Mini parked up and we made a beeline to the new customer. But we didn't get a chance to say a thing as a demented Chinaman hurriedly got out of the car and produced a large meat cleaver, threatening to chop all of us into little pieces and make a curry out of us if he found so much as a dirty fingerprint on his car when he got back to it. This had been our cue to move on, but not before Martin had left his calling card. The minute the Chinese man had walked out of sight, he was back at the car, sticking little pieces of discarded matchsticks into the air valves of each tyre, before we'd hurried on our way.

CHAPTER 13

Night Shadows

We arrived home at around nine o'clock in the evening, having collected three shillings and threepence. Helen and Maggie were at home, looking after Gosson, Michael and Kathleen, who were fast asleep on the old wooden-framed sofa, with its broken springs covered with a thick bed of flattened cardboard to prevent the old springs from poking through the thin cushions.

It had been a long while since the whole family had been in the house all at the same time, which only usually happened if there was a funeral, wedding, or some feud with another Irish family. Mammy and Daddy were in their usual place, at the pub, probably drunk with our aunties and uncles, grannies and granddads, keeping alive the old Irish tradition of carrying on their feuds from the last wedding or funeral, when the lot of them had been at each other's throats. Daddy would often come home on his own, leaving Mammy to stay away overnight with one of her brothers or sisters.

"Did yah bring home any wood for the fire?" Helen asked in her soft voice.

"No," the three of us replied guiltily and in unison.

Helen was fourteen years old and Maggie had just turned ten, though they both looked older. Helen took over most of the chores around the house when Mammy and Daddy went off for days on end and whenever Mary and Rose ran away from home, which became more often as time went on. And on those very few occasions when Helen also ran away, Maggie would take over from her.

Helen was the quieter of the two and often seemed to be far away in her own world. As she stared into the embers of the fire, I noticed how pale her skin was, which had made her pale blue eyes her most striking feature. I had always loved it when she gave out a smile because her face changed dramatically and she would radiate a genuine warmth that seemed to wrap itself around me in an instant. In those moments I could easily have curled up on her lap and and not cared if I ever woke up again.

Maggie, on the other hand, was forever telling us off. But only in the way a proper mother, one who cared for her children, would do. And I guess she had cared for us in the best way she possibly could. Both of them had. But when Daddy was around, they would hardly speak to us at all. It was as if they had been trying their very best to become invisible to everyone around them, including him.

Though the whole family were blue-eyed, Helen, Paddy and little Kathleen were the only ones in the family who had jet black hair. The rest of us were fair. Mammy and Daddy once got into a fight over us in the Rob-Roy pub when the drunken Gordon McKinley, who was Scottish, had announced to the packed bar, "If Adolf Hitler had chosen all the blue-eyed fair-haired Irish children for his master race, the whole world would now be full of gormless thick idiots!" The pub had erupted in laughter, which had incensed the Irish drinkers, with the inevitable riot erupting and the war of words and the usual threats going on for months afterwards, only coming to a truce after Gordon McKinley's eldest son, Connor, had been stabbed in both his thighs when the warring families had come together again.

Taking the money that we had collected out of his trouser pocket, Martin had placed this up on the mantelpiece in case Mammy and Daddy were to come home later that night. If not, Helen would use it the following day to buy something for the nine of us to eat. We never did have a clue as to when they would be coming home. And it hadn't been that unusual for them to be away for days on end, after having gone off to the pub for the one night. Sometimes, one of them would stagger into the house on their own for one reason or another, but mainly for rowing with each other, which wasn't all that unusual once the alcohol had taken hold of their senses. There had been many occasions when the pair of them came back to the house in the early hours of the morning with aunties and uncles in tow and all of them blind drunk and singing their Irish songs about missing the "land of their birth" or leaving a loved one behind. Or how they'd like to take up arms and murder the "Murdering Black-n-Tan bastards!" for what they'd gone and done to the likes of Kevin Barry and all the other Irish martyrs long since gone. And they'd sing and they'd dance and they'd reminisce about the good old days back in Ireland, Land of the Free, when there weren't enough spuds to feed all the starving people because of the potato famine and those blue-nosed bastards over in the North, hogging all the food to themselves.

Inevitably, someone would say just the one word out of turn, which someone else would always have to take offence at, or take the wrong way. Then they would be at each other's throats again, punching, kicking and biting, before staggering off out of the house, beaten and bloodied and swearing, "On the Little Flower of Jesus! I'll never be speaking with yah agin, as long as I've a hole up me arse!" Until the following weekend came along…

Nabby told us he was too tired to come out with us to collect firewood. And so Martin, Bernie and me made our way out into the backyard where we made ready the large pram. Bernie had bagged first ride and once she'd settled herself in, we made our way down the alley into the dimly-lit streets and down towards Stretford Road, where the electric streetlights smothered the area in bright light.

On our way, we passed an old woman sitting on the fifth concrete step leading up to a private bar. The night shadows cast an eerie look upon her face, with her left arm reaching upwards as her frail hand held the handrail of the ornate metal fencing running up along the side wall of the steps. It looked as if the old woman had just pissed herself, as a line of dark-stained liquid had slowly flowed from underneath her and ran all the way to the bottom of the steps, forming a small dark puddle on the pavement below. She'd probably drunk too much of the stout and couldn't hold it in, just like our granny when she'd drink herself into a stupor and suddenly drop off to sleep in the chair.

We spotted the small red purse nestling in the old woman's other hand, which was resting on her knee and Martin had taken it upon himself to see if he could steal it without waking her up. I woke Bernie and she hopped straight out of the pram just as Martin had dashed up the steps and grabbed the purse. But the sleeping woman had a firm grip on it and it didn't come out of her hand as easily as Martin had expected it to. Holding the purse even tighter, he gave it another tug and to our utter horror, the woman suddenly toppled headlong down the steps after Martin and landed on her back in a heap at the bottom. She was still firmly holding onto her purse and, oddly, hadn't made a sound, as she hit the deck.

"Jaysus Martin!" cried Bernie. "Yea've gone and killed her! They'll hang yah for sure!"

"I never laid a feckin' finger on her!" said Martin, who by this time was crying, which made me cry, too.

"For God's sake! Will the pair of yah shallup crying like a pair of feckin' sea lions!" snapped Bernie. "Or ya'll bring the whole show down on us!"

But it was too late. We'd been seen by the two young women coming out of the main entrance to the private bar. And now Martin was surely going to hang after all, a thought that made me cry even louder.

"Oh Lord! What has happened!" asked the blonde-headed lady as she rushed down the steps, with her dark-haired companion following closely behind.

"She just fell," I cried.

"She dropped dead right in front of us!" said Bernie.

"I didn't kill her!" cried Martin.

I had been taken by complete surprise when the blonde lady suddenly got down on to her knees in front of me, flung her arms around me and pulled me tightly into her. I was so gobsmacked, I didn't know what to say or do. "Is she your nanny, luv? Oh, you poor kids!" she said, pulling me even closer in to her. And I'd got to thinking, if I told the lady the auld woman wasn't my nanny, then she would probably stop hugging me. But on the other hand, if I said she was my nanny, I would probably have been digging us into deeper trouble. So I said nothing and let the woman think whatever she wanted to think as she pushed my face deeper into her soft warm bosom, affording me another whiff of her beautiful, perfumed skin, which for some reason had me imagining myself walking through a field of wild flowers - not that I can recall ever having set eyes on a field of wild flowers let alone walking through one.

I didn't feel the cold that much. But I was surprised to feel the heat from the woman's body creeping through my thin layers of clothing to touch my bare skin. And for the briefest of moments as I clung on to her, I felt what it must have been like to be held in the affectionate warmth of someone who genuinely cared for me - albeit us being complete strangers to one another. But in reality, if it had not been for the kindness of strangers such as her, life would have been much harder for us kids.

Martin stopped crying and I took a quick peek over the woman's shoulder to see him looking back at me with his big cheeky grin. Wrapped happily in the arms of the dark-haired woman, he winked at me before pressing his snotty nose right down into her cleavage, while Bernie had gone all agitated and stood there scowling at us.

It wasn't long before a large crowd had gathered around the dead woman who was just lying there, frozen in time and still gripping on to her purse for dear life. A man said he was a doctor and bent over the prone woman to examine her for a minute or two, before standing up and announcing to the crowd, "She is dead." This was plainly obvious even to an idiot, let alone people with no medical knowledge. Even we had known straight away that she was dead.

"She has been dead for quite some time now, probable heart attack," added the doctor, to my utter delight. And

I could see the relief on my brother's face, which lifted my spirits because he wasn't going to face the hangman's noose after all.

"She hadn't looked all that good, when I had passed here half hour ago with the dog," volunteered one man.

"Why didn't you call an ambulance?" asked a woman angrily.

"I thought she was asleep!"

"Asleep? On the pavement!"

"She wasn't on the pavement then! She was sitting at the top of those steps."

"And you thought she was having a kip, did yah!" said someone else.

With all the attention of the crowd directed towards the man and the angry woman arguing over someone they hadn't even known, we silently slipped away into the shadows. And as I took one last look back on the scene I was leaving behind, I saw the fair-haired woman who had held on to me so tightly, frantically looking through the crowd of people. Probably in search of the dead woman's grandchildren.

We made our way to the Town Hall, before crossing the Stretford Road and heading up along Lupton Street to an area near St Wilfrid's School, where the whole street was boarded off after the people living there had been moved out only days earlier. I would always get the same sort of feelings welling up inside me every time I walked through the empty streets that were

once alive with the hum of everyday noises and people
milling around. These streets, like most, were once the
children's playgrounds. Hopscotch. Chalk drawings
on the pavements. Racing bogeys up and down the
middle of the street. Swinging on the ropes tied to the
gas lamps. Playing football and all sorts of other games.
Here the front doors were all too familiar, doors that we
had knocked on countless times when pretending to be
collecting for charity, using the empty Oxfam envelopes,
or the books of Christmas raffle tickets or stamps we had
stolen from the school. And sometimes a door would
open and the people would put a few coppers in the
envelopes, or buy one of the raffle tickets, crossing their
fingers and hoping theirs would be the lucky ticket - with
us knowing full well it would be a miracle!

With it being much too dark to be scavenging inside
the empty houses, we went about collecting firewood.
Forever conscious about my recent encounter with the
Devil, I made sure I stuck closer than I would normally
have done to my brother and sister. Around one of the
corners, we came across a grey-haired Indian man sitting
on a small wooden box and looking into the flames of
a fire. He was in the company of a young Indian girl,
around Martin's age. The old man ignored us, not even
bothering to give us a brief glance to acknowledge
our presence, while the young girl had continued to
pull exposed copper wiring out of the fire with a small
piece of wood, leaving it to cool down while she threw

more of the rubber electrical flex onto the flames. She glanced over at us, the hint of a smile on her face. And I couldn't help but notice her eyes fixing on Martin for a few lingering moments. Admittedly, he did have a much grubbier face than me and Bernie, and I had supposed she could have at first mistaken him for an Indian boy!

We were unable to understand what the young girl was saying to us. But, when she had offered out the small brown paper bag of rhubarb-and-custard flavoured sweets, we knew our presence was not unwelcome. And so we had hung around by the fire. While Martin helped the girl to burn off the rest of the electrical flex, and we showed her how to cool down the hot copper wiring faster by pissing all over it! This made her laugh, the old man had seemed agitated and had gibbered at the girl in his strange language. I think Martin and the young girl had fallen in love! They kept throwing smiles at each other and as a sign of his affection, when we were leaving, Martin had even given her his two small round brass doorknobs, which he had found in the debris a short while earlier.

The house was in total darkness when we returned home with a heavy pram. We packed the firewood neatly into the makeshift lean-to Daddy had built to keep the wood dry. We hadn't a clue of the time. Not that time meant anything to us. But the streets were empty and all the pubs we'd passed had been closed and quiet. So it must have been late.

One of the chickens jumped off the dividing boundary wall, startling us. Martin grabbed the clucking bird by its neck and slung it over the gate into the back alley. Quick to spot the flash of the torchlight suddenly coming on in the back room of our house, Daddy had come up to the window, pressing his broken nose right up against the glass. We hid in the shadows of the outside toilet and watched as the beam of his torch had moved slowly around the yard, holding our collective breath as the light snaked its way across the walls in our direction, before touching the outer edge of the toilet block and passing us by, missing us by half a foot. Only after the torchlight had gone out and we'd given it a few minutes longer, did we dare sneak in through the back door, before quietly making our way through the house and up the stairs to our beds, with me following up last.

Just as I reached the top of the landing, I heard one of my sisters whimper, "I want Mammy." I tiptoed back down the stairs and stood listening in the dark at the door of Mammy and Daddy's bedroom. I was able to hear the soft, muffled voices on the opposite side of the bedroom door, with Daddy shushing my sister. I couldn't make out who it was wanting Mammy because the voice was muffled and low. But it wasn't unusual, when Mammy hadn't come home, to hear one of my sisters cry out late in the night.

I would go downstairs to listen at the door and would hear Daddy shushing them off to sleep. When I went back upstairs and hopped into the bed with the rest of my brothers, I was happy in the knowledge that at least he cared about them, if not the rest of us.

CHAPTER 14

Daddy's Right - Hand Man

Mammy and Daddy were having a blazing row. The cause of the row was the cause of the last row they'd had in the Red Rose pub, when Daddy came home on his own and Mammy hadn't. She had her big white Going Away suitcase standing next to her feet and was telling Daddy she was bailing out of the house for good.

"It's all over this time, Jim," she said tearfully. This would probably have been the twentieth time that year alone she had threatened to leave him for good. And as usual, none of us had taken a blind bit of notice of her threats to leave, as she would usually exit by the front door and arrive through the back door a short while later, as if nothing had happened.

Mammy accused Daddy of pushing his hand up a floozy's skirt in the pub the night before. She had told him, he was a "feckin' whore-man's bastard," adding, "Me eyesight might be bad, but I'm not feckin' blind!"

"On the little flower of Jaysus and the children's lives," swore Daddy, "I'd not shoved me hand up the floozy's skirt! I'd dropped fag ash on her knee an' was just brushin' it off! And that was all ta it!"

"She must have gotten the fag ash all the way up ta her hairy budgie!" Mammy hit back. "Because that's how far yer hand had gone up her skirt! I've had enough of yer womanisin' Jim. An' I'm not puttin' up with it any longer! I'm leavin' yah for good this time. There's no stoppin' me!"

"What about yea wigglin' yer big fat arse at all the men in the pub! An' throwin' yerself at that gimpy queer lookin' fella Danny Flanagan!"

"Danny Flanagan! For feck's sake! Him an' his brother are little' feckin' midgets!" said Mammy. "Sure the pair of them must be over eighty an' halfway in their coffins, if they've not already died durin' the night! An' where'd yah think the money came from for all them drinks? Not from your feckin' pockets!"

"Well yah started it all. Midget brothers! Jaysus yah must be feckin' desperate!"

"An' I'm finishin' it too, Jim! As there's a God up there an' I'm on bended knees, I'm finishin' it for good," promised Mammy. "An' where's them sheets off the bed?"

"What?"

"The clean sheets I put on the bed yesterday morning."

"Ah, them… I had to throw them out in the bin," lied Daddy. "The bed was full of bugs an' what-have-yah."

"Well they weren't my feckin' bugs!"

I knew Daddy was lying about the sheet, because I had seen him, from our bedroom window, in the early hours of the morning, making his way out of the backyard carrying what had looked to me, like a crumpled white sheet. I watched him as he walked up the alley, before he returned a short while later, empty handed.

Mammy gave us all her usual fond farewell handshakes and we had bade her goodbye as if we didn't give a damn. And she was off out of the house, slamming the front door behind her.

I stood watching Daddy roll himself a cigarette and light it, before blowing a plume of smoke in the direction of the nicotine-stained ceiling. He didn't seem to have a care in the world and I wondered to myself, if Mammy had really left him for good, would he have genuinely missed her or not? They seemed to get on well at times, and I loved to see them smiling and being happy, which would rub off on us, changing the atmosphere inside the house, for a while at least. But at times it was like treading on eggshells, with them rowing about almost anything and everything, especially the real issue of "not having two pennies to rub together".

Suddenly turning his attention to Martin and me, as if he had only just noticed we were standing there, he asked where we had been.

"Out," I said.

"I know you've been out, Tommy, Jaysus." He shook his head at me. "If yea'd half a brain yea'd be feckin' dangerous, I tell yah."

He must have spoken with Sister Joseph at one time or

another, because she had said the same thing to me some while back.

Daddy told us there was no food in the house and I'd felt a sudden urge to shout out to him, "The reason we've no feckin' food in this house is because yea and Mammy waste all the feckin' money yah get off the feckin Labour Exchange, as well as what we bring home, on booze and tobacco!" But the words refused to come out. So instead I told him, "Martin and me were just on our way out to get something to bring home."

Bernie smiled in my direction, appreciating the fact that I had said "Martin and me", which meant she didn't have to tag along with us, at least not yet. She looked tired and drawn, as we all were, from the endless hours we spent on the streets, walking for miles on end all over Hulme, Moss Side, Longsight, Gorton and the City. It was neverending.

"Here, before yah go off." Daddy held out a two-shilling piece and placed it into my outstretched hand, bringing to my mind the thought that the drink from last night must be still in his head, because he was giving us a treat. The drink always made the grown-ups do things they wouldn't normally do.

Father Murphy said alcohol was the ruination of all those that participated in its evil. "The Devil's poison" he called it, though it hadn't stopped him from swigging it back during Mass, or when he visited people's houses.

"Fetch back two bottles of ale, an' be feckin' quick

about it!" snapped Daddy.

The Red Rose pub was, conveniently, just around the corner from us and had a tiny off-licence. I hadn't long to wait at the counter, which I could barely see over, for the landlady to come out and serve me. Maureen was a big lady, with a beehive of bleached-dried straw hair sitting on the top of her head. She greeted me with a big warm smile and hadn't really fitted the description Mammy had given of her. She had long red nails, which had made me wonder how she could have kept them so nice and long with all the scrubbing she must have done all over Manchester. I told her the ale was for my daddy, Jim Rhattigan, and she said, "Oh, you poor thing!" as her eyes rolled up to the ceiling. Taking the threepenny piece change, I picked up the two bottles of ale and was about to head towards the door, when Maureen suddenly called me back.

"Here, have these on the house." She leaned across the counter and pushed the small pack of peanuts in my direction.

I thanked her politely, trying desperately to keep my eyes from gawking at her enormous knockers, which were resting on the bar top. Jesus! I'd thought Auntie Rosie's were big, but these must have been double her size. And when she asked me, with a big wide smile, if there was anything else that took my fancy, I nearly dropped one of the bottles of ale as I turned and hurried through the door.

Outside the pub, I'd put the two bottles down on
the ground before shoving the threepenny piece down
my left sock, thinking Martin and me could buy some
sweets when we went out later. I had thought, with the
state Daddy had seemed to be still in, chances were he
wouldn't remember the change. But if he did, I would
just tell him Maureen the landlady didn't give me any
change.

Pulling the cap off the beer bottle with his teeth and
spitting it over the fireguard into the fireplace, Daddy
took a long swig of the ale, which I could hear glugging
down his throat, before he suddenly put out his nicotine-
stained hand. "Change?"

"I didn't get any change, Daddy."

"What d'ya mean! Yah didn't get any feckin' change! I
want me change! Now, Tommy!"

"I didn't get any change, Daddy."

"Who served yah?"

"The auld scrubber."

"What auld scrubber?"

"The one behind the counter with the huge tits."

"Don't yah be talking about her like that!" snapped
Daddy. "Did yah tell her the drink was for Jim Rhattigan
did yah?"

"I can't remember if I did, Daddy."

"Yah can't remember if yah did! Yah lying humpy little
bastard, yah!" Daddy was off the chair in a flash.

Giving me a left hook to the nose, he knocked me

straight to the floor and there, with the blood pouring
from my hooter, he grabbed me by the arm and
dragged me out of the back room and out through the
kitchen. "The woman wouldn't have served yah with any
drink, unless yea'd given her a name first!" he screamed
like a madman. He grabbed the small hatchet hanging
on a hook by the back door, before dragging me out
into the back yard. And there, with me on my knees and
him holding my right hand down on the blood-stained
chopping block, which we used for chopping off the
chickens' heads, he raised the axe high into the air and
threatened to chop all my fingers off, one by one unless I
told him what I had done with his change.

Martin and Bernie were screaming at him to let
me alone, but their screams fell on deaf ears. Daddy
stamped down hard on my legs.

"I'm countin' ta three Tommy! An' if yah haven't told
me where me change is, your feckin fingers are gone.
One…"

I found myself looking up into the eyes of this
unrecognisable lunatic, seeing the hatred burning within
them. I was well aware that the chance of him carrying
out his threat was a real one. Just as I had known, if I
had have told him the change was down my sock, there
would have been an even bigger chance of him carrying
out the threat. Probably worse.

"Two!"

"Jaysus, Mary and Joseph! Jim! What the feck are yah

doing?" Mammy had suddenly walked in through the back gate. "Have yah lost yer feckin' marbles?"

"Keep out of this, Lizzy! I won't be havin' any thievin' little bastard of mine stealin' from me! An' if he doesn't say where me change is, I'll take both his feckin' hands off his arms!"

"Come on Tommy," said Mammy, attempting to coax the truth out of me, "Tell Mammy where the money is yea've taken."

"I didn't take any money Mammy! I swear on the Little Flower of Jaysus and on yer's and Daddy's lives!" I said, using one of Daddy's lines. "I never got any change from her. I swear."

"Three!"

"And how do yah know the auld feckin' whore didn't give him the money Jim?" Mammy brought a pause to the amputation, "She looks ta me like she'd steal the flea off a donkey's arse, if she'd half a chance, that one. And how would he be able to hump the wood or go beggin?" Have yah taught of that one?"

"He's a lyin' thievin' fecker is all I know," said Daddy. "Like the rest of them." Daddy let the hatchet drop to his side, giving me a swift kick up the backside instead.

"Get back ta the pub an' get me feckin' change! And don't dare come back to the house 'til yah have it! Or I'll be chopping yer feckin' legs off along with the hands! D'ya hear me?"

"Yes Daddy." I ran past Mammy and was out the

back gate and up the alley quick as a flash. I could hear
Martin calling after me and so I waited at the top of the
alleyway for him. He looked pale and worried and said
we had to go straight to the pub and ask for the change
and despite whether we got it or not, we should smash
all the pub's windows as well. But I had assured Martin
there wasn't any need to be doing either. Taking off my
sandal and sock, I shook out the brass threepenny piece
into my hand.

CHAPTER 15

A Tall Story

We spent Daddy's change on a handful of blackjacks from the sweetshop just a few streets away. The shop was run by a whole tribe of Pakistanis who made it impossible for us to steal anything because, like Mammy's mashed potatoes, there were too many eyes gawking at us. It had seemed our faces were either becoming all too familiar in the shops closer to home or, like a lot of the kids living around those parts, we just looked like the sort who would steal from their own grannies. Even on those rare occasions when our intentions were honest, we were still banned from entering some of the local shops. Tesco's just about tolerated us and only because they'd never caught us in the act. Though I did think they might have had their suspicions about us by the very fact that, once we had stepped inside their main doors, we would be met by a guard of honour in the guise of the three security guards who would escort us around the store on every visit.

We would walk the slow march and all three security guards would follow suit. Upping our pace to a quickstep and they upped their pace as well. It had taken them a long while to cotton on to Martin's fake fits and the fact, while they were dealing with him, we were helping ourselves before silently slipping back out of the store, unnoticed. When they had eventually cottoned on to our ruse, the guards changed their own tactics, cruelly ignoring Martin's fake fits and stepping over his prone body to hurry after us. And for a short while, this tactical change of theirs had worked in our favour. Because, while we were leading the security guards a merry dance around the store, Martin would suddenly make a miraculous recovery and get up to help himself before legging it.

There had been one time when Martin came out with this ridiculous plan to disguise ourselves before going back into the store. How we ever thought we could hoodwink anyone was beyond me. But as our auld granny had once told us, "Yea'll never know til' yah try!" And so we decided to disguise ourselves as an adult.

In the mouth of the back entry running down the side of the Tesco store, I slipped on the plastic Groucho Marx spectacles, complete with false hooter and moustache attached to them. I had borrowed Uncle Frankie's trilby hat, left at the house from his previous visit to see his favourite sister, Mammy. And then between us, we had worn Daddy's long raincoat, Martin adding the final touches with our brother Paddy's drainpipe jeans and shining black winkle pickers stuffed with a pair of undies to keep them on his feet. And hey presto! The two little kids had become a fully grown man!

We had practiced Martin's crazy plan a few times, with me sitting on his shoulders and him getting used to walking about the backyard holding my weight. And there we were, probably the weirdest looking gentleman in Manchester. Tall, skinny and handsome, with hands not quite able to reach his coat pockets and muttering directions to himself as he walked in through the main entrance of the store.

What a mind-blowing feeling it was to find myself as tall as an adult as I sat on Martin's shoulders. I felt the strange sense of confidence and power surge right through me as I was able to look down on people instead of having to look up to them. I stared down at six-year-old Joshua Lemon and his little sister Maura, who lived a few streets away from us, to see if they would recognise me.

"Hello children." My attempt to speak with a deep manly voice sounded like Mister Punch with a strangulated hernia.

"Pervert!"

Brilliant! The pair of them had not cottoned on to us. And everything went downhill from there.

Martin staggered as he walked across the rough surface of the floor mat just inside the main entrance. And for the briefest of moments, I felt that I was going to topple off him. But he somehow managed to retain our balance.

"Keep calm and just act natural," he called up to me.

"If yea'd stopped staggerin' around like an auld drunk,

I'd be fine."

"It's these feckin' shoes! I can't pick me feet up 'cos they keep slippin' off! Ah shite! One of them's come off!"

"Put it back on before we're corrupt!"

"I can't feckin' see it!"

Looking directly down to the ground, I wasn't able to see the shoe either. I watched with amusement, as Martin's foot, with the big hole in the dirty sock, snook out from under Daddy's old mac and searched blindly around for the shoe. "Forward a bit! To the left! To the right! Too far. Go back a bit!" I directed him. "Just a little more forwards. Come back a little - afternoon madam. Would yah care for a dance?" The words just sprang to mind when an old woman stared at Martin's left foot doing a jig, before she looked up at me, shaking her head and telling me I was a complete fool.

After a few more directions from me, Martin slipped the winkle-picker back on and we managed to get into the store and to the first aisle before he moaned again, "The shoes keep slipping off."

"Just shuffle yer feet along," I advised.

"Ah feck!" said Martin. "I'll have to undo a button so I can see where I'm going."

That's when I noticed we had an audience, with old Mrs McGinley and friend standing with their sour pusses gawking straight up at me. "Afternoon ladies." My polite, manly voice seemed not to have impressed the pair of them. And when I followed their gazes downwards, to the point where their beady eyes had firmly come to rest at, I was momentarily shocked to see Martin's finger poking out through the mac in search of a button as if beckoning to the two auld hens to come to me.

It was unusual for the devout Catholic Mrs McGinley to have been lost for words, as she was usually so full of herself, wanting the whole world to know all about her life past and present. But when I grabbed hold of Martin's little finger, her face suddenly turned scarlet. She turned and staggered off in utter disgust, having to drag her friend away, as the auld woman's eyes seemed to have been transfixed by the wriggling finger I held in my hand.

With Martin now able to see where he was going through the gap in the mac, we managed to get around the store without further incident, save for the odd look from some people as they nudged each other to take a look at the strange-looking fella. But Manchester was full of strange-looking people and it seemed we had gotten away with Martin's great plan.

Both shopping bags were filled and hidden beneath the mac and we were heading back down the aisle, in the direction of the main doors, when I spotted the security man's foot suddenly sticking out. It had happened so quickly, I'd no chance to shout a warning to Martin of our impending doom. I just managed to grab hold of the top shelf as Martin fell from underneath the mac, leaving me dangling there like a helpless, legless man.

Quickly dropping to the ground, I hitched up the mac

and legged it past the three confused security guards and over Martin's prone body, before dashing past the gawky-eyed Mrs McGinley and her confused companion and I was out the doors and up the high street to where Nabby and Bernie were waiting for us.

It didn't take long for our smiling brother to appear, barefooted and holding Paddy's winkle pickers. He told us the security guards had to let him go, on account they'd not seen him load the food into the bags, along with the fact that the food hadn't left the store. As for the midget who ran off? Martin told them, he'd never set eyes on him before.

On this particular day though, walking along with our blackjacks in our gobs, Martin spotted a large hessian sack resting up against the back wheel of scrap merchant O'Neil's lorry. We dragged it off around the corner into one of the empty houses and waited until he closed the yard's large wooden gates, getting into his lorry and driving off. Once we were sure the coast was clear, we hurried on our way in the direction of home, carrying the heavy bag of scrap metal between us down through the back alleyways and out of sight of prying eyes.

I had this daft notion that Daddy would be so pleased with what we'd brought home to him, he'd probably forget the matter of his threepence change and let it drop. Hurrying down the alleyway leading down to our house we'd met with Uncle Mike coming up from the other direction.

"What have you there lads?"

"Scrap.' We dropped the heavy bag to the ground so he could take a ganders inside.

"Where did it come from?"

"The bombed houses."

"You collected all this, today?"

"Yep," lied Martin.

"All on our own," I added.

"I'll give you ten bob for it?" offered Uncle Mike, searching around inside his jacket pockets.

"Twenty shillings," I heard myself say.

"Fifteen! And that's your lot." Uncle Mike handed the ten-shilling note and five shillings in odd change over to Martin, before picking up the sack, humping it on his shoulder and hurrying away to his house.

We agreed between the pair of us to give Mammy the five shillings in the odd change, after we had taken the threepence out of it to give back to Daddy, pretending that the landlady had made a mistake. We would hide the ten-bob note and spend it over the weekend, on all of us.

Mammy and Daddy were in the kitchen. Daddy threw out his hand, asking me for his change. Frozen with fear I looked over at Martin, silently pleading with him to quickly hand the money over, before Daddy found any excuse to start knocking me around again.

Fishing inside his trouser pocket, Martin took out the small handful of change to give to Daddy. As he did so, the neatly folded ten-bob note slipped out and dropped to the floor! You could have almost touched the silence, as all eyes stared down at the neatly-folded note lying on the stone floor. And when I looked up in Daddy's direction, I could see the coldness in his evil eyes as he glared, first at Martin and then at me. It may only have been fleeting, but in that moment, I had seen and felt his loathing, his hatred, the evilness of my Daddy who day by day, grew more and more of a stranger to me.

"We got fifteen shillings," said Martin, breaking the silence. Picking the ten bob note up off the floor, he deliberately handed all of the money to Mammy, to Daddy's obvious annoyance. "And your threepence change," he added, plucking the threepenny piece out from the pile of change in Mammy's hand and handing it to Daddy, who said nothing.

Putting the ten-bob note into her purse, Mammy handed the loose change over to Daddy. He counted it before shoving it into his trouser pocket. "Here." He flicked the brass threepenny piece in my direction, which, like a lizard's tongue catching a fly, I caught in midair and slipped straight into my pocket, before thanking him. The look he gave me in return told me it was far from being a reward, but merely a reminder that thruppence was probably about all I was worth to him.

CHAPTER 16

Miracle on Stamford Street

Two Truant Officers called at the house early one morning. Apart from Helen and Daddy who were up and about, the rest of us who were at home were still in our beds. I slipped out of bed and lay down on the bare floor at the top of the landing where I had a good view of the front door without being seen.

"Me Mammy and Daddy are not here." Helen told the man and woman standing outside. But like everyone else with an ounce of authority, they invited themselves in. They made their way into the back room with my sister hurrying behind them.

Straining my ears to the muffled voices downstairs, I couldn't make out what was being said and so I tiptoed down the stairs to stand on the bottom step, listening at the door.

"I swear on this Holy Bible -" I heard Daddy's muted voice going through his usual blasphemies, before Helen hurried from the back room and went straight into Mammy's bedroom.

"Mammy! Mammy! Wake up Mammy! The truant people are in the house!" she called.

When Helen saw me, she put a finger up to her lips and ushered me back up the stairs, following behind me to the top landing. "Quick Tommy, get the others out of the bed. Leave Michael and Gosson and come to the girls' room. Hurry!"

A couple of shakes and Martin woke. But I had to resort to the usual tactic with Nabby of dragging him out of the bed by his arm and letting him drop to the floor where, with his eyes still closed, he attempted to crawl along the floor and back into the bed. We pulled him to his feet and guided him along the landing. On the way, I knocked on Paddy and Shamie's bedroom door.

Giving Martin a tube of Mammy's red lipstick, Helen asked him to help her dab little red dots on all our faces and hands. "Just like this Martin." She made a few dots on Bernie's face to show him how it was done.

Shamie suddenly poked his head around the door, wanting to know, "What the feck is going on? An' why are yah puttin' all that shite on their faces!"

"The truant people are down in the back room talking with Daddy." Helen had kept her voice to a low whisper. "They want to know why none of us have been to school in ages. Daddy's only gone and told them we're all ill with the chicken pox. That's why I'm putting these spots on them. D'ya want some?" She offered the lipstick to him.

"Over me feckin' dead body!" he'd declined, "An' if them nosey bastards ask where I am, tell them I've gone."

"Ta where?"

"I don't feckin' know! Tell them I've died of whatever yea lot are supposed ta be dyin' of!" He silently closed the door behind him.

When Helen was satisfied we all looked diseased enough, she led us out of the bedroom and down the stairs, while Maggie stayed behind to spot her own face in the mirror. And there we all were, huddled in the back room like a group of lepers, staring at the two truant officers who took a big step backwards in the direction of the kitchen door.

"There yah are! Didn't I tell yah all me children were poxed! And yah didn't believe a word of it!" Daddy looked just as shocked as the two shocked Truant Officers. "Have yah ever seen a sight like it in all yer lives? Have yah, missus?"

"Well, no. I have not, Mr Rhattigan." The woman had her hanky almost wrapped around her nose, though I didn't smell anything out of the ordinary. "It is very odd," she said, as she studied us from a safe distance.

"That all my children are ill at the one time? Well it's catchin yah know."

"I meant the red blotches are odd. There doesn't seem to be a set pattern to them."

"Well they're not feckin' paintings by numbers are they!" growled Daddy.

"Mr Rhattigan! there is no need for that kind of language," interrupted the man. "What Mrs Burke is trying to explain is the fact that none of the red blotches on your children's faces are uniform. They seem to be in all shapes and sizes, which is very unusual indeed."

"Jaysus! Me children are dying of an unknown disease, like the plague! That's livin' in this poxty dump the Council call a home, it's the Council's fault for all this!" Daddy had gone on to blame everyone he could think of for our demise, naming them off one by one: The Rats, the Pigeons, the Police, the Welfare, the Government, the Pope, the Teachers, the Foreign Workmen, with a special mention for "the Blacks and the Pakistanis, who've never seen a shovel till they came over ta this country!" Adolf Hitler was also at fault for failing to blow the whole of Hulme asunder! And even the milkman got a mention, because he had refused to call at the house ever again, just in case he caught the lurgy! Though the truth was that he had refused to let Mammy have any more milk on tick until she had paid her last bill.

"Jaysus, Mary an' Joseph!" Mammy suddenly appeared in the doorway wearing her flimsy nylon nightdress, minus her two rows of false teeth, with a lit cigarette dangling between her lips. "The children Jim! They've been cursed!"

"They're not well, Lizzy."

"They don't look well either! What have yah done to them?" She glared accusingly at Daddy, only noticing we had visitors when she walked right in to the back room, giving us a wide berth as she did so.

"Who're the queer people?" she'd asked no one in

particular as she eyed the two Truant Officers.

"Ooh! I'm dying - I'm dead!" Maggie had suddenly staggered in through the open doorway with her arms outstretched in front of her, causing the two Truant Officers to take another step backwards, while Mammy took a few hurried paces to stand behind Daddy and peer out over his shoulder at Maggie, while giving out to him.

"Jaysus, Jim! Will yah get a look at her! She looks like one of them people that's died an' come back to life agin! What's the matter with her? Why's she walkin' like that! Ah God! The banshee's comin' after us!" Mammy reached down to the fireside and picked up the poker. "If yah come a step nearer ta me! I'll bourn this feckin' poker over yer feckin' head, God help yah, so I will!"

"Ah, feck, Lizzy!" cried Daddy, causing the lot of us to almost jump out of our skins, "Yer fags burnt a hole in me feckin neck!"

"I will be sending the Health Visitors around tomorrow!" Mrs Burke hollered, almost falling over herself as she rushed through into the kitchen after her companion, following him straight through the back door, out the back gate and up the alleyway without bothering to shut the gate behind them.

"Did yah see the faces on them two!" Daddy burst out laughing and we all followed suit - barring Mammy. She wasn't smiling. When Daddy had explained how we'd been codding the truant people all along, Mammy started a row.

"Why didn't yah give me the wink, instead of lettin' them gimpy eejits make a show out of me!"

"How could I give yah the wink, when yea'd stood behind me burning me feckin' neck an' threatening ta murder Maggie with the poker at the same time!"

"Jasysus! What are yah goin' ta tell the health people when the nosey feckers come breakin' the door down tomorrow?"

"Ah, don't be worrying yerself. I'll pop in ta the church on the way back from the Labour Exchange and I'll ask Father Murphy to pray for all our sick children and get him ta send a blessing."

"But there's nothin' wrong with any of them."

"Aye, we know that, but the queer people don't. It's about time the good Catholics of Hulme had a real miracle to talk about!"

Uncle Mike called in after Daddy had gone off to sign on at the Labour Exchange. It was the earliest Uncle Mike had ever called at the house. It had been some months back since he called to complain to Daddy that the chicken he had bought off him the previous week to make a curry had been off, laying up him and Auntie Rosie for almost a week with stomach aches and the scutters.

It seemed likely Martin had mistakenly given him one of the chickens that had dropped down dead on its own accord. But Daddy was having none of it. He'd patted Uncle Mike on the shoulder and advised him, "Yah shouldn't be eatin' all that foreign Chinese shite!" before closing the door on him.

A bit later, when Bernie answered the door to Uncle Mike, she slammed it back shut before running up the stairs to tell Martin and me, "Uncle Mike's at the front door, an' he looks ta be in a bit of a state!" As the loud banging echoed along the hallway, we hid under the big bed in the girls' bedroom.

We heard Nabby asking at the door, "Who is it?" and Uncle Mike's voice bellowing through the letterbox, something about, "Stringing the pair of bastards up by the bollocks!", confirming our suspicions he might have called because of us.

"Who the feck is it?" we heard Mammy ask Nabby.

"It's Uncle Mike come ta see yah Mammy," he said, before rushing up the stairs and into the girls' room. "Uncle Mike's at the door!"

"What would we do without yah Nabby!" quipped Bernie, as he joined us under the bed.

When we heard Mammy say, "Jaysus! What the feck has happened to yer face, Mike!", we crawled out from under the bed and took up a good vantage point at the top of the landing. We could see Mammy with her back to us, standing in the open doorway with the frying pan in her hand.

"Those two little fuckers of yours, Martin and Tommy, sold me a bag of scrap for fifteen shillings! They should have told me the truth and just said they'd stolen it, instead of lying and telling me they'd collected it from the bombed houses," ranted Uncle Mike. "I took the bag up to O'Neil's scrap merchants where those little bastards had fucking stolen it from! I thought it was a bit unusual when the big gorilla had asked me where I'd got it. And like a big fucking twat I told him I'd collected it myself. Then he showed me the little brass name tag sewn onto the bottom of the bag, stamped with O'Neil's name and the number fucking four, which tallied with the bag he'd noticed had gone missing. Not only did I get a few slaps, Lizzy - and he's a big fucker that fella - but he took the whole lot back and made me pay four quid on top! Four quid and fifteen shillings I've paid out for nothing! What are you going to do about it, Lizzy?"

"They must have forgotten were they'd gotten it from, yah know what children are like," said Mammy.
"I know what your fucking children are like Lizzie! Look at the state of me face! You can't say they'd forgotten they didn't collect it themselves can you?"

"I'll chastise them later."

But Uncle Mike was not satisfied with Mammy's promise to give us a good hiding, not that she would have done, as we'd given all the money to her. He wanted her to repay him the four pound fifteen shillings it had cost him, as well as allowing him the pleasure of being able to give us a good hiding. Or he was going to the police, he threatened.

"Yea can put that wife of yers on the game if she's not already on it and get double yer money back!" said Mammy. "Now feck off!". We heard the loud bonk as she hit him over the head with the frying pan, before slamming the door shut.

The rest of the day had dragged on because we had not been allowed out of the house due to the family's mystery illness. Daddy came home in the late afternoon. He had the hump, telling us to get all the shite off our faces, as we'd been miraculously cured by the new priest, "a young darkie." whose name he couldn't recall. He told Mammy, "The morning mass was commemorated to the family, along with the first church collection and I had to feckin stay and pray with the rest of the heathens just to get me hands on the money! The whole church was packed to the rafters and the first collection amounts to a shillin' and a feckin' ha'penny! Not even a piece of paper ta wipe me hole on! I tell yah Lizzy, not one of the humpy bastards could look me in the eye, except for that hunchback, Sister Gertrude, who handed over the collection plate with a feckin' big grin spread all over that face of hers. And there she was, telling me I should thank the feckin' worshippers for their feckin' generous gift! Humiliated Lizzy, that's what I was. I didn't know where ta put me face. An' there they all were, holding up their ten-bob notes an' wavin' them around like feckin flags, so as everybody could see what they were putting inta the second collection! All except for that tight-arsed auld cow Mrs Delaney. Always hiding her money in her hand so as no-one can see what she's puttin' in, when everyone knows it's a feckin' ha'penny."

"Poor Mrs Delaney," said Mammy. "She's so old and frail an' she can hardly carry her handbag, let alone lift her feet to walk."

"Aye! Because her feckin' handbag's full with all them ha'pennies!"

CHAPTER 17

The Danny Boy Debate

U ncle Oliver and Uncle Raphael, two out of Daddy's four younger brothers, turned up at the house one afternoon. Just home on Army leave from the King's Own Scottish Borderers, they were still wearing their uniforms and looked immaculate. Uncle Oliver's first ritual, whenever he came to visit us, was to dish out bags of sweets amongst his "favourite nieces and nephews". He threw his Army kitbag open on the floor and dished out sweets galore to the youngest of us, giving bottles of perfume to my elder sisters and a small Swiss penknife each to Paddy and Shamie.

It was Uncle Oliver's 26th birthday. And although much younger than Daddy, who looked a lot older than his thirty-three years, he and Uncle Raphael had what I can only describe as a boisterous quality about them, which would give us all a bit of a lift.

If there was one thing they'd all had in common, though, that would have been their toughness. All of them, including Daddy's other two brothers Christie and Paddy, were tough as nails. Which had to be an inheritance thing, because we were all tough, to a point.

..Whenever the five brothers were together they seemed to exude a confidence that was never there when Daddy was without them. In their company, he seemed to be able to put his miserable existence on hold and become a completely different person, albeit for a short while. Even for that short while, it was nice when the family got together.

We all knew Mammy thought a lot of our uncles, but she seemed to have a soft spot for Uncle Oliver. She got on really well with him, in a different sort of way, we noticed, than with her other brothers-in-law. And once, when Daddy was away from the house and Uncle Oliver was helping Mammy to "clean her bedroom windows", Martin and I took it in turns to have a quick peek in through the keyhole of the bedroom door and watch them having a kiss!

Many times I had wondered to myself what it would have been like if Mammy had not married Daddy and had married Uncle Oliver instead. I would often wake up in the mornings having dreamt the same dream about him suddenly announcing, "I am your real father!" and and us all rushing over to him, throwing our arms around him, crying in our excitement. I wondered if we all had that same dream.

A couple of hours and lots of beers later, we were following Uncles Oliver and Raphael, Mammy and Daddy up along Stamford Street to the Red Rose pub. And just as Uncle Oliver had walked through into the public bar, we were met by a loud screeching chorus of "Happy Birthday ta yaaaah!" from a large group of our relatives, which included his brothers Paddy and Christie, our Granny and Granddad - that's Daddy's mammy and daddy - and more aunties and cousins.

At first, the landlord, Fat Pat - so named because he was a fat man called Pat - was not happy about having too many children in his pub. After a few raised voices, Uncle Oliver smoothed things over by telling Fat Pat, "It's a special family gathering and the children will be no trouble." He went on to promise, "If they break anything, I'll personally pay for the damage." Fat Pat, although still not happy, had relented under duress, allowing us to stay as long as we behaved ourselves and kept the noise down.

People said he weighed in at twenty-two stone, which was two stone heavier than our cousin, Big Martin Rhattigan. But while Fat Pat stood around five feet-seven inches tall and had all his faculties about him, Big Martin was a giant of a man, standing at six-foot eight-inches tall and was apparently "a sandwich short of a picnic".

Though Paddy and Shamie weren't old enough to drink alcohol, they were given a pint of Guinness each. Helen was given a Babycham, which she pushed across the table to Paddy on account she never touched the "Devil's drink", while the rest of us had to contend with a warm glass of lemonade and packets of crisps. But me and Martin didn't like warm lemonade and were content to let Bernie and the others have ours while we had helped ourselves to the dregs of beer left in the bottom of empty glasses and the bottles.

As the evening wore on the pub filled with more drinkers, their cigarette smoke creating a misty haze across the whole room, making it difficult to identify the ghostly figures standing off in the far corners. And if the putrid poisons spewing from the chimneys outside hadn't managed to cut short people's lives, the shite floating around inside that pub probably did!

The whole family were enjoying themselves and seemed to have had plenty to talk about. Over to our left, the atmosphere was a little more solemn, with the O'Connor clan celebrating the life of their dear departed grandmother, Daisy. Big Martin was still standing after having already won his sixth bet, drinking down two pints of beer before his challenger could swig down just the one pint, with the loser having to pay for the beer. Mammy was standing just in front of us, propping up the bar with her two sisters MaryAnn and Brenda. Uncle Oliver, Daddy, Uncle Christy, Uncle Paddy and Uncle Raphael were standing not too far away, talking with a large group of other relatives, including my favourite grandad, Frankie Gavin.

Short and slim, Frankie was still able to knock out a man twice as big as himself with only the two punches. "That's all yea'll ever need Tommy! Just the two feckin' punches," he had once told me, when we were out in the back yard play boxing. "Yah keep dead calm and don't let the other fella git inta yer head. That's the secret, Tommy. Let the bastard shout out his anger while you let all yer anger go down yer arms an' in ta yer fists. And then, when the fecker least expects it, yah whack the bastard with yer surprise punch, straight in the bollocks! An' when he's doubled over with the pain of it all, yah follow up with a haymaker to the side of his head. And if that doesn't knock the fecker out, run for yer life!"

Just like the volume on a radio being slowly turned down, the chatter in the pub suddenly faded into silence as old Danny Doyle eased his frail body up off his chair to give his usual rendition of "Danny Boy". At the ripe old age of ninety-five, he was nothing short of a living miracle, considering he'd been part of the pub's furniture and had sat in the same chair, singing the same old song night after night for almost seventy years. And when closing time came along, he'd be off home sitting alone in his own world, just waiting for the pub to open up the following day so he could go through the same ritual. But he seemed happy with his lot. Daddy said, "In some way, Danny is living like royalty. Sure, didn't the Queen have ta sit in the same chair all day long and have ta listen to the same old boring song being sung to her!"

Just as Danny had come to the end of the song, an argument broke out as to which country the song belonged to, which escalated into an angry debate. George Campbell's family argued the song had been written by a Scot and therefore "Danny Boy" belonged to Scotland. Uncle Paddy had argued the bluenoses couldn't write such a lovely song and it had always been Irish. Mammy suggested old Sam Butcher, the know-all of Hulme, would know the answer and so she had sidled along to the end of the bar where Sam had been sitting, as usual, squinting through his gold-rimmed glasses at the Manchester Evening News.

"Tell these heathens the name of that Irishman who wrote Danny feckin' Boy, will yah Sam," said Mammy.

Taking his nose out of the newspaper, Sam took off his glasses, folding them neatly and placing them down on the newspaper before asking nervously, "If I give you the answer, will you all agree to abide by it?" to which the whole pub had agreed in unison.

"Sure we will, Sam!" smiled Mammy. "Just tell them blue-nosed eejits over there the truth."

"Well," said Sam, looking around the quiet room, "The lyrics of 'Danny Boy' were in fact written by Frederick Weatherly in or around 1913. He wrote them to an Irish piece of music called Londonderry Air."

"There yea are!" Mammy shoved two fingers up at George Campbell. "Londonderry Air! Only an Irishman could write such lovely words to that tune."

"Actually, Lizzy, he was an English lawyer," said Sam.

"Who was?"

"Frederick Weatherly. He was the writer of 'Danny Boy'."

"Ah well! His mammy and daddy at the least were Irish, so what's the difference?"

"South African."

"Africa? Are yah trying to tell us a feckin' Zulu wrote 'Danny Boy', yah gormless-looking gerky eejit yah!" With that, Mammy boxed the know-all in the gob, knocking him off his stool.

The free-for-all that followed had chairs, beer bottles and people flying all over the place. Paddy and Shamie ushered all of us out through the doors, behind those drinkers making good their escape so they didn't get caught up in the brawl. Once outside, our two brothers left us standing on the pavement, before hurrying back into the bar. A moment or two later, Martin and I went back in and immediately set about picking up the loose change falling out of the pockets of the people grappling and rolling about on the ground.

Fat Pat was sitting on the floor with his back propped up against the side of the bar, nursing a bloody nose. His wife Maureen was kneeling at his side, pressing down hard with one of the cloth bar-runners on the stab wound to his right thigh, while Paddy and Shamie were up behind the bar robbing the cigarettes. Mammy, too, was on her knees. She'd had the midget Willie Morgan - known to his friends as Wee Jock and to the Irish as Wee Joke - in a head lock and was beating the bejaysus out of the top of his head with one of the large tin ashtrays.

We saw our grandad, Frankie Gavin, kick a man straight in the bollocks. But, as he'd once advised me to do, he didn't run when the man hadn't doubled over as expected. Instead, he just stood there on the spot, glaring at him. Admittedly, the man looked to be in a state of shock, perhaps on account of his brain needing a little more time to register what had happened. But the same couldn't have been said about Grandad, when the man's wife whacked him over the head with the big beer bottle - he hit the deck like a sack of spuds.

The only person involved in the fighting who had not thrown or received a punch was our cousin Big Martin Rhattigan. And by the time he'd thrown the first two Campbells out through the pub's windows, the rest of their family and friends had already beat a retreat, scrambling out of the doors to safety. It was just after Big Martin lifted his own father high into the air and had thrown him through the window too, that everyone suddenly realised he'd completely lost the plot and the whole pub, including my family, had emptied within seconds.

There were no volunteers from us or anyone else to go back in to the pub and attempt to sweet-talk Big Martin to come out. And so he was left inside to help himself at the bar, until the police had arrived. It took eight coppers and their truncheons almost half an hour to eventually beat him into submission before bringing him out.

Fat Pat banned everyone from his pub that had been

involved in the brawl. He was incensed by Uncle Oliver's refusal to pay for all the damage as he'd promised he would. But our uncle had argued, "Even if it had been Lizzy who had thrown the first punch, I only promised yah I'd pay for any damage the children caused. And as the children had caused none, yah won't be gettin' a bean outta me!"

A few weeks later, after the pub had been fixed up and Fat Pat realised he'd banned most of his regulars, leaving the pub almost empty every night, he had a sudden change of heart and had lifted the ban to everyone - except the Rhattigans.

CHAPTER 18

Beware the Stranger

Just as there were lots of derelict houses to explore on the way to St Wilfrid's School, there were also many that had been reduced to mounds of rubble, though it was still possible to locate the coalholes and climb down into their cellars which, like the Radnor Picture House, had their adjoining walls knocked through, making it possible to walk along the whole street unseen. And it was here, in these coal cellars, on our way to school, that we had cruelly pursued a fat, ginger-haired fella who, without fail, would take the same route every morning. The fella would have been about sixteen or seventeen years old and he was afflicted with a large patch of thick purple skin covering the whole of his left eye. Whenever we saw him coming, we'd scamper like a pack of rats down the nearest coalhole and wait until he'd ambled past, before one of us would pop our head up out of the hole and call out to him, "Cookie-Eye!" Incensed, Cookie-Eye would rush towards the coalhole, grunting and throwing lumps of masonry at it, only for one of us to pop a head up from another coalhole further along. "Cookie Eye!" We would antagonise the poor fellow until we became bored, safe in the knowledge that he was far too fat to fit down any of the coalholes and come after us.

Our timing was pretty good, too. So when we eventually made it to the school, it would be around dinner time. And so we headed straight to the annexe, where the ever-smiling Mrs Moses, head dinner lady, would be waiting to greet us. I recall one particular occasion, when I noticed her looking over at me before she had suddenly leaned into the new dinner lady and had whispered something into her ear, causing a big grin to appear on the new dinner lady's face. It was cabbage on the menu that day, the one thing in this whole world that I had hated most of all.

I guessed what Moses may have been up to. And if they'd been thinking what I thought they'd been thinking, then I knew for a certainty it wasn't going to happen. Walking out of the line, I made my way up to where Sister Joseph was standing in the queue. "I'm sorry Sister Joseph, for all the troubles I've caused to you in your life," I said.

"What in heaven's name are yah gibberin' about!" she snapped. "Get back in line, there in front of me so as I can keep me eye on yah!" This is what I'd hoped she would say.

"Afternoon, Mrs Moses!" I said, keeping my eye fixed firmly on the large serving spoon the new dinner lady had raised in the air. But I was too quick for her and I swiftly moved my plate and myself out of the way, telling

In our last lesson of the day, Sister Margaret told us a story about a wedding that ran out of wine and how Jesus had worked one of his miracles to turn gallons of water into gallons of red wine. This got me wondering, if Mammy and Daddy and all my aunties and uncles made friends with Jesus, they could take him to the pub with only the need to be ordering pints of water all night long!

"Is there anyone who would like to ask a question, before we finish?" she asked. And my hand had shot in the air.

"Yes, Tommy?"

"Is it really true, Sister Margaret, that the Lord Jesus helps those people who help themselves?"

"Indeed it is true, Tommy. And a good question at that!" she smiled. "Those people who try hard at bettering themselves in life have the Lord Jesus behind them, supporting them in every which way that he can."

I was grateful for the information, which had dispelled any lingering doubts I had about stealing the charity envelopes from Sister Joseph's drawer. The money would certainly benefit us in some way and came with the blessing of the Lord Jesus. Things were looking up.

I waited for Martin and Bernie in my usual spot outside on Lopton Street and wondered what their reactions would be when I showed them the six full charity envelopes I'd helped myself to. Knowing the pair of them, they would probably want to go straight off to the nearest shop and buy some sweets, before taking the rest of the money home to Mammy and Daddy.

Martin and Bernie seemed to be taking a long time coming out. They would usually be amongst the first groups of children rushing out through the gates, but this day they were nowhere to be seen. I was sure I hadn't missed them and assumed they'd been held back in the school for one reason or another, which wouldn't have been that unusual. So I made myself comfortable, plonking myself down on the ground with my back resting up against the inner wall.

As I waited outside the school gates, I overheard a group of parents talking about the sudden disappearance of the sixteen-year-old girl some weeks previously. She had mysteriously vanished from Gorton while on her way to a local dance and had still not returned home. Everywhere we went in Hulme, the City, Longsight, Moss Side, Gorton, we would hear the name Pauline Reade crop up without fail. She was clearly in the thoughts of so many people, even after so many weeks had passed since she had gone missing.

Like Mammy, some people thought and hoped she would suddenly turn up out of the blue, wondering what all the fuss was about. But with nothing to indicate any reason why she would just up and go, and with the Manchester Evening News continuing to write about her mysterious disappearance, the name Pauline Reade was to remain in the public domain.

BEWARE THE STRANGER

On a warm July evening, at around 7.30pm, a vivacious and well-educated young lady of sixteen left her terraced home on Wiles Street, in Gorton, heading off to her local Friday night dance at the Railway Workers Social Club. Dressed in her new pink and gold striped dance outfit and white boots, the excited teenager had kissed her parents, promising faithfully that she would be home on time, unlike the previous dance when she had been late back after straggling behind with friends. From a close-knit, church-going family, Pauline worked as a trainee confectioner in the same sweet factory as her father. Like many other parents, Amos and Joan were very protective of their daughter and were coming to terms with their little girl's disappearing childhood. She had arranged to go to the dance with three of her girlfriends, but at the last minute, so it seemed, her friends had opted to go to the cinema instead, leaving Pauline to walk to the club on her own.

With no apparent worries in the world and probably with the tunes of the week's hit parade playing in her head, Pauline set off from her house, on the short journey. It would normally have taken her no more than five or six minutes to have walked up along Wiles Street in the direction of the Railway Social Club in Froxmer Street, some 500 yards away.

As she walked along Wiles Street, Pauline was seen by two of her friends who had opted to go to the cinema. Surprised that she'd had the bottle to go off to the dance on her own, the two friends decided they would follow her, taking a detour along a back entry so they could surprise their friend and be waiting for her outside the club when she arrived. Hurrying up along the back entry, the two giggling girls had reached the club within minutes, where they waited outside in expectation of their friend appearing around the corner. But, Pauline Reade never turned up for the dance. She had vanished without a trace, with only one of her discarded gloves lying on the pavement to show that she had been on her way.

Having waited by the school gates for around half an hour or so, with no sign of Martin and Bernie, I had decided to make my own way home. I was positive I'd not missed the pair of them and if they'd come out through the other entrance on Rutland Street, I was sure they would have come looking for me here. But with no good reason to be hanging round the school any longer than necessary, especially with the charity envelopes stuffed down the front of my trousers, I set off in the direction of home.

On the way, my heart nearly jumped into my mouth when sirens suddenly blared out and the police car roared past with its blue lights flashing. And if it had not been for the ambulance following close behind it, I would probably have thrown my hands up in the air and given myself up.

Further up the street, I could see the police car and ambulance, still with their blue lights flashing, by a row of half-demolished houses. A small crowd had gathered and as I walked over to them to have a nose, I could see Cookie-Eye standing with two uniformed policemen. He was crying uncontrollably and talking gibberish, which no-one seemed to understand. The two policemen then walked him over to their police car, where I caught a glimpse of his bloodstained hands and coat! Pushing my way even closer to get a better look to where the two ambulance men were kneeling on the rough ground, the shock of seeing the sight before me made my heart miss a beat and my legs turn to jelly. "Martin! Bernie!"

CHAPTER 19

Headless Chickens
and Burnt Bottoms

Martin and Bernie were discharged from the hospital a day later. The pair had taken a good beating, for no other reason than to have been in the wrong place at the wrong time. They told the police they had never before set eyes on the two older fellas who attacked them, though they were able to give out rough descriptions of the evil bastards and said they had Scottish accents. A few cuts and bruises and a gash on the side of Martin's head, needing six stitches, and they were otherwise on the mend from their ordeal.

The police told Daddy if it hadn't been for Cookie-Eye chasing Martin and Bernie's two attackers off before raising the alarm, things could have been a lot worse.

"Well, ye'd better hurry up and find the bastards! Because I'm tellin' yah now, the description my kids gave won't be what they'll be looking like if I get me hands on them first!"

Mammy and Daddy had told the coppers they had not known anyone or any reason why someone would have a grudge against the family. But when the police had left the house, the first person they accused was Uncle Mike because he'd still had the hump over the stolen bag of scrap. When that was eventually ruled out, they blamed Fat Pat, the landlord from the Red Rose, before moving on down the long list of other names who had a grudge against the family.

Martin and Bernie were taken by the police to see Cookie-Eye, so they could personally thank him for helping them. The police had bought a big bunch of flowers and a huge box of chocolates with a red bow tied across the corner for them to give to him, because Daddy had told them, "I couldn't even afford ta buy me wife a Milky Bar and bunch of dandelions, for her birthday! Let alone for a stranger!"

When the pair returned, they told us Cookie-Eye's name was Gordon and described how he had hidden behind his mammy, bawling his eyes out, when he recognised the two visitors to his house. When I heard this, I felt quite sad. And for the first time ever I realised pain came in many different forms and not just from the physical beatings we suffered at the hands of our parents, or strangers, or from the everyday cuts and bruises we sustained throughout our daily lives.

Bernie laughed as she told me how, when Cookie-Eye's mammy had told her ginger-haired son to give them both a big hug for bringing him the chocolates and the flowers, he had completely ignored her, ripping open the box and shoving handfuls of chocolates into his gob like there'd been no tomorrow.

I'd often heard people say, "Time is a good healer," and "They'll soon get over it." Some much quicker than others. The previous summer, when Auntie MaryAnn had married Uncle Frank who wasn't our Uncle Frank until he'd married her, I had seen her sitting on her own at a table, with tears in her eyes. I'd gone over to her and gave her one of my biggest hugs and I'd told her, "Time's a good healer Auntie MaryAnn. You'll soon get over it." She had suddenly burst into fits of laughter, making me feel really good about myself for having cheered her up even though she'd seemed sad about marrying Uncle Frank.

Vowing to myself that I would never ever call Cookie-Eye, Cookie-Eye again, I wished for him to hurry up and find the time to get over the pain we had caused him as well as getting an agreement from the others not to antagonise him ever again.

The following morning, as we sat waiting for our breakfast, Daddy told Martin to kill three chickens and take them to Ali Baba, over at the mosque in Longsight. "An' make sure yah get the money from the tight-fisted cheatin' Jew before ya hand them chickens ta him!" reminded Daddy, plonking hot mugs of dark tea down on the table before making his way back into the kitchen to fetch the bread and dripping.

Mammy managed to crawl out of her bed and walked into the back room, looking bleary-eyed and the worst for wear. She had a lit fag dangling from her gummy mouth, one of the eighty or so she smoked every day. Still in her nightdress, the smell of the perfume Uncle Oliver had given to her as a present was overpowering. She had a habit of spraying the stuff all over her, especially when she was going out, making Daddy exaggerate his normal cough, as well as complaining the stuff was getting into his lungs and killing him.

As always, Mammy stood with her back to the coal fire before hitching up her long nylon nightdress, exposing her bare bum to the flames. She stood there in silence, staring down at the floor as if she had been put into a hypnotic trance, her subconscious mind probably far off to some distant land, where her arse was warm and she didn't have the burden of us to contend with.

When Daddy walked in with the plate of dried bread and the bowl of dripping, Mammy was just lighting her second fag when she'd suddenly given out an almighty shriek, like a scalded cat.

"Ah Jaysus Jim! I'm burning to death!" Mammy's nightdress had suddenly caught alight. She hopped around the room like a wild banshee and we had instinctively thrown our tea at her in our attempts to douse the flames. My tea had hit the radio, which had suddenly stopped working, possibly blowing a valve. Martin's tea had hit Churchill the cat full in the face. After doing a backward somersault, the cat had climbed up the wall, stripping off some of the damp wallpaper as he went, before the deranged animal settled to hang from the top of the net curtains. Luckily for Mammy, everyone else's tea had hit their intended target and the nightdress had been doused out.

"Ah Jim! Jim!" she cried. "Me poor hole!" She was lying on her front with a few little pieces of burnt material stuck to her backside.

"It's out Lizzy! It's out!" said Daddy. "God Jaysus! Didn't I warn yah about standin' close to the poxty feckin' fire!" He set about easing off the pieces of scorched matcrial from her skin. And then, grabbing the bowl of dripping off the table, before we'd even had a chance to use any of it, he rubbed the whole lot of it on to her bare red bum - which meant dry bread for us.

"I'm scarred for life! I'm cursed! I'll be walkin' like a duck and never able sit down agin for the rest of me life!"

"Ah give over will yah!" said Daddy. "It could've been a lot worse." He gave her a gentle pat on the bottom, which had only caused Mammy to howl out all kinds of obscenities at him and us. She cursed everyone barring the Catholic Church, Jesus, the Virgin Mary, and her usual band of favourite saints, His Holiness Pope Paul VI and the Shaw family living at No19, who'd always had the time to lend Mammy a cup of sugar or a few coppers when she hadn't two pennies to rub together, as well as the times Mrs Shaw and her daughter, Anne, had given the family sanctuary when Daddy had wanted to take his temper out on us.

Daddy told us to scarper before Mammy swung for the lot of us, which was a blessing as we could barely hold back our laughter. Paddy and Shamie came out into the yard. It was no surprise that they were not on speaking terms with each other again. Paddy headed straight out through the back gate, without so much as a second glance at us, while Shamie paused briefly to ask what was wrong with the auld woman.

"She caught fire and nearly died of the pain," said Maggie. Our big brother just shrugged his big shoulders before heading off in the opposite direction to Paddy.

Maggie volunteered to take Michael, Kathleen and Gosson to Auntie Brenda's, as she wanted to stay out of the way for as long as she was able. She was not wanting to take responsibility for Nabby. As young as he was, she couldn't handle him. Every time she'd tell him to do something he would refuse to do it, unless it was something he had wanted to do. She said he was more stubborn than a dead donkey. And I suppose, in some way, she was right. But if she had put some effort into finding out the secret to his stubbornness, she would have realised it was simply that you had to ask him to do something for you and not demand it.

Tagging along with us, he helped us to corner the three petrified chickens in the yard. Martin went about cutting their throats with Mammy's serrated bread knife, while I held them down on the wooden cutting block, the same one Daddy had used when he had threatened to chop off my fingers. Normally we would just chop their heads off with the small axe and let them have a run around the yard, until they keeled over with the shock of suddenly realising they'd lost their heads. But Ali Baba's chickens had to have their necks slit, but not cut right off, before being hung up on the hooks to bleed to death.

"Can I have a turn?" asked Nabby.

"Okay," said Martin. "But yah have to be careful not to cut right through its neck." Martin handed him the knife. But our little brother's enthusiasm to show us he was up to the job without any problems caused us a big problem when he cut the neck clean through and the head fell off the chicken.

"Now look what yah done!' moaned Martin. 'We'll have ta get another one. Jaysus! If Daddy finds out we've killed a chicken when there'd been no need, he'll beat the shite outta us!" He certainly would have done, despite the ordeal Martin and Bernie had recently been through.

"Have yah done with the chickens yet?" called Daddy through the open back door, causing Martin to panic and throw the headless chicken over the wall of our next door neighbour's back yard.

"We're just waiting for them to stop bleeding!" I called back.

"Hurry up about it!"

The bald head of Mr Sands, our Welsh neighbour had made a sudden appearance up over his boundary wall. "Would you believe that!" he told the whole of Hulme.

"A flying chicken's just landed in my yard, missing my head by an inch!"

"What's wrong with the two-faced nosey town-crier, who's nothin' better to do than stand starin' out of the window all day long!" shouted Daddy, loud enough for Mr Sands to hear. "Yah can't stop chickens escapin' over the walls now and again. It's their natural instinct."

"Well, perhaps you might like to have a quiet word in their feathery ears and advise them not to cut their heads off before trying to escape to freedom. They'd probably be better at seeing where they were going."

Lucky for us, Daddy hadn't any time for the Welshman and he'd had already gone back into the house, slamming the door behind him so he didn't hear his last rejoinder.

"Yah can keep the chicken for a shillin' if yah like?" offered Martin.

"A shillin' is it? Now that's a bargain! I'd love to have it for a shillin'!" grinned Mr Sands, leaning further over the wall and offering his empty hand out to Martin. "Come on then boyo! Give us the shillin' then!"

Mr Sands laughed at Martin before his bald head disappeared back over his side of the wall.

We set about chasing down another chicken. And with no objections from Nabby, Martin slit its throat open. But with no time to hang the third chicken up to bleed, I volunteered to carry it by its feet, leaving a trail of blood up along the back entry and along the streets for about a mile, until all the blood had drained from it and I slipped the bloodless chicken into a bag.

Ali Baba's shop wasn't a proper shop, in the true sense of the word. Although it looked like one from the outside and was probably once used as a shop, it had nothing inside it to sell. In fact, it was completely bare inside, except for a few small coloured mats spread around on the floor. Stranger still, Mr Ali wore a long white dress and a small circular white cap on his head, but no shoes. Mammy said he was a Himshe, which meant a cross between a man and a woman. Though to us, he didn't look much like a woman, with his long grey straggly beard. Before he would allow us into the shop, he told us to take off our shoes, which we did before handing over the three bagged chickens once he had paid for them. And then we watched in amazement as the large group of beardy shoeless men ambled into his shop. Some were wearing white dresses like Mr Ali and some carried small coloured carpets, like the ones already on the floor. Mr Ali invited the four of us to stay for prayers but the air inside the shop was becoming pungent with the smell of cheesy feet and we had made our excuses not to stay.

"We are good Catholics," said Martin.

"Mammy only lets us pray to St Martin, her favourite saint," said Nabby, "An' we're not all Himshes like yea lot! An' yah wouldn't be catching any of us wearin' them dresses."

"Sister Joseph said we'd be breaking the first

commandment if we'd prayed to false gods," I informed him.

I think Mr Ali's friends were unhappy about something, because they started babbling loudly and pointing their fingers in our direction. Perhaps they thought, we were the cause of the pong? Mr Ali asked us politely to leave and we left quickly, screwing up our faces and holding our noses just to make the point.

CHAPTER 20

Sister Michael in the Buff

Heading across Alexander Road, our first port of call was to the convent of Our Lady of the Cenacle where we would often call in the early afternoon to beg for food. After banging the large metal knocker against the thick oak doors, we stood back and waited patiently for a few minutes. When no-one answered, Martin hammered the knocker against the door continuously for what seemed like an eternity, letting those inside know we were not going away until they'd answered it. Even so, when it was eventually answered there would still be a fifty-fifty chance of getting something to eat, depending on who opened the door to us.

Last time, it had been the Irish witch herself, Sister Michael, the miserable skinny auld walking skeleton of a Mother Superior. "No feckin' wonder she's married herself to God!" said Mammy. "There's not a livin' man that'd go near that, not even the Devil himself!" Without fail, Sister Michael would shoo us off with a wave of her long bony hand while dictating her same boring sermon, word for word.

"The starvin' children of the African nations are more

deservin' than the likes of yea lot of Irish tinkers, with
yer lazy good-for-nothin' fathers who've never worked an
honest day in their miserable lives - save for breedin' like
rabbits! An' yet they still have the means ta go off an' get
drunk every night!"

She also had a few choice words about our mammys:
"With their IQ levels below zero an' the decorum to
match! An' whose idea of a full-time occupation is
forever lyin' on their backs and getting pregnant year
in an' year out, with most of them havin' never seen
their dirty feet since they were children themselves!"
After she'd drawn breath, she'd finish off with her usual
slamming of the door in our faces.

This time, the door had been answered by a fresh-
faced young nun aged around twenty. She smiled, which
was a good sign for us, even if it was an apprehensive
smile as she looked us up and down without saying a
word.

"Is there any food after meals, Holy Sister?" asked
Bernie. The use of the word Holy was deliberately
patronising, acknowledging we recognised her as being
on par with all the saints in heaven and leaving it to the
said individual to prove us wrong, just as the miserable
Mother Superior always did. But unlike the walking
skeleton, the new novice had blushed at the very thought
of being called holy. "I am Sister Rosemary," she said
in a soft, almost timid, Irish voice. "If yea'd like to wait
just there, I will go and see what I can do for yea." She

disappeared behind the door which, to her cost, she left slightly ajar.

To seek out and seize opportunity is a risky business. "But if no-one is prepared to search for opportunities, then the whole world would stop revolving and come to a standstill," said Father Murphy at Sunday Mass. He would also remind us constantly, "Seek and yea shall find." But as he had never set out the criteria as to what it was we were supposed to be seeking and finding, I assumed he was saying, grasp at any opportunity that might arise and which might sustain you in life. In other words, Help Yourself!

Telling Martin and the others to wait outside, I slipped in through the gap in the doorway with every intention of seeking out and finding any opportunities that came my way, being a firm believer in Daddy's own saying, "Finders Keepers".

Hurrying along the hallway's highly polished wooden floor, I tiptoed past an oak-panelled door that was slightly open and I headed down the corridor towards the larger than larger-than-life statue of the Virgin Mary, who was smiling down at the Baby Jesus in her arms. Approaching the statue of Our Lady, I couldn't help but notice the small plain white cardboard money box at her feet. Making the sign of the cross, I bowed my head in respect to Our Lady and her baby, before looking up into her face to see her smiling down at me through her half-closed eyes. And for the briefest of moments, as I had stood looking up at her, I got to wondering what this saintly woman must have been thinking of me, a poor kid, about to steal from under her very nose. Surely, I thought, she wouldn't begrudge me for seeking and finding my opportunity. And the Baby Jesus, all snug and warm and sitting comfortably in his mother's arms and smiling up at her without a care in the world: would he miss a few coppers here or there?

That was when I had heard the inner voice uttering the words, "Take of me as you will. For what is mine, is yours." Although I was unsure as to whether the inner voice was that of Father Murphy or the Divine Lord himself, I was certain it had been the voice of a man, thus ruling out Our Lady. Not that it had really mattered to me who had uttered those divine words. They must have been the words of the Lord Jesus himself and this made me feel all the less guilty when I snatched up the money box and had headed out.

Halfway along the corridor I suddenly heard footsteps up ahead. Stuffing the money box down the front of my trousers and making sure it was safely tucked inside Bernie's pink, flowery knickers, which were the only clean undies I'd been able to find three days earlier, I pressed myself up against an oak-panelled door with a small sign hanging off its handle. Since I couldn't read I didn't know what the sign said, neither did I care. I was much more interested in Sister Rosemary, who appeared in the corridor carrying a large oven dish laden with food. The tantalising aromas wafting in my direction made my mouth water so much I began dribbling from the corners of my mouth. I readied myself to tiptoe out from my hiding place and follow behind her, when a nearby door suddenly creaked wide open. I then had just the two alternatives, either to get caught by whoever had opened the door, or to take another opportunity and turn the handle of the closed door behind me so I could hide until the danger had passed.

Nothing could have prepared me for the sight that met my eyes, when I slipped through into what turned out to be a large bathroom. There, in front of me, was Sister Michael, dripping wet and stark bollock naked! Never having seen a sight like it in all my life, I just couldn't stop my eyes from gawking up and down her wrinkly skeletal body. There wasn't a hair on her head. Not onc strand. She was as bald as a coot. But what she lacked on the top, she made up for down below, with a huge grey beard around her budgie, rising all the way to her belly button. For some obscure reason, it reminded me of the grey-bearded Ronnie Drew, Mammy's favourite singer from the Dubliners. And I could bet if either Paddy or Shamie had been cursed with the opportunity of standing where I was standing, they would not have wanted to write home about her saggy breasts, which looked like lumps of lead in a pair of nylon socks.

"Lord have mercy!" cried the stunned Sister, cupping said bosoms in her hands.

I had a feeling that the shock of seeing me looking her up and down might have filled her with indecision, because she let go of her upper bits and covered up her budgie with her hands, before cupping up her bosoms again, then letting them droop and covering up her budgie again. She could easily have slung her drooping breasts over her shoulder and out of sight, thus saving herself a lot of stress.

"Don't yah be thinkin' of gettin' that thing out yah dirty little divil yah!" she hollered at me.

I hadn't a clue what the crazy nun was going on about until I followed her gaze downwards to the large bulge in the front of my trousers. I wondered how she could have known I had the money box down there in the first place, let alone why I should want to get it out and let her see it, after having gone through all the trouble of getting it for myself. Well, she wasn't having any of it and I tapped the bulge with my hand, giving the auld witch a knowing smile, just to let her know it was all mine. And that was when she started to holler all kinds of obscenities at me, before picking up a large brown lump of carbolic soap, about the size of half a brick and hurling it straight at me, missing my head by a whisker. I managed to hurry out of the bathroom and back into the main hall as a smaller lump of soap whizzed past my left ear. And it was here, in the main hall, where I suddenly found myself confronted by a huge nun.

Short, fat and snarling, she reminded me of Mick

McManus, the famous wrestler. She stood with her shoulders hunched and her legs apart, her huge hands, the size of dinner plates, dangling at the end of tree-trunk arms, which I imagined were just waiting to trap me in a bear hug and crush me half to death, before picking me up and slamming me back down to the ground and bending my legs all the way back over my head in a full Nelson...

Looking past the huge nun, I was able to catch a glimpse of the others through the open front door. Bernie and Sister Rosemary were in a tug of war with the tray of food and I could only assume the young nun must have had a change of heart and had decided to keep the food for herself, while my - now less pious - sister Bernie cursed her with every swear word she could think of. It was only after Nabby took the initiative and stamped on the poor nun's left foot that she let go of the tray, sending Bernie flying backwards onto her bum, amazingly without spilling any of the food.

I turned to see Sister Michael wrapped in a big white towel, rushing towards me and hollering something about castrating sex maniacs, "No matter how little they were!" or words to that effect.

She obviously hadn't seen the small lump of carbolic soap on the floor until she stepped on it, skating freestyle on the one leg before colliding into me, with the pair of us ending up on the floor in a heap. When she finally dragged herself up off me, I found myself staring up at the Mick McManus lookalike standing above me as she suddenly grabbed one of my legs.

I conjured up this terrible thought of her swinging me around her head and bashing my head on all four walls, like Daddy had done to the cat. But Martin, my hero, came to my rescue again. Running into the hallway, he kicked the unsuspecting nun right up her backside.

Leaving the wailing nun dancing around on her tiptoes, we scurried off back up along the Convent's cinder path, with Bernie leading the way whilst holding firmly on to the tray of food. We rushed out through the main gates and headed straight across Alexandra Road towards the park. I don't recall which sound came first, the car horn or the screeching of the brakes, as the black cab had borne down on our sister, hitting her.

I saw two wood pigeons fly off the branch of one of the huge trees in Alexandra Park and swoop straight over our heads. I heard Martin and Nabby scream louder than I had ever heard them scream before. And then I heard the people around us shouting and crying. All except for me. I wanted to scream. I'd tried to scream out a warning but it just wouldn't come out. I'd seen the look of terror in Bernie's eyes just before she was hit when she looked across at me and I had known I was helpless to do anything for her.

A dead leaf floated down from a tree and landed next to my sister's still body lying in a heap in the middle of the road. All three of us rushed to her side where strangers were already flocking around her like vultures. A black man was on his knees stroking my sister's hand. Incensed, Martin shouted at him to leave her alone. The man was sobbing uncontrollably and told Martin and anyone else listening, "She ran straight out in front of me!"

We stood emotionless just looking down on our sister, not knowing what to say or do. There were many tears from the strangers gathered around Bernie, but there were no tears from us. We had wanted to pick her up and take her home, but we knew we couldn't do this, as off in the distance we could hear the sirens. Looking over in the direction of the convent gates, the distraught Sister Rosemary, followed by the Mick McManus lookalike, rushed out of the main gates and across in our direction, where they fell to their knees down by the black man, who was still holding Bernie's hand. And Sister Rosemary then blessed herself with the sign of the cross before praying over Bernie's prone body.

Picking the metal oven dish up off the ground, I automatically began retrieving the cooked sausages and roast potatoes. An old woman picked up two sausages and had placed them into the dish and I thanked her. A man picked some of the roast potatoes up and had placed those into the dish and then someone else did likewise. I'd thanked each one in turn and I thought of how Sister Joseph and Sister Gertrude must have felt saying all those Thank yeas, when passing the collection plates up and down the aisles and the people putting their money in them.

Once all the food had been retrieved I'd made my way back over to Martin and Nabby who were standing over the two nuns still kneeling at Bernie's side. "As we won't be needin' it now, yah can give it to the starvin' children of Africa!" I thrust the oven dish full of gritty food into Sister Rosemary's hands and she suddenly burst into tears.

CHAPTER 21

When the Sh** Hits the Fan

Daddy and the black man walked back along the hospital corridor in our direction. Daddy was carrying a huge black doll which the man had bought for Bernie and which Daddy had later sold on to the rag and bone man for three shillings. "Apart from a broken arm and a few scratches, she's goin' to be fine," he told us. We were overjoyed that our little sister would be back shoplifting and collecting firewood and scrap metal with us very soon.

Daddy introduced the black man to us. He was the driver of the cab that had hit Bernie. "Samuel says Bernie just ran out in front of him and he wasn't able to stop in time."

"She looked right and left and right agin before crossin'!" lied Martin.

"Bernie never looks anywhere ta see what's comin'," said Daddy. "She walks straight out in the road and expects all the feckin' traffic ta suddenly stop dead in their tracks just for her!" It was true, but that wasn't the point.

The man, called Samuel, gave us a big white smile but we fixed him with accusing eyes, which he took as his cue to leave, promising Daddy he would come to visit Bernie at the house, which he did a few times, until Daddy got into a drunken row with him and accused him of deliberately trying to murder his little daughter. I think he must have been after another doll to sell.

"Yea lot have ta see the doctor," said Daddy. "As yah might all be in a state of shock without knowing it. Though yah don't look any different ta me." He waited outside the examination room as all three of us marched in and stood in front of the long desk, gawking open-mouthed at the sight of the chocolate-skinned midget sitting behind it. We'd seen the odd midget now and again, but never a black one, so it came as a bit of a surprise to us all. Just as surprising to me was the reminder that the money box was still hidden down my trousers, it having slipped my mind until one of its hard edges dug into my soft dangly bits.

"Well, you all seem to be very undernourished and anaemic," said the little doctor. His observations did not really impress any of us, considering we always looked pale and hungry. He seemed to pay particular attention to me and asked, with his eyes dropping down to the bulge in my trousers, "Is there anything you would like to share with me?"

"No!" I said firmly. Jaysus, they were all at it! "I don't have anythin' I'd like ta be sharin' with yah!"

"Well, if you wouldn't mind going behind the curtain, I'll examine you first."

"Can't yah examine me brother Martin first?" I suggested. "He's the eldest, and the eldest always goes first."

Martin was pretty peeved with my suggestion and stood there scowling at me, but the doctor was adamant it was me he wanted to examine first. And so I hurried behind the curtain, hoping I'd be able to whip out the money box and hide it somewhere before the doctor came around the curtains. But I never got the chance, because the little dwarf was right behind me, breathing down my neck.

"Right," he said. "If you would like to undo your trousers and slip them down around your knees." He kept his eyes firmly fixed on my bulge.

Reluctantly I slipped down my trousers to reveal Bernie's pink pair of flowered knickers. And it was just as he was peering down them, that I had suddenly noticed the smiling faces of Martin and Nabby peeping up at me from underneath the curtain.

"Hmm? That is the most odd-looking penis you have there," said the doc. He was just slipping his podgy little hand down to investigate the cause of my bulge as the curtain suddenly flew along its rail to reveal my Daddy, eyes blazing and red-faced with anger.

"Yah big feckin' perverted leprechaun yah!" he bellowed, before his fist made contact with the doctor's mouth, the force knocking the little fellow straight across the floor. "What has playin' with me son's flute got to do with shock!" he raged. Martin and Nabby rushed to the door, ready to run if Daddy had completely lost it.

"Git yer kecks up Tommy!" ordered Daddy, before turning on the doctor, who was on all fours. "Y'er a disgrace to this profession, so y'are!"

"Please let me explain Mr Rhattigan! I'd noticed your son had an unusual bulge in his trousers and -"

"- yah wanted ta have a good feel around with him, did yah? Yah dirty fecking homo ya!" Daddy landed a few good kicks up the doctor's backside, as the midget scurried away across the examination room, managing to take refuge under his desk. "Go on! Git back to Alexander Park where yah feckin' belong with all the other bush perverts!"

"But Mr Rhattigan -"

"Don't be buttin' me!" bellowed Daddy. "I'll feckin' see yea'll never work in a circus, let alone a feckin' hospital again!"

The doctor insisted he wanted charges of assault and battery brought against Daddy. But, as the little doc had his mouth fixed by another doctor, Daddy warned them, "When the shite hits the fan, some of it will always stick - him being a midget and all." We never heard another word said about the incident after that, apart from Daddy being told he wasn't welcome at the hospital again, barring emergencies.

Martin once used the same tactic on Father Duggan, from St Anne's church over in Longsight when the old priest caught the pair of us in his church, attempting to force open the metal cover of the wall offertory box with a rusty old butter knife. At the time, the priest had been in the company of John Carson, a plump twelve-year-old we knew from Shamie's gang. Carson, with his bloated red face, had seemed a bit awkward when he had first seen us and hurried out of the church without so much as a hello or goodbye.

When he'd called after Carson to remind him that his next Bible lesson was 'Three o'clock next Friday", Father Duggan turned to us and spewed out his bile on our sinful desecration of his church and how we would be forever damned in hell's fire.

"Once the shite hits the fan some of it sticks!' said Martin, with me adding a knowing wink.

To our amazement, the flustered Father Duggan pushed his hand under his cassock and produced a half-crown, which he held out to Martin whilst demanding that we get out of his church and never to show our demon faces in it again.

It couldn't have been long after this when I tried the same tactic on Sister Joseph. At the time, she was about to give me three whacks of the ruler in front of the whole class, for calling that bastard Paul Morgan a bastard. I just couldn't understand why calling him a bastard was wrong in the eyes of God. I'd been called it so often, it had become more familiar to me than my first name. And once, when we were walking up along Philips

Street, where Morgan lived, his mammy had suddenly come to her front door and had shouted out to him in her foghorn voice, "Git in here, yah little bastard!", so I couldn't really see what his problem was to be snitching on me to the nuns. Anyway, Sister Joseph was having no excuses and so, as I had held my hand out to her I'd looked her straight in her good eye and warned, "Just remember Sister, once I've shit on the fan it'll stick all over yah," or words to that effect. Besides the class erupting into fits of laughter, the old dragon gave me an extra three whacks for my insolence.

Home from the hospital, we waited until Daddy had headed off to the pub before I finally relieved myself of the bulge in my trousers. Bernie had to stay in the hospital overnight, just so as they could check to see if she'd suffered any damage to her brain (though Daddy said, he wouldn't be able to tell the difference anyhow).

Having agreed between the three of us to spend whatever money there was in the box on goodies for Bernie, Martin and Nabby peered eagerly over my shoulder to get a better look as I tore it open and tipped the contents out on the table top. Three halfpennies, two farthings, fourteen black buttons and five Irish shillings! "The tight-arsed auld witches!" cursed Martin.

"Jaysus! It's a collection for Sister Bernadette's retirement!" laughed Maggie, who had come into the back room and read the side of the money box. "She wouldn't have been gettin' far on that lot!"

"Neither are we!" said Martin. "We were going to get something for Bernie! Ah feck it! We'll just have to go and see what we can steal for her."

"I was just on me way inta the city, if yah want ta tag along with me?" offered Maggie, knowing full well she would have a better chance of getting what she wanted if we were there as a distraction for her. She tried to make it clear to us that she was in charge and although Nabby didn't give out too much, he had made it clear to our big sister that she wasn't in charge of him. Needing us more than we needed her, she didn't argue and our journey on foot into the city was a reasonably peaceful one.

I'm not sure if it was something about the way we had walked or talked, or whether it was just my imagination, but there was something definitely odd about the people who worked in the city's large department stores. They never seemed to smile, at least not when we walked through their doors! It had always seemed to me, our very presence had an impact on these people as all eyes would automatically roll upwards, quickly followed by their noses!

We'd been taught one old proverb, amongst a lot of other old proverbs, that said, "Never judge a book by its cover." It seemed that this didn't apply to the likes of us. Just because our clothing was old and grubby and ill-fitting and falling apart, it didn't mean we didn't have two pennies to rub together. And if we'd actually had two pennies to rub together, surely our money would have been just as good as anyone else's? If we'd been minded to spend it, instead of helping ourselves to what we wanted...

It hadn't been too difficult spotting the two store detectives pretending to be a married couple out shopping, considering the pair of them were pointing straight at us from the top of the escalators, before rushing down them in our direction. How we loved the challenge of the chase! To us, this was just another game of cat and mouse. Only the two chasing cats were more like a pair of stout bulldogs. We took the lift up to the clothing department where we spent a few minutes swiftly choosing new outfits before we bundled into the changing rooms and changed into our new clothes, leaving our old rags in one neat pile on the floor. As we followed Maggie back towards the lift, I wondered whether anyone would recognise us as being the same children who had walked in a short while earlier. But no one, it seemed, paid us any particular attention as we hurried along one of the aisles, with Maggie plucking some blouses off the hangers and stuffing them inside her new yellow polka-dot blouse. She followed up with three packs of ladies' knickers, four brassieres and a handful of woolly gloves. She was attempting to squeeze a pair of pink slacks down her already full skirt, when Martin shouted the warning.

"Scram! We're corrupt!"

The two store detectives were on to us. As they

hurried along the aisle in our direction, we immediately separated, Martin and me in one direction, Nabby and Maggie in another. Using one of our diversion tactics, Martin snatched a red blouse off its hanger and, in full view of the two detectives, stuffed it up inside his new green jumper before we dashed off into the large furniture department. With the two bulldogs in hot pursuit of us, Nabby and Maggie made good their escape, knowing we would be meeting up with them shortly.

"In here," said Martin and I followed after him into the large wardrobe, closing the doors behind us.

"How can the little sods just vanish into thin air?" said the female voice between heavy breaths.

Said the male voice: "The little bastards always manage to give us the slip!"

CHAPTER 22

Jesus in a Campervan

Bernie was soon out of the hospital. The doctor said, "Except for the slight limp, which should go away with time, she seems as normal as she is ever going to be." For her homecoming treat we had boiled goose eggs which Daddy had stolen and looked twice as big as the swans' eggs he'd stolen for us the previous Christmas and which he said he would never steal for us again because we had complained so much about the stench of them.

After our goose eggs, we could hear Mammy talking at the front door with Mrs Gough, who lived on one of the streets up near the bathhouse in Leaf Street. We'd known it was Mrs Gough without even having to set eyes on her, because when she laughed it sounded just like a demented donkey. She had large stained teeth, which Daddy once said, were like the keys on an old piano. I thought her browny-green teeth were more like the teeth of the donkeys at Belle Vue, which you could ride for threepence.

I remember that little jerk Jonathan McGee riding the donkeys there. He'd had enough money to buy the whole fecking donkey, let alone pay for him and all his chums

to ride them! I'd never been able to see what enjoyment
he could actually get out of riding a stinking, flea-ridden,
hee-hawing donkey - except to show off to his friends. I
was also incensed with the little weasel when he'd offered
to share a donkey ride with Cathy McCarthy. "Oh my
sweet dar-link Jon-a-thon! That's very kand of you to
pay for dear Cath-ay, to rade with you!" said the snooty-
nosed Mrs McGee in her best plum-in-the-gob voice.
Well Cath-ay didn't get to rade the feckin' donkey with
or without the dear sweet darlink Jon-a-thon. Though
the creep did get the ride of a lifetime and one that he
hadn't bargained on.

I always carried a tiny penknife around with me, which
had its many uses, such as unscrewing the tiny brass
screws of the window catches and brass doorknobs in
derelict houses; cutting worms in half so it would rain
(and it did work, no matter how long it took for the
heavens to open up); cutting away the chewing gum we
had pressed up into the "return" slot of public telephone
boxes to block any of the returned monies to its rightful
owners. And last but not least: sticking it in a donkey's
arse when you want it to bolt off with a big jerk sitting on
its back.

Mrs Gough was laughing at one of her own jokes
as Martin, Nabby, Bernie and me made our way out
through the front door.

"Where yea off ta?" asked Mammy.

"School," said Martin, which, for some unknown

reason, had Mrs Gough in fits of hysterical laughter. We could still hear her hee-hawing as we turned the corner at the longest end of Stamford Street, heading off in the opposite direction from the school. With Halloween approaching, we wanted to get our costumes in as early as possible, so we could go off on our begging sprees in the guise of Trick Or Treat. But when we got to Woolworths, we were disappointed to find they were out of stock, though we had been informed by one of the assistants that thc Longsight store still had plenty.

On most occasions we walked the route, but because of Bernie's limp we'd decided to catch the bus into Longsight. How we were going to pay for the fare was something we would only think about when, and if, the bus conductor came asking. Planning something in advance wasn't something we were particularly good at, finding it much easier to think on our feet and on the spur of the moment rather than confuse ourselves with trying to follow a set plan. The only plan we ever did have on any given journey was to pick a landmark to meet back at if we ever became separated.

Walking was our preference, mainly because we could see more on foot. It was the not knowing what was just around the corner that made our travels all the more exciting. The streets of Manchester had much to offer its children like us. Though not quite feral, we were often called "Fucking animals!". We didn't miss the warmth of a mother's hug or the kind words from a father, or the pampering and kisses outside the school gates, or the "Happy Birthday to You", because we had never experienced such things. And the only difference between us and those kids who had experienced all those things was the fact that we could survive without them. People were just a hindrance to our lives and, if push had come to shove, we could easily have survived off the streets, alone and without any human contact apart from each other.

When the black bus conductor came up the stairs for the fares I reached inside my trouser pocket and pulled out the foreign coins I'd stolen from the convent a while back.

"Yagga googa pleezy!" I handed the coins to the conductor with no clue as to what foreign language I was talking in. And neither, it had seemed, did he.

"Yagga googa? What sort of language is that man?"

"We A - fri - ca."

"Africa! You lot! You're not even black. Well, apart from the dirt."

"A - fri - ca," said Nabby, getting in on the act.

"Ok then. What part of Africa do you come from?"

"The coldest part," said Nabby, quick as a flash. The three of us could only glare at him.

"The coldest part? That's why you're white! I like it!" laughed the conductor. "So you're able to speak some English then? At least the little white African fella can?"

We said nothing and sat staring blankly up at him.

"Okay, if I'm to believe you're all from Africa - and there's no reason to disbelieve you - how much are these Irish coins worth? So I know what change I have to give you back?"

"Two shillings," I said.

"Five shillings," said Martin.

"Ten shillings," said Nabby. Bernie had opted to shake her head at us and say nothing.

"Right! If the inspector gets on the bus, you lot get off it, okay?" The conductor gave us a smile as he slipped the two Irish coins into his jacket pocket.

"Did we have any change to come out of that?" Only Nabby had the cheek to ask.

"Yagga googa!" came the swift reply.

Standing outside the Woolworths store in Longsight, we agreed between us, it was better to go in one at a time so as not to bring any suspicion upon ourselves. Martin was first, coming out a few minutes later with a skeleton outfit stuck down his trousers. I went in next and bagged myself one of the two remaining skeleton outfits, which I hid up under the armpit of my jumper. Bernie and Nabby went in together, coming out moments later with Bernie having bagged the last skeleton outfit and Nabby, sulking as usual, having to make do with one of the last two remaining witch's outfit. He argued, "As Bernie is the girl, she should be the Witch."

"The last of the two witch's outfits were too small for me to wear, Nabby, as well yah know! Anyways, my nickname's Skeleton."

"Well yah don't need a costume then, do yah!"

On our way out of Longsight we donned our costumes, leaving off the masks, not that Nabby had needed one, before hitching a lift back home. A campervan pulled up.

"Hi guys! Which cemetery are you from!"

"We're just heading there," said Martin, walking over to the smiling young man with shaggy hair in the front passenger seat.

"Are yea Jesus?" asked Bernie.

"You've found me!" laughed the man, introducing the young pregnant driver as his wife Mary! He'd offered us a lift to anywhere we had wanted to go and without any hesitation we hopped into the back of the van.

"So where is this cemetery of yours?' asked Jesus.

"Hulme," said Martin.

"It's not a real cemetery," said Bernie.

"It's worse," I added.

"Have you two ha'pennies for a penny?" asked Nabby, holding out the penny.

"Don't be askin that!" scolded Martin. But Jesus just laughed it off as he rolled himself a cigarette and lit it, before taking a deep drag and then putting the fag into Mary's gob as she drove along.

The whiff from their cigarette smoke was nothing like the suffocating smoke from Mammy and Daddy's cigarettes, which sometimes had us in coughing fits, especially when the whole family were together smoking inside the house, which forced us outside into the back yard. The smell of their smoke was so different, even nice!

"Look Martin!' Bernie suddenly pointed through the van window as we headed down the Stretford Road past the Eagle pub. "That's them two bastards that hurt us!" But by the time we looked, all we saw as the van drove past was the back of a fella walking up the big step into the pub.

"Are yah sure it was them, Bernie?"

"I'm as sure as I'm sittin' here Martin! I swear ta God it was them two!" Bernie was so adamant we couldn't just ignore her, or the tears that welled in her eyes.

Martin promised he would tell Daddy the second we walked into the house. For the rest of the journey, we listened in silence as Jesus told us stories of their travels to distant lands such as Scotland, Wales, Liverpool, London, Margate, and now Manchester. By the time we were dropped off, I'd got this notion in my head that one day I, too, would go on an adventure to these far-off places.

"What name do you think we should call our new baby?" asked Jesus as we climbed out of the van. Bernie suggested Joseph was a nice name and Martin said Moses was much better. I said Tommy was the best name of all and Nabby said, "Have yah got two ha'pennies for a penny?"

"Yah shouldn't be begging off people who have just helped us Nabby," said Martin. "It's not right."

"Don't ever be afraid of asking for anything," advised Jesus, "or you'll never get anything. And even if you don't get anything, at least you asked." To our surprise, Jesus reached into his inside coat pocket and brought out a pound note, which he handed to Nabby. "Keep the penny," he smiled and then gave us a wave as the van drove off.

CHAPTER 23

Trick or Treat

After donning our Halloween costumes and Bernie making up Nabby's face with some green eye shadow she found in Mary's make-up bag, we hung around the house for a little while longer, waiting for Daddy or Shamie to come home with the news they'd found the two bastards who had beaten Martin and Bernie.

"There'd be more chance of the cat walkin' in off the street with a rat up his hole than seein' them two before the night is out," said Mammy.

We made our way down into Philips Street before we started knocking on the doors. We never had a set list of tricks to play on anyone that refused to give us a treat and were just content as usual to do things on the spur of the moment. One of our favourites was making a poo parcel and setting it alight on the doorstep, before knocking on the door again and then, from a safe distance, watching the occupier stamp out the fire. Coating a door handle with dog turd, or shoving a banger through the letter box were other silly little things we did. I loved being out in the dark, especially late at night, when there was hardly anyone about. Hulme in the dark belonged to us.

It always baffled me how people could stand at a window, peering out through their net curtains while pretending not to be in. After about an hour, we stopped for a quick tot-up of what we had collected in the old metal treat bucket. This amounted to three pennies, two stale fairy cakes, a Blackjack sweet, a sweet wrapper wrapped around other sweet wrappers to make it look like a sweet, a silver medallion of the Virgin Mary, nine assorted biscuits, most of them broken as they had been thrown in the bucket before front doors were closed quickly in our faces.

Turning the dark corner into Daisy Street, we bumped into Frankenstein and his strange floozy friend. They frightened the lives out of the lot of us, barring Bernie, who immediately recognised our two older cousins, Paddy and Francis Doherty.

"Why haven't yah dressed up for Halloween, Paddy?" Bernie asked him, all seriously, which had us all in stitches except Paddy.

"Who's the laughing floozy with yah?" joked Martin.

"I'm a Zombie! Not a feckin' floozy!" protested Francis. But disguised in his mammy's blonde wig, with his eyes coated in black eye shadow along with his reddened cheeks and lips, he looked more like a floozy than himself.

"Jaysus," said Paddy, "we've been on the go for ages and nothin' ta show for it so far! We've had the usual threats an' the one large welly, which some auld miserable bastard from number thirty-three slung at us. But that's about all."

"Why'd he go and do that?" asked Martin.

"We stuck a couple of lit bangers through his letterbox for wastin' our time, we weren't ta know the eejit was standin' behind the door."

"What's the point of keepin' the one welly, when yah can only put it on one foot?" asked Nabby.

"It's a left-footed wellie," said Bernie, "and as he only has the one left foot he can only wear it on the left foot."

"But even if he'd had the two left feet, he can only wear the wellie on the one foot!" argued Nabby.

"He could cut off the toe end and wear it on any of his feet," I said smugly.

"What good's a welly if water can get in?" countered Francis.

"Anyway, we're keepin' the welly just in case we get another one thrown at us," said Paddy, "and then we'll have the pair."

"Unless yah get another left one!" laughed Nabby.

Sitting down together on the cold ground underneath a gas lamp, we shared out all the biscuits between the six of us. I bit into one of the fairy cakes and nearly broke a front tooth, so I handed it over to cousin Paddy, who shoved the whole lot into his gob and devoured it in one go. I gave him the other one.

It seemed strange sitting in the cool night air, with the

silence around us almost deafening. The mist by now had dropped to cover the grey damp rooftops, though it was still possible to see the dark grey smoke spewing out of chimney pots from those fires that had been lit. I'd no clue as to the time. And even if I had, it wouldn't have mattered to me because time meant nothing to any of us. We only knew the time by the space between different events. Getting up in the mornings, having school dinners, going to church, begging on the streets, searching for scrap or firewood. I had always felt much safer and more at ease at night, more so than at any other given time. Perhaps because there was hardly another soul about, except maybe other children like us. And it was much easier for me to escape from the harsh realities of life hidden under a thick blanket of darkness.

"Shall we see if the auld bastard will give us the other wellie?" asked Martin, breaking the silence, "He might throw the other one at us if we annoy him long enough! And then Paddy will have a pair!"

We all thought Martin's idea was a good one, they usually were! Save for that time the pair of us were seen in the early hours of the morning, rummaging through the milk float parked inside the Allied Dairies yard up on Mulberry Road. Like the little early birds so often did, we had been helping ourselves to the creamy tops from the milk bottles to tide us over for the day. But just as we had got to our seventh or eighth bottle, we'd been spotted by a couple of milkmen who had headed over in our direction, only for my clever brother to quickly come up with his idea.

"Sit tight!" he'd shouted, before slamming his foot hard down on the pedal and driving the float out of the main gates of the dairy!

I'd screamed across at Martin, "How the feck do yah know how ta drive one of these tings!"

"Easy, it's just like driving them bumper cars at Belle Vue! One pedal for the accelerator and one pedal for the brake!" Only he'd forgotten to use the brakes at least twenty-three times, which, according to the arresting police officer, was the amount of cars we hit before we'd come to an abrupt halt outside the Mulberry Street Primary School.

Another of Daddy's sayings was, "There's no use crying over spilt milk," and I'd wished he could have been with us at the time, if only to have told this to the lynch mob who'd had us surrounded. If it hadn't been for Mrs Regan, the headmistress of the school, coming to our rescue and waiting with us until the police arrived, we'd probably have been strung up! So we were grateful to her and the fact she hadn't been aware at the time that her car was the fourth we'd hit on the way down to her school!

Martin led us back along Daisy Street to number thirty-three. He told Paddy and Francis to wait with Bernie and Nabby across the street, warning them to be ready to make a run for it if needs be, while him and me went to the front door. I'd only just knocked when the door swung open, as if the smiling man on the other side of it had been expecting us. But instead of getting the verbal abuse we were anticipating, along with, hopefully the other wellie, he seemed really pleased to see us!

"Just wait there while I get you a nice treat," he said, before hurrying off back along the narrow corridor in his bare feet. I spotted the lone wellie standing just inside the front door.

We smiled across at our bemused cousins. Before long, the man reappeared with the barrel of an air rifle pointing straight at us.

"Here's your treat you little fuckers!"

I'd never seen Martin move so quickly. I snatched up the spare wellie just as the man fired off a shot. It obviously missed me because I felt no pain as I ran off down the street, following the two skeletons, the witch, the floozy and Frankenstein, who was hollering something about having been killed.

Outside the coalyard, Paddy was holding his nose. His brother Francis had taken some old newspaper out of a rubbish bin and had walked in to the shadows of the alleyway.

"Here's the other wellie!" I threw it on the ground next to the other one.

"I've been feckin' shot!" moaned Paddy. "The bastard has killed me!"

"Where'd he get yah?" asked Bernie.

"Me hooter! Just get a look at it!"

"Take your mask off and let me see it then!"

"I've taken me feckin' mask off!" screamed Paddy. "Are yah sayin' I'm ugly are yah, Bernie?"

"Course I'm not saying that! Who told yah that?" asked Bernie.

"Yah recognised me with the mask on."

"That's only because I'd recognised yer voice - and the way yah walked."

"I was walking like feckin' Frankenstein!"

"Hold still and let me see yer nose."

Unable to hold back our laughter, Martin, me and Nabby walked over to the entrance of the alleyway where we saw Francis take his last four bangers out of his pockets and stick them, like candles into a birthday cake, into the warm turd he had just deposited. Then he wrapped the whole lot up into a tidy poo parcel.

We waited in the shadows and, with a heaving fog slowly rolling towards us, watched Francis as he dropped to his knees outside number thirty-three. A moment later, we saw the sudden flash of yellow light and him giving the front door a couple of good heavy kicks before the blanket of thick fog engulfed him. We heard the first two bangs go off followed by a loud shout, "Ahh! My fuckin' foot!" instantly followed by the sound of grotesque laughter and then Francis, like a scary vision, suddenly appearing out of the gloom.

"I think I blew his foot right off his leg!" he said happily.

As we hurried off, we heard a third bang and more

shouting, only stopping when we had reached Dixon Street, where our two cousins lived.

We promised Paddy, if he should die of lead poisoning during the night, we'd say a prayer for him at Sunday Mass. He'd told us to feck off, telling Bernie he didn't like her anymore because she'd said he was ugly. Bernie said, "If yah take yer mask off I'll give yah a peck on the cheek." This only infuriated Paddy more because he wasn't wearing the mask.

Not long after leaving our two cousins, we became lost to the thick murky-yellow smog, which we had never seen as bad before. We couldn't even see a hand in front of our faces. Martin said to hold hands tightly so we didn't lose each other. And there we were, three skeletons and a witch walking in a straight line, not able to see or be seen.

We listened out in the eerie silence for the odd muffled sounds, attempting to follow in the direction we thought they'd came from. But we had been too disorientated and found it impossible to concentrate. Ghostly figures crossed our paths and as we reached out to them for help, they shrugged us off. Then we suddenly heard the voice of our guardian angel: "Pavement! Bus on the road!" Out of the smog, the dimmest of lights from a ghostly red giant was inching in our direction to save our sorry souls. "Bus on the road! Pavement!" The conductor's voice continuously called out his warnings to the unseen pedestrians as he walked along the edge of the pavement, letting the bus driver know where the wheels of his bus were so he was able to safely drive along the edge of it. Following the voice, we safely navigated our way to the bus and settled ourselves on the top deck.

I watched Nabby, Martin and Bernie fall asleep and with nothing for me to see out of the windows, I got to wondering if purgatory, as described by Father Murphy, could have been like this. Just moving around in the thick smog hearing voices but unable to see a thing, with nothing else to do but bump into each other until St Peter decided to open the gates of heaven and let us in to meet with the rest of our dearly departed. If any of us were allowed in.

CHAPTER 24

Bible Lessons

A couple of days had passed since Daddy, Paddy and Shamie, along with our uncles, had taken Martin and Bernie - with me tagging along - down the Stretford Road to the Eagle pub on the off-chance they might be able to spot the two fellas who had beaten them up. They'd been back to the pub three times and had not been able to match the description Martin and Bernie had given to Daddy.

But this time they got their chance. Mick O'Brien, a fella Daddy had known for a long while, gave Daddy the names of Pat and Jimmy Boyd as likely possibilities.

"This is just between me and yea Jim. If their father Cliff gets wind it was me that told yah, I'll be dead for sure".

"Well I'll be sayin nothin' to no one so don't worry!" assured Daddy.

"Some while back now, I heard the pair of them talkin' in here with some of their friends," said O'Brien. "They were bragging on about givin' a hiding to a couple of Paddys up near St Wilfrid's Church. Sweet Jaysus, if I'd known it was two defenceless little children, I'd have said something earlier." O'Brien seemed genuinely shocked. "Cliff and the rest of that family are over there in the corner," he said, with a slight nod of his bald head. Then he warned, "Yea have to be careful. The whole lot of them are feckin lunatics! An' believe it or not, that wife of his is the worst outta the lot of them. She won't have a bad word said about any of her brood."

"Have a pint on us," offered Daddy by way of thanks, though he did not stay at the bar to pay for it. Instead, he and the rest of the family headed over in the direction of the Boyds who were sitting in the corner, chatting amongst themselves.

"Which one of yea is Cliff Boyd?" asked Daddy, stopping a few feet away from the table. Martin, Bernie and me had stayed back hiding near the piano and behind our brother Paddy, while Shamie, always wanting to be in the mix, had stood alongside Uncles Oliver and Christy at Daddy's left shoulder, with Uncles Paddy and Raphael on his right flank.

"An' who is it that wants ta know, Paddy?" said Helen Boyd. While she glared at Daddy, her husband Cliff sat looking us all up and down with a grin on his face.

"I think yea'd better put yer falsies in Jock!" retorted Daddy, "I can't understand a word yer sayin'! An' the name's Jim fuckin' Rhattigan ta yea!"

"Well y'er all fuckin' Paddys ta me!"

"Aye, an' yea should know! Yea've charged plenty of them for your services I wouldn't wonder!"

"I'm not sittin' here listening ta this!" Helen Boyd was up on her feet, which was the cue for the rest of her family, about eight in all, to stand. Two women and six fellas, and not much difference in size, except for Cliff Boyd, who was probably about the same height as Daddy and my uncles but much wider across the shoulder, with a huge beer belly almost bursting out of his shirt. He looked like someone who could handle himself if the need arose.

"Are yah goin ta tell us what all this is about then? Or do we have ta beat it out of yah!" threatened Cliff Boyd.

"Like yah beat feckin' innocent little children!" said Daddy.

"Now just yea fuckin' wait -"

"Aye! I'm talkin' about yer two poxty-eyed sons that beat me two little children senseless. I just want yah ta know, I'll be feckin' swinging for the pair of them when I git me hands around their scrawny Scotch necks!"

Shamie landed the first punch that started the brawl that had caused the whole pub to erupt into a free-for-all. I saw him crack a beer bottle over Helen Boyd's head as she pushed her way past some of her family to get at Daddy, while holding in her hand a carving knife as long as a sword. Then I was smacked with a punch I didn't see coming. It turned my legs to jelly and, as I hit the deck, I saw thousands of stars dancing in front of my eyes, before the hands came around my neck and squeezed the living daylights out of me. Martin later told me how big brother Paddy had dragged the man off me then half kicked him to death, only stopping when Uncle Christy grabbed hold of Paddy and pulled him outside.

But, as usual after a big brawl, some people liked to tell it the way they had wanted to see it and said Cliff Boyd had thrown the first punch, knocking Daddy clean out. Someone else said it was the mother, Helen Boyd, who knocked Daddy out with a single punch. Uncle Christy told us how Uncle Oliver had called the whole family of Boyds, a "bunch of feckin' blue-nosed child-battering bastards", before knocking Cliff Boyd out with just the one left hook straight up his hooter.

But at the end of the day it didn't matter who had said what, or who had thrown the first punch. The end results were still the same. The pub was wrecked and there were lots of broken heads, while Cliff Boyd had ended up playing the piano with his face. Not surprisingly, there were no arrests because, as usual, no-one had seen a thing. And Daddy, still incensed by the fact he had still not got hold of Pat and Jimmy Boyd, warned the family that matters hadn't ended until he got his revenge.

The following day our youngest sister, Kathleen, had rushed in off the street to tell Mammy, "Father Murphy an' Sister Joseph are comin' up the street!"

"Did yah all go ta church on Sunday?" asked Mammy. Half of us said, "We had," and the other half said, "We'd not."

"Oh Jaysus! Didn't I tell the lot of yah ta git ta church!

Jim! I'll be thrown out the feckin' church because of these gormless bastards of yers."

"Father Murphy and his church are all hypercritical auld feckers!" said Daddy. "He calls us sinners and heathens and tells us our children are bastards. An' yet, these righteous feckers still take the money and the food from out of the mouths of those same sinners and bastards! The Church is a mockery! I tell yah Lizzy. They're like the feckin' Mafia, only instead of shooting yah they feckin' blackmail yah with God. Debauched thieves and liars and whores and queers, the whole lot of them!"

When the knock suddenly came at the front door, Daddy had told Martin to answer it: "But take yer time so I can think of somethin' ta say."

Martin slowly walked off in the direction of the hallway, placing one foot in front of the other like a tightrope walker crossing the rope.

"Jaysus Martin! What the feck is the matter with yah?"

"Yah told me to take me time, Daddy."

"A few minutes, not a week!" he shook his head in utter despair. "Bernie, go and answer the door. And if it's them nosey auld bastards just stand in the way and act all gormless! It shouldn't be hard for yah ta do that. Just try and slow them down ta give me a minute ta think. The rest of yah can git down on your knees and pretend y'er praying for once in yer miserable lives."

We dropped to our knees and Daddy had pulled out

the big family Bible just as Father Murphy and Sister Joseph came through into the back room.

"Ah! Hello Father!" said Mammy, genuflecting to the old priest and scowling nun. "We were just in the middle of our usual daily prayers."

"It's a shame the family are not saying their prayers in church Mrs Rhattigan," said the priest. "Sister Joseph here tells me we haven't seen any one of you at Sunday Mass for a few weeks now, isn't that right Sister?"

"At least two weeks Father."

"An' yea've been at the church these last two Sundays ta have not seen us, have yah Sister?" asked Daddy.

"Well, I was there last Sunday but not the previous Sunday, though Sister Gertrude was. She always is."

"An' I suppose Sister Gertrude didn't bother ta tell yah, it was my ten-shilling note in the collection box? Not this Sunday gone, but the Sunday before, hmm?"

"What happened last Sunday gone?" asked Sister Joseph.

"Tell them Lizzy," said Daddy. "Tell the good people here why we'd not been to church this Sunday gone."

"We'd been robbed!" blurted out Mammy. She broke into her crocodile tears, which started the lot of us off, barring Daddy.

Father Murphy seemed genuinely concerned and told Sister Joseph to take Mammy into the kitchen and make her a cup of tea to calm her nerves.

"And if you can help her to write a list of the items

she'd had stolen, so as we can put a message up on the church notice board for the parishioners to read, perhaps they might feel obliged to help replace as many of the missing items as possible." He'd gone on to promise Mammy he would present any offerings to her and Daddy at the end of the next Sunday Mass.

"What is it you have there?" asked Father Murphy, suddenly taking a keen interest in the large leather-bound family Bible Daddy was holding.

"The family Bible, Father," said Daddy proudly. "An heirloom handed down from one generation of Rhattigans to the next. Better than any book on the shelves." In reality he had never read the Bible and had not opened its pages since writing the name of the last addition to the family, which was Michael, three years previously.

When Father Murphy began flicking through the book, he pulled out a set of photographs stuck between the pages. "What are these?"

"Ah now, they'll be just a few of the family photographs. We like ta keep some in there so as they are close ta God, if yah see what I mean."

Daddy had no notion that the priest was looking at images that had nothing to do with our family or God. There were eight photographs in the set. All of men and women - and a donkey - doing dirty things with each other. I knew this because I had seen Shamie hiding them in there some weeks back and I'd taken a quick peek for myself.

"These are all members of yer family?" asked the incredulous priest.

"Aye they are that Father. All Irish families couldn't be closer and that's what we are. Can I get yah a drink? A glass of sherry will it be, Father?"

"W-w-well yes, I think I'd better have a large one at that!"

I couldn't help laughing inside and I wondered what Daddy would say when the flustered priest eventually showed him the porno pictures. But it seemed Father Murphy wasn't in any particular hurry to be discussing the photos with Daddy and was already into his third peek at them while swallowing down a half-pint glass of sherry. "May I take these pictures for a while? I mean, it's not really appropriate to be keeping them hidden away in the Bible." He held his empty glass out for a refill and Daddy obliged.

"Y'er welcome to have them Father. It's not as if I can't take any more of them, is it?" asked Daddy. "I suppose yea'll be wanting to put them up on the church notice board alongside with all them other pictures of the parishioners and their families?"

Father Murphy didn't answer that question. He slipped the photographs into his cassock pocket and threw a quick blessing over all of us.

When the auld priest eventually left, he had seemed a little worse for wear, though much happier than when he'd first arrived. As for Sister Joseph, there wasn't any change in her mood though she must have had a sore hand writing out the long list of items Mammy had suddenly recalled having been stolen. And by the time she and Father Murphy left the house to go off and save more lost souls, she'd had her work cut out to save him from his usual drunken antics.

The gossip around the streets a few days later told how Father Murphy had gone, blind drunk, into Mr Jordan's house, telling both him and his wife that their eight children were all bastards in the eyes of God because Jack and Hilda hadn't taken the sacrament of marriage. Flooring the drunken priest with a punch to his purple nose, Jack Jordan had reminded Father Murphy he'd married him and his wife at St Wilfrid's Church some twenty years earlier…

CHAPTER 25

Boy Overboard

Me and Martin were outside the house playing on our own makeshift swing - an old car tyre attached to a piece of rope hanging from the crossbars of the lamp-post outside our front door - when Bunny Lewis came and said hello. One of Manchester's best-known drag queens, Bunny was dressed on this occasion in his normal clothes, but it would have been nothing out of the ordinary to have seen him walking into the Marsland pub on the Hyde Road dressed as a lady.

"Go fetch your Mammy will yah luvvie," he asked Martin. "I just want to have a quick chat with her."

Daddy said Bunny was a homosexual and warned us to keep our backs to the walls and away from the likes of him otherwise he'd be giving us his big sausage. But all the kids around here loved Bunny. He would often say hello or kick a football around with us or he'd have a turn at hopscotch as he passed by. We all knew he was a singer and an actor and sometimes he would be in character when we'd see him and he'd stop and sing us a song and play up to his image. But it was all in good fun and he made us laugh.

"What can I do for yah?" said Mammy, looking like she didn't really want to do anything for Bunny. She remained standing in the middle of the open doorway with her arms folded across her chest, which is how she always stood when she wasn't inviting anyone in (though the police would just push her out of the way). Daddy had told Mammy she could invite the whole street into the house if she liked, but he forbade her to ever invite Bunny Lewis in, as he'd not wanted to be associated with "bendy boys and shirttail lifters". He'd often complained about Bunny pretending to be a woman, dressing up like a "feckin' tart an' wiggling her fat arse in men's faces". He even said he was going to have a quiet word with Father Murphy about it, until he'd seen the old priest and another fella in a dress coming out of the pub where Bunny lived, laughing and joking and worse for wear. "Debauched, Lizzy! The whole feckin lot of them," said Daddy to Mammy. "Whores, lesheens an' feckin' puffs!"

Mammy told Daddy, his problem was not being able to get over the night he couldn't keep his eyes off Bunny when he came to perform at the Rob Roy pub, "Offering ta buy her all them drinks an' goosing her big feckin' arse, while pretending ta help her back up on the bar stool! Only yah found out later she was a man. Jaysus, everyone else in the whole place knew it was a drag queen barring yea, yah humpy bastard yah!" How Mammy loved to rub salt in to his wounds and shame him. "The truth only hitting yah, after yea'd shoved your hand up the auld floozy's dress for a grope at her budgie, only to get the two biggest surprises of yer life! She had a flute! An' you wakin up in the bed the next morning with a big fat lip and a loose front tooth!"

The reason for Bunny's visit was to ask Mammy if he could use some of us to star in his Christmas pantomime, Peter Pan, which was opening in a few months. He'd pay of course and he handed her a large bottle of sherry, her favourite drink, as a goodwill gesture. Having almost snatched off his hand for it, Mammy disappeared back inside the house.

"No he can't borrow any of the children for his pufty Christmas pantomime!" Daddy's answer came back within seconds and was bawled so loud that the whole street could hear. "It's bad enough being a homo pretending ta be a woman at the same time! But playin' a grown-up man who can't grow up an' wants ta hang around with a gang of little children, is an even bigger pervert!"

By the time Mammy had come back to the front door, minus the bottle of sherry, Bunny had already stepped away from the house and had walked off back down Stamford Street.

Pushing his way past Mammy and out of the front door, Shamie told Martin and me we were going rafting with him. We made our way up to the derelict warehouses near the Bridgewater Lock canal where we collected long pieces of wood, three doors and four discarded car tyres lying about the place. Then Martin and me sat back and watched our older brother set about building his vessel, which took him about an hour to complete.

As we were dragging the heavy raft to the edge of the water, we suddenly heard loud urgent voices calling out Shamie's name. We spotted our cousins, Paddy and Martin Power, on their own makeshift raft, moving at some speed on the water as they had been chased down by two other rafts that were slowly catching up with them.

"It's them Delaney brothers and their scanky crew from Moss Side!" said Shamie, immediately recognising the lads chasing after our cousins. Heaving our heavy new craft into the water Shamie shouted at Martin to jump on, which he did.

For the briefest of moments I'd thought the whole thing was going to sink as the top of the wooden platform had suddenly disappeared beneath the dirty water, before rising back up and settling about an inch above the surface.

"Chuck us over some duckers, hurry!"

Keeping a tight hold on the string holding the bobbing platform to the canal bank, I picked up fist-sized lumps of broken bricks and concrete and passed them to Martin.

"That's all we need." said Shamie. "Yea can let go of the string."

"What about me?" I wailed.

"I don't want yah getting' in the way an' no arguments! An' if them feckers try to head over to this side, bomb them ta death!" he ordered. And with that, the raft floated out across the canal away from me, with Shamie using the piece of floorboard as a paddle to move the cumbersome vessel in the direction of our two cousins.

The thought of putting up any kind of argument or protest about not being allowed onto the raft with my two brothers hadn't even entered my head. If anything, I was really chuffed Shamie had made the decision for me to keep my feet firmly on dry land, saving me from having to show myself up. I'd been frightened to death of water since I could remember, and like Martin, I couldn't swim to save my life, though he had seemed comfortable enough with being on the raft. I don't know why I had a fear of water. It wasn't as if I'd had a bad experience.

With a pile of my own duckers at the ready, I watched Shamie and Martin float off across the canal in the direction of our two cousins. It only took them a few minutes to draw alongside their raft out in the middle of the water, before the gang of five from Moss Side started their bombardment, raining their duckers down on my brothers and cousins who immediately returned a bombardment of their own.

It had been a strange, almost surreal image that I had found myself watching as the battle intensified.

Martin just managed to duck out of the way of a flying missile about the size of a brick, which missed his head by a whisker before one of the other rafts collided with theirs. Shamie and our two cousins seemed to be in their element as they whacked at their enemy with lumps of wood. A fat kid of about fifteen had suddenly let out a cry of pain before dropping to his knees, as cousin Martin caught him a whack across the back of his legs.

What I had been witnessing was ordinary teenagers who played football on the streets, swung off lampposts, stood outside the picture houses for Saturday matinees, smashed the windows of derelict houses and played every other game teenagers play. And yet here on the canal, it was not a game. This was a war, albeit a kid's war. But it was for real. And the intent to hurt one another was also for real.

Then, my worst nightmare began to unfold. I felt the panic rush through my whole body as I watched Martin suddenly lose his balance and topple into the murky water. I watched in utter horror when his head disappeared beneath the surface and didn't come up again. I was almost killed with fear when I realised suddenly that my two cousins and Shamie weren't even aware Martin was missing.

"Shamie! Martin!' I shouted at the top of my voice. My heart was racing so fast I'd expected it to suddenly give out on me and stop dead, I wasn't able to breathe properly, my legs turned to jelly and I felt the nausea rising up into my throat. I wanted to jump into the canal to help my brother but I was paralysed at the very thought.

"Shamie!" I screamed as loud and as long as my lungs permitted me. And then I stood silent, helplessly transfixed to the scene set out in front of me. I saw Shamie drop to his knees after a whack to his head; the Moss Side crew steering their raft back up the canal while holding their bloodied heads; Shamie looking back over his shoulder realising Martin wasn't on the raft; Shamie and our cousins on their knees, with watcr up to their shoulders, hands searching blindly for Martin. Frame after frame, the pictures flickered through my mind's eye likc a series of still photographs as I prayed out loud to Jesus. Then the last scene: Shamie - my hero - pulling Martin, coughing and spluttering, back up to the surface.

It would usually have taken a lot of physical pain to make me cry but, as I watched Martin sitting on the raft and puking his guts up, I cried like a baby, making no attempt to hide my tears.

"Cop hold, Tommy," said Shamie, throwing the thick piece of string across to me. I pulled the raft close into the side of the canal and held it there for Martin, helped by Shamie, to scramble back onto dry land. Then like a true captain of his ship, Shamie had stayed on board his own vessel, while he had seen our two cousins safely on to shore before hauling himself up onto the bank and letting both rafts float off down the canal.

"Jaysus!" said Paddy, putting a consoling arm around our Martin's shoulder. "Yer guardian angel was with yah today, for sure Martin."

"Shamie's no angel he's our brother!" I snapped.

"Oh thanks for that, Tommy."

I smiled at my big brother, pleased for having said the right thing - for once.

"Yea'll have to get out of them wet clothes," said Paddy. "We saw some workmen's old overalls in one of them bombed warehouses over there, I'll go get them."

"Why were them humpy bastards after yah in the first place?" asked Shamie. Cousin Martin was reluctant to give an answer until Shamie told him he didn't give a shite what they'd done wrong, he'd still stick up for them because they were family.

"It's not me they were after," confessed cousin Martin. "It's me eejit brother Paddy, he's madly in love with Mary McGovern."

"So what's up with them puttin' out about Paddy being in love? Sure he's only thirteen an' he'll have been in love with all the girls in Moss Side by the time he's fifteen. And so will yea, just wait and see. Yea'll be chasing after the girls with yer tongues an' little mickeys hangin' out!"

"That's the reason why they're after us."

"Jaysus, yah dirty fellas! See Tommy, y'er not the only one running around all the time showing your little worm to all the girls!"

I ignored him, as he'd only have another answer. And

anyway, I wasn't going to tell him I would probably have let Cathy McCarthy take a quick peek. But only if she'd wanted to. I mean, I wouldn't have just walked up to her with my mickey dangling out of my trousers and say, "Hello there Cathy darlin', how are things with yah today? Here, take a look at me flute!" It probably would have given her the shock of her life, just as it had done to old Mrs Turner, who had lived in the house directly across the street from us. One Saturday afternoon we caught her peering out through her upstairs window and into our sister's bedroom. She'd been standing there for a long while just peering across, so me and Martin had taken off all our clothes and pressed ourselves right up against the window pane. By the look on her face she seemed to have been shocked by the sight of us, though she hadn't moved an inch and just stood there gawking at us. Daddy explained later how the ambulance people had told him she had died of a heart attack while gawking out of her bedroom window.

"Promise yah won't say anythin' ta Paddy if I tell yah?" said cousin Martin.

"Yah know me, Martin! I'm not one for talking," said Shamie.

"Paddy's been humpin' Mary McGovern," smiled Cousin Martin. "An' her brother Mick is jealous, that's what it's all about."

"Yer Paddy is humpin' fourteen-year old Mary McGovern!" laughed Shamie. "What a show-up for the books!"

We all watched in silent admiration as Paddy hurried back, handing our Martin the grubby workman's overalls, before opening the green canvas lunch bag he'd stolen from one of the demolition workers huts. Shedding his wet clothes, Martin donned the overalls, turning up the long legs and arms, before slipping his wet sandals back on his feet. Shamie divided the doorstep Spam sandwiches amongst the five of us, letting our Martin have the two hard-boiled eggs and most of the dark stewed tea, which none of us made a fuss about, considering the ordeal he had been through.

"Heard y'er pokin' Mary McGovern then?" said Shamie, despite his promise not to.

Paddy went up the wall. "Was it yea, Martin?" he asked. "Jaysus, you'd tell the whole fuckin' world somethin' happened when nothin' even happened, so you would that!"

"The whole of Hulme, Longsight and Moss Side put together already know about it!" lied Shamie.

"But yah were humpin' her!" said cousin Martin. "We were havin' a peek at the pair of yah through the bedroom door only last week when Mammy and Daddy were at the pub. We saw you lying on the top of her with your spotty arse going up and down in the air."

"Who the feck's we!" said Paddy.

"Our Bridget was peekin' in too."

"Well, it was only the once," confessed Paddy. "But

never again, not after all this feckin carry on!"

"Only the once is all yah need Paddy!" laughed
Shamie, "Before yah know it she'll be tellin' yah yea've
got her up the duff, and her mammy an' daddy will be
marryin' yah off with a shotgun."

"I'd emigrate back to Ireland if they started any of that
larky!" promised Paddy.

As we had headed back off in the direction of home,
our Martin had looked none the worse for swallowing
a bit of the Manchester canal, though he was a little
worried he might have swallowed rat shite floating about
in the filthy water.

"Well I wouldn't worry too much about that, Martin,"
reassured Shamie. "Just keep an eye on the palms of
yer hands an' if yah see any little hairs starting ta grow
on them, yah have to tell someone otherwise they'll be
putting yah in a place like Belle Vue Zoo."

another ten-bob note out of me, she's another think coming,' said Mammy. Outside the church door, Sister Mary was standing in her usual spot with her begging bowl at the ready. "Keep yer hands in yer pockets, Jim," warned Mammy, "or she'll be dippin' inta yer trousers."

"The only ting the auld hen will find in me trouser pockets will be dust and tin air!" said Daddy, "An' if she digs deeper, she might be lucky and find a pair of hairy bollocks to play with!"

"Jaysus!" said Mammy. "Yah shouldn't be blasphemin' like that outside the church! He's feckin' got ears yah know!"

"Who has?"

"The Almighty has!"

"Isn't it just amazin' how the Almighty can hear me feckin' blasphemies, but can't hear me prayin' for me horse ta win a race!"

"Whisht up and walk in front of me! I don't want ta be talking with that one."

"Good morning to yah, Mr and Mrs Rhattigan! It's so lovely to see yah all here today." Sister Mary, the lying old hen, was going through her same old ritual. "Ah, will yah get a look at all those lovely children of yours. Thirteen angels this time," she said, counting us off on her crooked fingers.

Daddy stumped the remnants of his rollup into the nuns' empty begging bowl, before hurrying into the church with the rest of us tagging close behind.

...looking at the
...st on the list we
...d a finger on the name
... in big bold lettering,
...ked proudly through into
...he church. It was the first time
...m-in-arm as they strolled down
...ke a strutting pair of chickens. The
...d come close to holding hands was a few
...lier, when they were both arrested for being
...d disorderly and were handcuffed together
...e being carted off to the local police station.

It wasn't unusual to see the church full on a Sunday and this was no exception. Cathy McCarthy turned to give me a wide smile as I walked in, before her mother noticed and nudged her to look back to the front. My biggest dream was to one day see her walk down this aisle with me waiting at the altar for her, while her miserable mammy and daddy looked on, unable to tell me to bugger off out of it, as they often did. Every time I saw Cathy, I had an urge to fall down on bended knee, like I'd seen in the films and ask her for her hand in marriage - just to spite her parents!

When me and Martin sat down in the pew, the people sitting there had kindly slid along one by one and eventually moved off to another pew so the whole family could have the row to ourselves. Martin dropped a smelly fart, which vibrated all over the church, with a sea of

---

sense of security by
...had spilled the beans
...en absolved and my
...ll it up again, but
...d, I would have to
Catholic, because
"It's only the
confess their
...an to put on a
...ink of any sins
...laying with

Sister Mary
...thing into h...
...face, bef...
...ddle ...
...gl...
...do wi...
and then the bike...
McCarthy'...
...ly's good books.

...ly seven years of age, I ...
...wn way what Father Michae...
...of us who had stayed awake to ...
...ond, he was telling us, "If we confessed ...
...e would be absolved from all of them." And ...
...other, he was also telling us, "We will have to ac...
...the Almighty for all our sins." So my take on this w...

acc... eyes ...
was t... e every ...
sneeze...
an objec...
all eyes w...
pointed an ...
us, to let the ...
Martin and Na...
fingers pointing ...
out of the church ... tears ...
on us for upsetting t...

Father Michael, a y...
and informed the cong...
Mass in the absence of F...
feeling too well".

"Pissed more like!" Daddy...
loud enough for the two old w... in th...
of us to look over their shoulder...

The Mass seemed to go on for a...
minded listening to the priest dron...
of the world being doomed to hell a...
voice seemed to have a calming effect...
the congregation having either fallen as...
into an hypnotic state of religious calm, a...
on about a time when we would all have to...
the Almighty God and give an account to hi...
we had lived our lives on this earth.

He didn't say whether this was to be through...

the Church had led me into a false...
making me believe that every time I...
and confessed my latest sins, I had b...
sin slate was wiped clean, so I could...
this obviously wasn't the case!
Sometimes, when I hadn't even sinn...
make sins up just to prove I was a goo...
Mammy said that Father Murphy said,...
good Catholics who go to Confession t...
sins," and so we'd had no choice other t...
good show.

Once, Shamie told me, "If yah can't th...
ta confess, just tell the priest you've been j...
yourself. He loves those sort of sins!"

With the Mass nearing its end I noticed...
lean into Sister Gertrude and whisper som...
ear, which had brought a smile to Hoppity's...
she lurched off to the vestry door and opene...
low murmur of voices rippled around the m...
as those people sitting in that area got a quic...
of Father Murphy sitting in a chair and swigg...
on a bottle of the church wine, before Sister G...
steadied herself and slammed the door shut be...
A few muffled voices and the sound of breaking...
later, the vestry door opened a touch and Siste... rude
reappeared, squeezing herself out through th... small gap
she'd left in the doorway. She was carrying a handful
of small brown envelopes and hobbled back over to

Sister Mary. The pair of them had a short exchange of sour looks and ear whisperings, before she'd handed the envelopes over to the Mother Superior.

During final blessings to end the Mass, Father Michael asked, "Will those parishioners on Father Murphy's list on the noticeboard wait behind. Sister Mary and Sister Gertrude will deal with you."

We waited. While most of the congregation left the church, there were still thirty people sitting in the pews, although there were only five names written up on Father Murphy's list.

"Nosey auld bastards," muttered Daddy, peering around the church. "Look at them. It's not enough for them ta be givin', they want us ta bow down an' kiss their feckin' arses, too! Well I won't be thanking any of them for sure."

"Would Mr and Mrs Delaney like to come up to the altar," called out Sister Mary. 'Flasher' Delaney's parents were halfway down the aisle before the Sister had even finished her sentence.

"Look at them," scoffed Daddy, "Like a fat pair of pigs running ta the trough!"

"Will yah give over Jim!" snapped Mammy.

Three medium-sized boxes were carried out of a side room and placed to one side of the altar.

"These are the lovely gifts specially donated for yea from the parishioners of this church," smiled Sister Mary. "Now, as there is too much for yea to carry on yer own we've arranged ta have them delivered to yer house. Oh! And there's this, too." She dug deep into the pocket of her habit and pulled out two small brown envelopes, which she said contained monetary offerings. She invited the pair of them to address the congregation, which they milked for all it was worth. They thanked everyone for this and that and by the time they had finished their thankings, it seemed they'd thanked everyone in the whole of Manchester, barring the Rhattigans. Not that we'd given them anything.

Another two names were called out before the one name we, and I suspected many others, had been waiting to be called. "Would Mrs Cooper like to come to the altar?"

"She'd like to feckin lay on the top of it as well!" snapped Mammy, not even bothering to keep her voice low as the stunning dark-haired young woman had made her way out of her pew and past us, with the heels of her stilettos clippety-clopping out a rhythm like Mr McCarthy's cart horse Goliath when he was coming down our street.

Wearing the shortest of skirts, Mrs Cooper smiled and waved a delicate finger in the direction of Daddy, plus Paddy and Shamie, as she headed down towards the altar. With the exception of my two brothers, whose tongues almost hit the ground, Daddy and the rest of the male congregation seemed not to have noticed Mrs Cooper as they searched out imaginary spots on their shoes to stare at while she had passed by.

She wiggled her bum all the way up the aisle while
the three church wardens and the two nuns struggled to
bring through the six large boxes of goodies gifted to her.

"Donated by all the dirty feckin auld men in Hulme, I
wouldn't wonder!" said Mammy.

Just as she had done with the Delaneys and everyone
else, Sister Mary, minus her patronising smile, had
informed Mrs Cooper she would have her boxes
delivered to her front door, before presenting her with
the handful of brown envelopes, one of them slipping
from her grasp and falling to the ground. Without
ceremony, Mrs Cooper bent over from the hips upwards
and retrieved the envelope in one swift movement, to a
chorus of loud gasps.

"Yah feckin' auld whore yea!" called Mammy as the
young woman walked past us. She acknowledged Mammy
with a wide smile and a flutter of her false eyelashes,
before blowing a kiss towards Daddy and the rest of us,
which had only antagonised Mammy even more.

"And last but not least, would Mr and Mrs Rhattigan
like to come to the altar," said Sister Mary. All week,
there had been a sense of expectancy about Mammy
and Daddy, which was understandable seeing as no one
had ever given them anything. And with a long list of
items on the stolen property list, even if they'd received a
small percentage of the items, it would have amounted to
a tidy sum. They looked relaxed, as they calmly walked
out from the pew and headed down the aisle, as if they'd

been out for a Sunday stroll. Mammy clippity-clopped along in her high heels, easily outdoing Mrs Cooper, until the heel of her right shoe suddenly collapsed and fell off, with Mammy having to walk the rest of the way doing an impersonation of Sister Gertrude and accompanied by the titters of the congregation.

The sound of squeaky wheels broke the silence as we watched Sister Gertrude, hobbling backwards out of the side room, guiding out the old long metal clothes rack which was burdened with the weight of assorted second-hand clothes. Barring a few men's overcoats, which looked as if they'd seen better days, most of the clothing was creased-up children's clothes that looked as though they had been pulled hurriedly out of bags and slipped onto coat hangers. Sister Mary asked Daddy if he'd wanted to say a few words to the congregation.

"I wouldn't be able ta find the right words ta tell them what I thought," said Daddy. And judging by the way his jaw muscles kept tightening up as he ground his teeth together, this was probably a blessing in disguise.

CHAPTER 27

Bang to Rights

There had been no brown envelopes on offer for Mammy and Daddy and no offers to have the clothing delivered to our house either, perhaps because it would have been just as easy to push home the old squeaky clothes rack, which Sister Mary had told Daddy he could also keep.

"Wheel that lot of rags down ta the back of the church and wait there with them," Daddy ordered me and Martin.

With Martin pulling from the front and me pushing from the back, I stood on the bottom cross rail, letting him do all the donkey work. The clothes rack suddenly stopped moving and my end swerved across the aisle. Martin fell over Mammy as she bent over to retrieve the heel of her shoe, causing the rack to tip over. It had taken only a few moments to right it back on to its four wheels and for the angry Mr Arnold to remove the old raincoat from off his wife's head. But that was all the time needed for me to have swiped her purse out of her open handbag and slip it into the pocket of the other old overcoat hanging on the rack.

Pushing the squeaky-wheeled clothes rack along the wet streets in the direction of home, wasn't as easy as pushing it along the smooth surface of the church floor. Our eldest sisters and brothers had disappeared, while Mammy had gone off to her sister Brenda's house with some of the others, leaving Bernie and Nabby to tag along with Martin and me. Daddy was in a bad mood and wouldn't stop going on about being shown up in the church. "A few miserly feckin' shillin's ta tide us over, that's all we needed! An' they roll out a pile of feckin' rags! Good Catholics' of Hulme me arse! A pile of auld rags none of them greedy bastards would be seen dead wearing, let alone their own children!" He walked a few yards ahead of us with his head hunched into his shoulders and his ears sunk into the turned-up collar of his jacket, in a vain attempt to stay dry in the drizzle.

The rain didn't bother the rest of us. We were used to being out in all kinds of weather and didn't feel the cold that much, with the exception of the winter just gone, which had lasted right up until March, freezing the ponds and the lakes and the extremities of all the brass monkeys! I loved being out in the rain. For me, the heavier the better. The fine drizzles never seemed to have much impact other than to make a damp miserable atmosphere even more damp and miserable. On the other hand, the heavy rains were glorious! They cleansed everything: my hair, my clothes, my skin, the dust-covered grey-slated rooftops and the grimy buildings.

And the puddles galore. We would splash through them to our heart's content, saturating ourselves and any passerby, who could hardly complain when they had already been soaked to the skin by the downpour.

As we headed up along Clopton Street, Daddy was having a chat to Billy Smart, a rag-and-bone man he'd known for some while.

"Leave the rack there an' clear off with yah!" said Daddy. My attempts to tell him I wanted to keep the big black coat fell on deaf ears, needing only the one angry glare from him to tell me to scarper or I was in for it.

Hardly able to tell him in front of the rag-and-bone man, I had stolen Mrs Arnold's purse from the church and had hidden it in the pocket of the black overcoat hanging on the clothes rack, I said nothing and hurried off after the others. Martin and I went off on our own and when we finally got home that night, just after midnight, Daddy was at the kitchen sink, naked and washing himself down. "Feck off ta bed the pair of yeah!" was his drunken greeting.

Early the following morning, as the rest of the family slept on, Martin and I decided to go off into Longsight and meet up with some of our cousins. On our way out of the back gate we bumped into Mammy coming along the alleyway. She looked the worse for wear and didn't even bother to acknowledge us as we stepped aside for her to pass by us. We said nothing to her either, mainly for our own safety. She had obviously had another big row with Daddy the previous night and so everyone would have to be treading on eggshells for a day or two before they made up again.

We came across a couple of empty houses on the edge of Longsight and although these had already been stripped to the bone, we were able to crawl down through a small gap leading into one of the cellars where we found electric cables still attached to the wall and running across the ceiling. I always felt a sadness whenever I searched inside an empty property. As I walked through the silence of each room, seeing a discarded family photo, or a birthday card to Joan or Donald or Fred, I was forever mindful that I was walking through someone's past.

Working quickly together, we managed to tear down all the electric cable before Martin crawled back out of the hole and I passed the thick flex up to him. And by the time I had managed to get myself back out into the open air, Martin had already lit a small fire and a black cloud of smoke was spiralling up into the grey sky as the rubber burned away to expose the copper wiring - Daddy's gold. When all the copper had been exposed, we pulled it out of the fire with a stick and urinated on it to cool it down, before twisting the cooled copper into lumps and hiding it from view in the old pushchair, before going on to search another house.

When we arrived back home, in the early hours of the afternoon, there were three policemen inside our house. Two of them were dragging Daddy head-first down the stairs as a third, a sergeant, looked on. One of the coppers gave Daddy a sideways glance across the side of the head with his truncheon, causing his head to split open and blood to spill. I found myself silently applauding the policeman, even though I hadn't a clue as to the reasons why they were arresting him in the first place. But it was a good feeling to look on as he was being bashed by someone while he was unable to fight back. I remembered how, at the top of these same stairs, I had witnessed Maggie and Rosemary struggling with our drunken father. I discovered much later that he was trying to take our sister Maggie to his bedroom. Daddy had his hand around Mary's throat and had her leaning backwards over the rail before Rosemary pulled a mirror off the landing wall and smashed it over his head before he'd staggered off back down the stairs. And then there was I praying the policeman would hit Daddy again, just for good measure.

"Ah Jaysus, I'm dying!" moaned Daddy, as his bleeding head bounced off the last few steps. One of the coppers lifted him up by his arms, the other took his feet and they carried him out of the house like a captured animal ready for the slaughter, before throwing him into the back of the meat-wagon.

Maggie's face was very pale and drawn, much whiter than I'd ever seen before and her whole body was trembling. Mammy was shouting all sorts of names at the sergeant, telling him that someone who had known they were going to be out during the night must have come in through the unlocked door while everyone was fast asleep and hurt our Bernie.

"Come on Lizzy. We've every good reason to be arresting your husband on suspicion of assault," said the sergeant. "It was the young child herself who said she thought it was her father who'd attacked her during the night."

"I swear on the little flower of Jaysus and all the saints alive, he wouldn't lay one finger on the children!" protested Mammy. "An' if he ever did smack them it was only ta chastise them for doin' somethin' wrong. Anyways, the child's disturbed in the head. She'd say anythin' if she can't remember the truth." In her desperation to protect Daddy, Mammy went on, "The back door is never locked! Anyone could have come in ta the house while we were out."

"Did you hear anything unusual in the night?" said the sergeant to Maggie. "Your Daddy?"

"Don't yah be putting words into her mouth!" snapped Mammy.

"No, I didn't see Daddy!" said Maggie, before bursting into tears once more.

"Go back ta bed an' get some more kip!" said Mammy. Maggie didn't need a second invitation and hurried off up the stairs, not bothering to avoid the bloodstained steps.

I wondered why Maggie had not just told the coppers

how Daddy would sometimes come and take her, or one of our other sisters, downstairs to his bedroom to comfort them if they'd been scared in the night when Mammy hadn't come home. Perhaps she'd not wanted people to know she had a fear of the dark, which was nothing to be ashamed about. Almost everyone had fears. Everyone who had known me, especially the Manchester Fire Brigade, knew I suffered with heights.

Every time they came to fetch me down from a rooftop, the chief fireman would threaten, "This is your very last time! We're leaving you up there the next time and we won't be bothering to come out!" But they always came. Martin too had a phobia, he couldn't sit down on a toilet so he'd stand up on them. Our uncle Sean apparently had a fear of women, which had always confused me because if Uncle Sean had a fear of women, why then did he always dress up like a woman? Even Daddy, as tough as people liked to think he was, had a fear of the debt collectors.

Before leaving the house the police sergeant told Mammy that Daddy might be home later in the evening. "If no charges are preferred, that is. Otherwise he won't be coming home for a long while."

It was Mary who had raised the alarm after coming home in the late morning to discover Bernie still lying upstairs in the small bed on her own. She had been burning a fever which is why no one had bothered her. But when Mary had pulled back the bedcovers to lift her up into her arms, she'd noticed the blood on the mattress. She'd sent Paddy running off down the street to a neighbour who owned a telephone and they called for the ambulance. Later in the afternoon, when Mammy had got back from the police station after Daddy's arrest, she told us Daddy had admitted to hitting Bernie a couple of times during the night, but only with the back of his hand, because she'd been cheeking him. But he had sworn blind he'd done nothing else to her, continuing with Mammy's argument that the back door was always left unlocked. This was true, though none of us was convinced a stranger had just walked down the back entry and into the house to attack our little sister.

CHAPTER 28

Secrets and Lies

After Daddy's arrest, later that evening, Mary and Rose started a blazing row with Mammy. She had gone on and on so much about Daddy that anyone who hadn't known him would have thought she'd been talking about a heavenly saint! My two sisters told Mammy they were leaving the house for good. They already had their bags packed and waiting in the hallway, but before they left they were going to have their last say, whether or not Mammy liked it.

"The problem with yea Mammy," screamed Rosemary, "is, not only do yah believe the bastard's fuckin' lies, yah believe in yer own fuckin' lies as well."

"I was here with yer father the other night so yeah can't go accusin' him of things he hasn't done!"

"Yah were not here with him the other night!" snapped Mary. "Yea'd had another fight in the pub with the auld bastard and left him again."

"An' how would yah know that? The pair of yea are never here ta know what goes on in this house! Out all the nights with no shame on yah, whorin' yourselves ta yer fancy men! Get a look at yea! How can yah afford all them nice clothes and that fine jewellery ye've drippin' off yah, while we're sittin' here starvin' an' wearin' the same auld rags!"

Maggie, wrapped in her moth-eaten blue blanket, had joined us to listen on the stairs as my two sisters spat their venom at Mammy.

"It's called fuckin' gettin' a job! Which that auld bastard wouldn't know the meaning of!" snapped Mary. "We gave yah money an' yah both pissed it up the four walls of this house, instead of spendin' it on the kids, which is what it was intended for! Yea have our Martin, Tommy, Nabby and our little Bernie out on the streets beggin' all hours of the day and night an' the pair of yah piss that away, too! An' if yah want to know how we know yah weren't with the bastard yesterday night, Auntie Brenda told us yea'd had another blazin' row an' stayed with her all the night an' yah didn't leave til seven in the mornin'! That's how we know! And if yah want to know how we know you weren't here all the other fuckin' nights..."

"Jaysus! Why are yah sticking up for the fuckin' bastard?" Rosemary asked Mammy. "He's done for us! Just like he did in Ireland! Yah know that don't yah? An' the chances are, he's done for the others as well. An' he's beaten the livin' daylights out of yea too. An' yah stick up for him through thick and thin. Yah can't see past yer own nose Mammy that's yer problem. Either that or yah know what's been goin' on but yah don't want to face the truth."

"And why would yah believe someone just walked into the house and up the stairs to attack little Bernie in the bed?" asked Mary. "Only for Daddy to hear her giving out and come up the stairs to chastise her! Where was this stranger at that point? Hiding under the bed?"

"There's no such person! It never happened an' yah know it," said Rosemary. "Yah made it up to save the bastard's skin. That's what yea've done. But yea'll be the one that'll live to regret it - I tell yah. And yah will regret it Mammy. You will regret it!"

"If yah don't stop with all the lies about yer father I won't be responsible for me actions," said Mammy. But her threat fell on deaf ears, as Mary and Rosemary laid bare their demons.

"The poxty bastard should have been castrated and jailed a long while ago!" screamed Mary. "It might have been the gypsy way, on the roads in Ireland, with all their interbreedin' and what-have-yah! But we're not in Ireland anymore! And we're not putting up with it anymore."

"Yea've no rights talking about yer Father like this!" said Mammy. But the venom in her own voice was lost as she searched for the words to throw back at my sisters. "He's clothed yah - he's fed yah! He's..."

"...used and abused us in every fuckin' way that he could!" spat Mary.

"Get outta my house yah pair of feckin' whores! Get out!"

"Oh, we're going! There's no fear about that!" screamed Mary. "We wouldn't stay another minute under this poxty roof! And if you or the auld bastard come looking for us again, I swear as there's a God in heaven, I'll tell the police an' anyone else that wants to listen what he's done to us. And he'll fuckin' swing for it!"

The three of us watched from the stairs as our two sisters snatched up their bags and hurried off along the hallway and straight out of the house without a backward glance, slamming the door behind them.

The next afternoon, Mammy took me and Martin with her to see Daddy on remand. On the bus, chain-smoking her way through a pack of ten Woodbines, she told us, "If anyone asks about yer father tell them he's gone off and left us." We hadn't dared tell her the whole of Hulme already knew he was in Preston nick for hurting our Bernie.

Getting off the bus on Southall Street, Mammy took us straight across the road to the corner shop opposite the prison. She asked the larger-than life-shopkeeper, who had what looked like a tatty-haired ginger cat sitting on the top of her head, for a packet of ten Woodbines and an ounce of Old Holborn tobacco. The woman told Mammy she had only just run out of the Old Holborn, before asking her, "Are you new to these parts, or just visiting someone?"

"I'll have an ounce of the Golden Virginia, then," said Mammy.

"Afraid we're out of that as well. I seem to be selling it by the bucketload these days!" she quipped.

"Well, I was only after the ounce," said Mammy, which got the shopkeeper laughing.

"That's a good-un, missus! I like a woman with a sense of humour! Here." She took a packet of tobacco from the shelf behind her and dropped it on to the counter. "Black Shag. A tad cheaper, which most of them over there have a preference for. Unless you'd like the special packs?" She lowered her voice, "With the pound note inside -" she coughed. "If you're inclined that is?"

"Do yea two want anything?" asked Mammy. We were stunned by the question and I looked deep into her eyes, unsure as to whether or not she had only been codding us. I looked at Martin for confirmation that my imagination wasn't playing tricks on me and he, too, seemed to be having some difficulty taking it in. "Here!" she offered out the silver sixpence to me, which I was hesitant to take. At no time, in my living memory, had Mammy ever bought any sweets for us, let alone offered us the money to buy them! The fact we knew that she knew we didn't need money to buy anything, had only added to our confusion and my thinking was that she'd gone funny in the head. But she thrust the sixpence into my hand and shooed the pair of us off out of earshot, leaving her and the shopkeeper to chat in low whispers about her special packs of tobacco.

We wandered around the shop, eventually choosing

two penny boxes of Captain Scarlet sweet cigarettes. We handed the four pennies in change back to Mammy, which the shopkeeper thought was really sweet of us.

"You can see those two little lovey-doveys of yours have been brought up proper missus. Not like some of the snotty thieving little buggers we get in here at times, trying to steal everything in sight while their mothers, some looking as if they've just managed to drag themselves out of their beds, turn a blind eye to them."

Stuffing the special pack of tobacco into her pocket, Mammy left the shop, with us close behind. We walked across the main road, following alongside the towering wall until we reached the main entrance to the prison. Before we went in, me and Martin shared out all the sweets we'd nicked from the newsagent's shop.

Daddy seemed genuinely pleased to see us, which, just like Mammy back at the shop, took us by complete surprise. He had told us so many times in the past he wanted to see the backs of us and yet there he was, with his two black eyes and swollen bruised conk, arms outstretched and expecting me and Martin to come running and jump straight into them. There was no way I was jumping into his arms. So I stood back, inviting Martin to go first, which he declined.

"Ah Jaysus! Will yah get a look at them beautiful children of mine!" Daddy raised his excited voice so everyone in the visiting room heard and looked over in our direction. "It's me two favourite boys!"

I had a feeling the policeman's truncheon bouncing off his head must have done something to his brain, just as I also sensed something different about him beyond his paleness and the black eyes and the broken nose. To me, it seemed his confidence, as bold and assured as it had once been, was now diminished and he was not so cocksure of himself.

"Martin!" Taking a long stride forward, he grabbed hold of my brother and lifted him up in his arms before whispering something into his right ear, to which Martin nodded his head. I thought most likely he'd promised to give Martin sixpence to spend on himself or to share with me like Mammy had done. And if this was the case, then he wouldn't be getting any change back.

"Ah! Tommy, Tommy! Me little monkey yah! Still climbing up the drainpipes I hear."

Well I wasn't climbing up into his arms for sixpence or anything else if that's what he'd been expecting. But he had no intention of giving me a choice. In one swift movement my feet were off the ground and he was holding me tightly to his chest! "D'ya see the big black gorilla gawkin' over this way? Do yah Tommy?" The stench of strong tobacco on Daddy's breath made me want to retch because it brought to mind my encounter with the Devil in the bombed house. Looking beyond Daddy, I could see a big black man staring over in our direction. His showed his huge white teeth as he smiled at me and I quickly turned my gaze away to avoid any further eye contact with him.

"He likes to gouge out children's eyes from their sockets and place them on the kitchen stove so the eyes can watch him as he chops the children into little pieces, and throws them into his cooking pot to make himself a stew! Then he sucks on the eyes and throws them into the pot, too. So if yah don't listen to me carefully and do what me and your mother tells yah ta do, I'll be sendin' King Kong to the house for the pair of yea. D'ya hear?"

Just like my brother Martin, I nodded and then Daddy placed me gently back down on the ground, scuffing my short hair with his nicotine-stained hand, before telling us to smile, sit at the table and open our big ears.

"When the pair of yea came home the night yah saw me washin' meself in the kitchen sink, where was yer Mother?" questioned Daddy. "An' before yah say anythin', let me tell yah the answer. Yer Mother was sitting at the table in the backroom waiting for the pair of yah ta come home, that's where she was! An' don't feckin' forget it! So. Where was yer Mother when yea'd both came home late that night and saw me having a wash in the kitchen sink?"

"Mammy was waitin' in the back room for us to come home, because we were late," said Martin.

"An' yah never saw or heard anyone else, did yea?"

"No, Daddy."

"An' you Tommy, with the scowery puss?"

It had been too good to be true for Mammy to be

giving us money to buy sweets and I should have
realised there must have been a catch to it. Lying for
Daddy wasn't anything out of the ordinary for us. It was
something we did all the time and came naturally. But
having to lie for him against my own sister, especially
when it was Bernie, who meant the whole world to me
and Martin, that was difficult. And just as hard to come
to terms with was the fact that, if he wanted us to lie for
him about the night we'd seen him washing himself in
the kitchen sink, it only showed Bernie must have been
telling the truth about him hurting her that night.

"Mammy was sittin' at the table in the back room
waitin' for us to come home," I heard myself saying,
while in my head I was asking Bernie to forgive me for
lying. I was sure she would have preferred me to lie,
rather than having to go through the ordeal of having
my eyes gouged out and placed by the side of a cooker
and having to watch the big black man chopping me to
pieces to make me into a stew, before sucking my eyes
like gobstoppers and throwing them in the pot after me.

"Good boys!"

"An' yah heard nothin' after yea'd both gone to bed,"
added Mammy. "Stick to the truth and everythin' will be
all right, d'ya hear?"

CHAPTER 29

Penny for the Guy

It was almost Bonfire Night and Martin, Bernie and me were outside in the backyard making up the Guy Fawkes. It was the middle of the morning and the sun was shining. Mammy hadn't been home for the past few days, not that we had been overwhelmed with grief by her absence. We knew she was staying at Auntie Brenda's. She'd been staying away from the house more frequently since Daddy had been away, coming home whenever and hardly talking to any of us, save to have a good moan about the house looking like a tip - before getting on her hands and knees and scrubbing the floors clean.

I wondered if Mammy resented having all of us, or had it been that she couldn't cope with looking after all of us on her own that made her stay away. Every time she left the house did she intend to stay away for good? It was perhaps only the fear Daddy had instilled in her that made her come back each time. Perhaps she felt incapable of doing everything for us on her own, if she even cared. It wasn't as if he'd been around to start any rows with her and the house had been more peaceful without his presence. These were questions I asked myself to try and understand my Mammy. But having a Mammy who had no bond with her children, what was there for any of us to understand?

We made the body of the Guy from old rags stuffed into the workman's blue overalls and the one-sleeved donkey jacket we had found in one of the derelict houses the previous night when we were out collecting firewood. Bernie drew a face on the yellow balloon for the Guy's head, but Nabby decided to add a few extra touches around the eyes with a pencil - and promptly popped the balloon.

"That's the only balloon we had Nabby!" scolded Bernie. "Right, y'er going ta have ta be the Guy, til we get another one."

"Yea'll not be seeing me dressing up as a Guy, that's for sure, so yah won't!"

"Well if yah don't, I'm telling Mammy it was yea that took the shilling off the mantelpiece a couple of days ago," threatened Bernie.

Nabby took the part, albeit reluctantly! We stuck him in the smaller old pram and Bernie had a go at making his face up with Mammy's rouge, black mascara and deep red lipstick. She fancied herself as a good drawer and was better than us, if that was anything to go by. She added a set of weird-looking eyes to his eyelids, so he could shut them when people approached and they still looked open, so it was less obvious he was alive.

When she stepped back to admire her handiwork,

Martin and me forced ourselves to agree she'd done an
amazing job, otherwise Nabby would have kicked off!
In truth, we both found it difficult to keep straight faces!
The extra pair of eyes had one bigger than the other and
they were grotesquely crooked, with one looking towards
his nose every time he closed his eyes. Nabby wasn't too
happy, dressed up in the old clothes which, he had kept
complaining, stank of cats' pee. And he did have a point.

"How d'ya know its cat's piss, it could be any kind of
piss?" questioned Bernie.

"It doesn't matter if it's cat's piss, dog's piss, or pig's
piss! They stink of piss and I don't like it. That's what
counts!" said Nabby. Catching sight of his reflection
in an old broken mirror resting up against the wall, he
added, "An' look at the face yea've drawn all over me! I
look more like a big whore than Guy Fawkes!"

"Since when have yah seen a Guy with the same face?"
Martin had asked.

"Well I want a mask ta wear or I'm not doin' it!"
Nabby was about to hop out of the pram.

"I've got an idea!" said Martin. He rushed back into the
house and reappeared with Mammy's perfume bottle and
one of her old stockings. He set about spraying plumes of
the pungent-smelling liquid over Nabby, almost suffocating
the lot of us with the fumes before offering the stocking to
Nabby. "Shove that over yer head."

Nabby threw it back at him. "Since when have yah
seen Guy Fawkes wearing a woman's stocking over

his head? It's bank robbers that do that, an' we're not robbing a poxty bank! Jaysus! I smell like a whore's jockstrap! I'm not wearing Mammy's auld feckin' stockin' over me head an' that's final!"

"We'll go down ta Woolies and steal a mask for yah straight away," promised Martin. That, and letting him look after the small petrol lighter we used for lighting our small fires to burn electric flex, seemed to satisfy Nabby. He slouched back in the pram and Martin quickly manoeuvred it out the back gate and down the alley towards Stretford Road, before our little brother could change his mind.

On the way, we had to put up with him complaining about how the streets were too bumpy, his back was hurting and he was starving hungry. Thankfully, by the time we got to Woolworths he'd dozed off to sleep, though to the passers-by he still appeared wide awake, his crooked eyes glaring down at his nose.

Martin's suggestion that we should leave him sleeping was a good one. We left him outside the main store entrance as we went inside, heading straight to the fancy dress aisle to find him a mask. But when we got there, all the Guy Fawkes stuff was already sold out, or stolen, barring a couple of long rubber witch's hooters.

"Guy Fawkes had a big conk like them, didn't he?" said Martin. He pulled one of the six inch noses off the hook and was about to shove it into his trouser pocket, when the voice of the assistant manageress suddenly called down the aisle. "If one has no means or intention of paying for that item, one should replace it back on its hook!" Or words to that effect. We immediately recognised the assistant manager's voice even without having to look, as she had been the only person in the whole store, perhaps in the whole of Manchester, who spoke the way she did. Not that we could understand half of what she had said anyway!

"Did yah pay for that hooter yer wearing?" I asked her. To my surprise, she ignored me. We were waiting for the usual barrage of verbals along with our marching orders, but instead she rushed off in the direction of the main entrance as the distant sirens become louder and we saw the flashing blue lights of the ambulance that had pulled up right outside.

As the stampede of shoppers and staff hurried towards the exit for a nose at what was going on, we couldn't help noticing that the jewellery counter had been left unmanned! And being children never to miss out on an opportunity, Martin and me dived behind the counter while Bernie kept a look out for us – or so we thought!

It was like walking into an Aladdin's cave! My hands shook in trepidation and I found it difficult to contain my excitement at being amongst the glittering array of gold and silver diamond rings and necklaces that stared back at us from the display cabinets. My first thoughts were, "It's gonna be Belle Vue every single day for some months to come! And catching a bus every time instead of walking." But my dreams were soon shattered when we discovered all the display cabinets were securely locked. As a consolation we found a small, unlocked cupboard filled with boxes of watches and cigarette lighters, which we swiftly removed from their packaging before stuffing as many of them as we could into our trouser pockets.

At one point we'd had to quickly drop down on our hands and knees as two middle-aged men suddenly walked close by the counter. And although I suspected at least one of them had spotted us and had made the briefest of eye contact with me, he and his companion had continued past the counter as if nothing out of the ordinary was happening.

When we slipped out from behind the counter, our little sister was nowhere to be seen, which was the reason we hadn't received the expected warning call about the two passing men. We found her in the next aisle, attempting to stuff a boxed Sindy doll down her knickers.

"Take the feckin' doll out of the box first!" suggested Martin.

"I found this for Nabby, sticking out from under the shelf." She showed us the torn green cardboard Guy Fawkes mask.

"Yea were supposed ta be keeping an eye out for us," I scolded. "We could ALL have been arrested because of yea!"

"It wasn't me behind the counter, so they couldn't have

arrested me for anything!" said Bernie with a smile.

CHAPTER 30

A Fair Cop

Outside the Woolworths we could see Nabby still snoozing in the pram. Which I suppose was a blessing in disguise, considering that the long-haired, bearded lunatic and the cause for all the commotion was standing right next to him with a lighter in his hand and a large assortment of fireworks strapped to his body. He was threatening to blow himself and the whole street to kingdom come if he wasn't taken to the Houses of Parliament straight away, so he could finish the job he had set out to do a few hundred years previously!

Holding the cigarette lighter up for the crowd to see, the man flicked it into life a number of times to show he meant business. We weren't able to squeeze through the packed crowd to get to our sleeping brother. Meanwhile some onlookers were egging the madman on to do what he'd been threatening to do.

"Nabby." I called out softly to him, not wanting to shout too loud in case the lunatic took fright and set off the fireworks. But Nabby did not hear me.

"Wake up yah Scalpy bastard yah!" screamed out Bernie. Scalp was one of Nabby's hated nicknames, along with Patch, Sitting Bull or Red Indian, and had been bestowed on him by the family on account of the patches Daddy would sometimes leave in his head when he'd gone mad with the hairclippers. The secret to a pain-free crew-cut, as we kept telling Nabby, was to "keep feckin' still!" while Daddy quickly ran the blunt hair clippers over our heads. If you didn't, the clippers would snag, tearing the hair out by the roots. Nabby just couldn't hold still, resulting in him being virtually scalped every time. Hence the nicknames!

Bernie's shout did the trick and when Nabby's eyelids slowly opened, they fixed immediately on the suicidal maniac standing next to him. I half expected my little brother to leap out of the pram and run for his life. But instead, we watched as he slowly reached into the side pocket of the smelly one-armed donkey jacket and pulled out the cigarette lighter Martin had bribed him with. Flicking the lighter into life, he slowly offered the small flame up to the fuse of one of the large Catherine-wheels. An eerie silence descended as a streetful of shocked faces gawked at the Guy Fawkes who had suddenly come to life! The silence was broken by the Catherine-wheel whooshing into life and the screams of the lunatic as he fled down the middle of the street towards the crowd, just as the police arrived.

The three of us rushed to Nabby's side, only for him to be slouched back in the pram with his arms folded across his chest and looking pissed off with everything. "Why d'ya have to be callin' me names for?" he moaned, more put out about that than the fact that he could have been blown sky high.

"Yah should be grateful I saved yer life instead of pullin' the long face!" said Bernie. She pushed the pram away from the crowd, with Martin and me following behind. "Anyways," she continued, always having to get her say in, "I didn't call yah names, I only called yah the one name." Luckily, Nabby couldn't see the grin on Bernie's face.

Turning off Stretford Road into Upper Jackson Street, we made our way up to the old school building where we hid in the shadows of the tall archway out of view from prying eyes.

"Did yah get anythin'?" asked Bernie, struggling to get the Sindy out of her knickers.

"We got these!" I excitedly showed her the seven watches, slipping them onto my left arm one by one.

"An' these!" Martin pulled six watches and three silver lighters out of his trouser pockets.

"What do yah want all them watches for? Sure, yah can't even tell the time with only the one!" scoffed Bernie, as Martin slipped them onto his arm.

"Sure I can tell the time! I taught meself," said Martin, looking down his nose at Bernie.

"But all the watches' hands are pointing at different numbers," said Bernie. "So which one is telling the right time?"

"I know," piped up Nabby. "Our Paddy taught me how to tell the time."

"Go on then, clever clogs." For a short while Nabby sat studying all the watches on Martin's arm, before suddenly announcing, "They're all the right time!"

It'd seemed all those bangs our brother Paddy had delivered to Nabby's head with Mammy's alarm clock hadn't taught him a thing about telling the time. When Paddy first hinted he'd be willing to teach all of us how to tell the time, it had seemed an exciting prospect. After we'd witnessed his teaching method of bonking Nabby over the head with the clock whenever he got the time wrong, we'd decided that time, after all, wasn't that important to us.

"Here." Martin slid a gold-coloured watch off his arm and handed it to Nabby. "Yah can get some more practice while yer sittin' there doing feck all."

It never bothered me that I couldn't tell the time. For me, time was meaningless and had no beginning and no end. Any given morning would follow its usual course into any given afternoon and on into any given evening and a night, before ultimately drifting back into another morning, another afternoon and so on. And as long as it kept doing that, there was nothing for me to worry about. The same for the four seasons. Spring into summer saw all the flowers and the trees in full bloom, with the majority of moody people smiling again and giving away their pennies. Autumn into winter and all the blooms died off, with a penny much harder to come by as the majority of people walked around with their heads hunched into their shoulders.

Christmas, too, always came along without fail, with the carols and Christmas trees and all the bright twinkling lights that went with them. And Father Christmas coming to see all the good girls and boys, which was the reason why he never came to see us - not that any of us really cared. While the pot-bellied miserable bastard brought the odd toy to all the goody-two-shoes, we were out stealing our own Christmas presents. And lots of them, too.

"Okay you lot! You can hand those over right now." The taller of the two fellas we'd seen walking past the jewellery counter in Woolworths stood in front of us with one hand raised in the air, like a policeman holding up the traffic. Only he wasn't holding up any traffic but a small leather wallet with a silver star-shaped badge attached to it. His companion stood alongside him, trapping us underneath the arched entrance and blocking off any escape route.

"Hand what over?" Martin had put on his blagging face, looking so innocently confused, he had "guilty" written all over it.

"The items we saw you helping yourselves to from the jewellery department in Woolworths, that's what!"

"You're not having me feckin' Sindy!" yelled Bernie, "I paid for it, so yah can fuck off!"

"Well, if you paid for the doll, it isn't a problem, is it?" said the tall policeman, giving Bernie a smile.

"We paid for all the watches, too," said Martin.

"And the three lighters Martin has in his pockets," said Nabby. If looks could have killed, he should have died on the spot as the three of us glared at him.

"Right! You have two choices," said the tall policeman, who had clearly become agitated. "You can either hand over everything you've just stolen from Woolworths and clear off, or we can take you down to the nick!"

"Just give him the poxty tings!" said Bernie. But Martin had other ideas and had suddenly thrown himself to the ground, faking a seizure, which caused the two policemen to take a cautious step backwards as they watched him writhe on the ground like he was in his death throes.

"He's having a fit!" I shouted.

"He's not having a fit!" scoffed the tall policeman.

"He's dying, so he is!" pleaded Bernie.

"He's always doing that," said Nabby.

"What, dying?"

"Puttin on - I mean, having one of his fits!"

"Hurry an' call the ambulance!" said Bernie, scowling at Nabby.

"If he were having a real fit, his feet would be shaking." The tall policeman stepped forward to take a closer look down on Martin, whose feet, right on cue, had suddenly gone into spasm like a tap dancer tapping out a dance.

"Faking it! Just as I'd thought!" The tall policeman set about sliding the watches off my brother's arm before groping in his pockets for the lighters.

Incensed by this, I took a run up and was about to kick the thieving policeman in the gob. But his short fat companion was far too quick for me and managed to get his podgy hand around my throat. "Okay son!" he snarled, "Let's be having them." He searched my trouser pocket, before pushing up the sleeves of my jumper and shirt and forcing me to take off all the watches on my arm.

"I'm not your feckin' son!" I snapped angrily at him.

"No you're not! Otherwise you'd have got one of these!" He cuffed me across the side of the head before letting go of my throat. "Now clear off or you'll be in serious trouble."

We watched as the two policemen, laughing and ignoring the names we were calling them, ambled back down in the direction of the Stretford Road.

"At least I still have me Sindy doll," said Bernie, pleased with herself.

"Only because yea'd stuffed it down your knickers," said Martin.

"Then you should have stuffed all the watches down yer pants, Martin! They might have let yah keep them!" retorted Bernie.

"We've still got this," Nabby held up the gold-coloured watch Martin had given to him earlier.

CHAPTER 31

Close Call

There were a lot of comings and goings at the house. First thing one morning, two detectives called to speak to Martin and me separately. They wanted to know about the night we came home and saw Daddy in the kitchen having a strip wash, while Mammy was sitting in the back room waiting for us to come home. They said Mammy and Daddy said we could vouch for this.

Like proper robbers, we asked the two detectives to show their police badges to us just to prove they were real detectives, before we would agree to talk to them. We had seen the baddies do this in the films. Their badges looked nothing like the star-shaped sheriff badges the other two policemen had shown us, which made me suspect that the first two 'officers', who had walked off with our lighters and watches, were fake.

When these real policemen questioned me I wasn't going to let them catch me out telling them something completely different to what Martin might have already said. I was much too clever for that. Before answering any of their questions, I got them to confirm the answers Martin had already given.

"Did Martin say, when we saw Daddy washing himself in the kitchen sink, he had some blood on him?" I asked.

"Something similar," said one of the detectives. And so I agreed that was the case.

Easy peasy! I even stuck up for Daddy and told them how he would often bring one of our older sisters down into his bedroom to comfort them when they were upset and when Mammy stayed away from the house after another of their drunken rows.

"Was your Mam waiting in the house when you came home that night?"

"Did Martin say we passed her coming home early the following morning?"

"Something similar."

"Then she wasn't in the house that night," I said.

The two detectives thanked me for helping them with their enquiries. and I was only too pleased with myself for being cleverer than them.

Not long after they had gone, Uncles Paddy, Oliver, Christy and Raphael, showed up at the house with Father Murphy in tow. We'd had no idea what was going on as the priest set about blessing the house and everyone in it, before turning to Uncle Oliver and asking him, "Will yer late Father be joinin' us at the house? And of course, your dear Mother?"

"Aye, they'll be here for sure," Oliver assured the priest. And knowing our Grandad, who was always up for a good family booze-up, he'd be here, even if he was a little late!

Turning down the bottle of ale from Uncle Oliver, the priest accepted a glass of sherry from Mammy, which he blessed before downing it in one gulp and holding the glass out for a refill. Mammy obliged, before whishing us all out of the house. "This isn't the place for children ta be listenin' to grown-up talk."

While Martin, me, Nabby and Bernie took the pram and headed off to collect a few more pennies for the Guy, Maggie took the younger ones off to Auntie Maureen's, who only lived a few streets away in Philips Street. Nabby said he wasn't going to be the guy again and I was only too pleased to volunteer. My stomach had been feeling queasy and walking the streets hadn't been such a good idea. I donned the one-armed donkey jacket, the old cloth cap and the broken Guy mask Bernie had found in Woolworths and off we went.

By late afternoon we had seen only the odd few pennies pass through our hands, which Martin suggested we might as well spend on blackjacks. The three of them left me outside the corner shop, only for me to be stolen by a bunch of thieving little kids, who rushed off with me up along Rosmond Street with Bernie and my two brothers in hot pursuit. I, meanwhile, desperately fought to keep the cheeks of my bum squeezed tightly together.

"I think we lost them!" said one of the kids and the pram slowed to a much gentler pace. Having never been stolen before, I was unsure what to do next. I didn't know how many kids were involved in my theft and so I wasn't sure if I stood up, whether they would make a run for it or bash me up? Even worse, would my bowels drop in the process? Not wanting to tempt fate I continued to lay back in the small pram without moving a muscle.

"That's a fine-looking Guy Fawkes you have there, John."

"Yes, Mrs Mullins. Our dad made it for us."

"Yah lyin' fecker! Yah stole me!" I was a whisker away from shouting.

"Almost lifelike."

Squinting through the mask I saw Mrs Mullins open her purse before bending over the pram to have a good look at me. "Almost lifelike," she repeated, while reaching a hand out with the threepenny piece between her two fingers. Enough was enough. I snatched the threepenny piece out of the shocked woman's hand and sprung up out of the pram, pushing it hell for leather back up the street. Before long I bumped into Martin, Nabby and Bernie and we headed over to a group of derelict houses.

I just managed to scramble hurriedly over the loose debris and squat inside the entrance to what was once somebody's kitchen, when my bowels finally emptied. Jaysus, the stench! "Can any of yah see any auld rags?" I called out to the others, who were searching the house.

"I've found some electric flex!" said Martin.

"I can't wipe me hole with a lump of flex!"

"I've found tuppence!" called Nabby excitedly.

Spotting the edge of a dirty net curtain poking out from the debris a foot or so away from me, I gave my bum a good wipe and while others searched around upstairs, I stepped outside and away from the stench I'd created.

I always found it easy to drift off into my own world when visiting those empty places, conjuring up images of a forgotten time, of smoking chimneys and children swinging off lamp-posts, chasing after the ice-cream van, playing football, jumping on the back of a moving lorry and generally enjoying their lives. But I was soon snapped abruptly out of my reveries.

"Oh Jaysus!" cried out Bernie. "It's them! The Boyds!"

Running back over the debris and into the house, I went upstairs into the front bedroom to find my panic-stricken sister. Through the dirty cracked window panes, I could just make out Pat and Terry Boyd, heading straight across the croft in our direction. The pair of them were in the company of a little blonde-haired lad, around the same age as myself. And though none of us had ever set eyes upon him before, it was easy to tell he was a Boyd, even from that distance. The young kid seemed to be having a good time throwing his toy parachute high up into the air and watching it slowly drop back to earth, as Pat Boyd took aim with his air-rifle and fired off a shot at it.

"Oh God! They're going to shoot us!" cried Bernie. "What are we goin' ta do?"

"Keep our gobs down for a start!" snapped Martin, placing a finger on Bernie's lips. "Anyways, we don't even know they'll come right over this way."

"But the pram's outside!" said Bernie.

"Shit, I left the guy's clothes and the mask in it!"

"I'll get it," volunteered Nabby.

"Leave it!" said Martin. "Get the bricks over there and pile them next to the stairs at the ready. If them feckers start to come up, we'll bounce the lot off their heads!"

Martin didn't seem too bothered about our approaching doom, or he did a good job of keeping it to himself, probably putting on a brave face for Bernie's sake, which was the sort of thing he would do. Poor Bernie. She had already wet herself with the fear and to be honest, I was grateful I had already opened my bowels.

"Yah missed again!" We heard the little boy's excited voice.

"Throw it up higher then!" Pat Boyd's voice sounded very close to the house. Another sharp snap, and we could only sit and watch in silence as we saw a mouse dangle upside down from its makeshift parachute, which had snagged on the jagged edge of the broken window pane. It didn't seem to have been injured though it had desperately wriggled in its feeble attempt to free itself. I hadn't really felt anything for the plight of the mouse, having an acute hate for them. And under normal circumstances I'd have probably whacked it with a lump of wood. Not that it was normal in Hulme to see mice dropping from the sky in parachutes.

Another crack and the mouse was dead. "Gotcha!' Pat Boyd sounded very pleased with himself.

"I want my parachute back!"

"Well yah can go fetch it yerself, I'm not gettin' it for yah. An' don't expect us to be waitin' for yah either."

To our relief, we heard footsteps walking away from the house, only for our joy to be short-lived when a moment later we heard someone approaching. Putting a finger to his lips for us to keep quiet, Martin tiptoed out of the bedroom and picked up two of the bricks from the small pile, holding them at the ready.

"Augh! It stinks like a skunk in there!"

We listened as the kid hurried away over the debris before we dared stand up. We saw him catch up with his brothers and we watched them through the broken window pane until they eventually disappeared from view.

CHAPTER 32

What's Up With Grandad?

Shamie was throwing down large chunks of old lead from the old church roof when we came across him for the first time in almost three weeks. We asked him if he wanted us to give him a hand and put some of the lead on the pram and take it home for him.

"Fuck off and don't mention a word to the old woman about seein' me," he said, climbing down from the small side roof. "I've left for good and won't be coming back to that poxty dump any more!" I supposed this wouldn't make any difference to Mammy considering she was hardly at home herself to miss him. It was the same with our eldest brother Paddy, who'd run off not long after Mary and Rose had left, leaving Helen, aged thirteen and Maggie, aged ten, to take on the responsibility of looking after all nine of us that were left.

"Is it okay if me an' Martin ta have yer's and Paddy's bedroom? Since yah won't be needing it any more?" I asked.

"Jaysus Tommy!" said Shamie, picking up lumps of the lead and taking them to the small wooden entrance gate of the church. "Yea'd jump in me coffin before I got cold!"

A rusty grey old van pulled up and Shamie's mate Jaffa jumped out of the driver's side. He began loading the lumps of lead into the back of the van and we lent a hand, picking up the smaller pieces and throwing them in.

"Yea can have the bedroom.," said Shamie. "An' I'll also throw in two bob, if yea'll do a favour for me later on tonight."

"Two shillin' each?" I asked.

"A fuckin' shillin' each! Or nothin', not even the bedroom. Take it or leave it, I'm in a hurry."

We immediately agreed to the deal even though we hadn't the slightest clue as to what the favour was going to be. Shamie arranged for us to meet him on the corner of Park Street at around seven o'clock, when he'd tell us what we had to do and give us our dosh.

"I didn't know St Philip's Church was derelict?" said Bernie, which for some reason made Jaffa burst out laughing.

"Hurry up Jaffa and get us outta here!" ordered Shamie, hopping into the passenger side of the van, which looked as if it was about to collapse any minute under the sheer weight loaded into it.

"You'd better fuck off outta here!" warned Jaffa, handing me a shilling piece. "And it isn't!"

"What isn't?"

"The church isn't derelict – shit!"

Following Jaffa's gaze, we saw some people, five in all, hurry out St Philip's School gates and head towards us.

But as we had done nothing wrong, we decided we were going nowhere fast.

"Don't forget Martin. Seven o'clock on the dot tonight!" shouted Shamie through the broken side window of the passenger door. The old van chugged off, coughing and farting its way along Newcastle Street, with three of the posse from the school following close behind it but not fast enough to catch up with the old heap. Meanwhile two women had stopped next to us and were giving out about stealing the lead from off the church roof and of how we should be ashamed of ourselves. We said it was nothing to do with us and got out of there.

Later in the afternoon as the darkness started to slowly creep in on us, we made our way back home. There had been some discussion about whether or not we should be going to Auntie Maureen's or to our own house. Bernie seemed minded to believe Mammy had wanted us to go and stay with her sister indefinitely. Or at least until she had sent word for us to come home. But she had been outvoted by the other three of us who'd decided we should go home first and see what Mammy had meant us to do. I had wondered out loud, if Grandad had got to the house on time, but the others were more interested in wondering about the favour Shamie wanted.

One of Daddy's favourite sayings was, "It's better to be late than never." Not that the lady sitting behind the counter at the Labour Exchange had seemed all that impressed with him, when he had turned up two days late to sign on and had tried to use his two "very ill boys" - Martin and me - as his excuse for being late. The woman had laughed in his face, telling him, "Not only would it take you a million years to convince me your two sons are seriously anaemic, sir! But it is obvious to everyone looking in this direction, their faces have been powdered white!"

We had smugly shrugged our shoulders at Daddy, as if to say, "We told you so!". It had been as plain to us as the plain flour he had used to coat our faces that his idea was doomed to failure. Daddy wasn't impressed by the woman's attitude or her catching him out. "Why don't yah feck off back to the jungle and play with yer coconuts!" he suggested to her, which had gotten him arrested and fined by the magistrate. The fine had originally been twenty shillings, but Daddy complained this amount was far too much for him to pay, saying that such an amount could feed a whole tribe of Zulus and suggesting the Magistrate ask the woman from the dole office, who'd given evidence against him, to back this up as "she is one of the tribe!" His fine was increased to forty shillings.

Arriving outside at our house, we found it in total darkness. This wasn't that unusual if there was no-one at home, but given it was only about six o'clock, it was unusual for no-one to be home. Martin tried the back door and found it locked so Bernie and Nabby had gone around to the front of the house, coming back with the news that the front door was also locked.

As luck would have it, the latch on the sash window to the back room was not completely pushed home. And so with a few bangs against the window frame with the side of his clenched fist, Martin was able to work the latch across and pull the bottom half of the window upwards until it hit the two small blocks of wood Daddy had screwed to each side of the runners to stop the window from opening too far. With Bernie being the skinniest, she agreed to squeeze in through the small gap so she could unlock the back door for us.

"Get on yer knees Tommy and I'll get up on yer back," she ordered. I could hardly feel her weight as she stepped up on my back and attempted to squeeze her tiny frame through the gap in the window. "There's loads of beer bottles on the table," she called back to us. "And there's a kinda box, too."

"How d'ya mean a box?" asked Martin.

"A box."

"But what kind a box?"

"A feckin box-box, Martin! What other kind of box is there!"

"A small box? A big box?"

"Let's have a ganders," said Nabby as he stepped up on my back. "I can't really see much but yep, it's definitely some sort of a box all right. A biggish one."

"Didn't I already tell yah it was a poxty box?" yelled

Bernie.

"Can't yah push it out of the way then?" snapped Martin.

"Jaysus! Me back's goin' ta break in a minute!" I warned the pair of them as they walked all over me like I was a doormat.

"It won't budge, it's too heavy," said Nabby.

"An' so are yea two! Will yah get off me back!"

"Out the way," said Martin. "I've an idea."

"Don't yea be jumpin' on me back, too!"

"There's no need." Martin told the other two to get off me, much to my relief.

Fetching a length of wood from the pile of firewood, he shoved one end through the window. We all got behind him and pushed on the wood until the large box slowly moved across the table taking most of the empty bottles with it, before it fell off the table with an almighty crash.

Up on my back once more, Bernie managed to squeeze herself through the small gap this time and a few moments later, we were walking through from the dark kitchen into the dark backroom. Nabby flicked the light switch up and down, but no light came on, concluding, "The electric's gone, or the bulb's broke."

"That's clever," quipped Bernie.

"Well, it's obvious!" snapped Nabby.

"Exactly!"

"I can't see nothing."

"That's cos it's dark Nabby."

"Well that's feckin' obvious, too."

"Exactly."

"Will yea two give over?" I said.

"Light the lighter Nabby an' we'll be able ta get a better look," suggested Martin.

When the lighter flicked into life and Nabby held out the tiny flame in front of him, we were just able to make out some flickering reflections off the empty beer bottles lying about the place, but not much else. In the dim shadowy light my eyes had homed in on a plate with a couple of biscuits still on it.

"It must be someone's birthday," said Nabby as he moved the small flame slowly around the room, casting shadows everywhere. "Fuck me sideways!" he shouted suddenly. He dropped the lighter, leaving us in pitch dark, with me choking on the two biscuits I'd greedily shoved straight into my gob.

"What the feck's wrong with yah Nabby?" said Martin

"There's someone lying on the floor! I think its Grandad! Where's the poxty lighter!"

"What's Grandad up ta?" asked Bernie.

"Not much," said Nabby, "Grandad! Are yah alright? He's fast asleep in a heap! An' the stench of drink!"

"D'ya think he missed the others an' fell asleep waitin' for them to come back?" I asked. "That could be the reason why the back door was locked?"

"An' drunk all the party beer ta himself!" laughed

Martin.

"What was the big box that fell? Can yah see it?" asked Bernie

"I can't even see me hand. Aah he's got hold of me!" screamed Nabby.

"It's me that's got yah! I'm down on the floor!"

"Feckin Jaysus, Martin! Yah scared the life out of me!"

"Here it is!" Martin flicked the lighter back into life again. The small glow had given us enough light to barely see each other, "He's obviously drunk himself silly or that box we pushed off the table has hit him and knocked him out cold," concluded Martin.

"Oh God! He'll swing for the lot of us when he wakes up! An' if he doesn't, Mammy will!" said Bernie and she started crying.

"For God's sake will yah shallup!" snapped Nabby.

"We'll have to put him somewhere out of the way." By this time, the lighter had run out of petrol so there wasn't even a glow to light our way.

"In Mammy's bed" was Bernie's bright idea! Nabby thought we should throw him down the cellar steps, so as it would look like he'd knocked himself out by accident. I suggested taking him down the alleyway to the Red Rose pub and leaving him propped up against the wall, "which wouldn't be unusual, being it was Grandad".

Martin said Bernie's idea was the best of the lot, as he would be much safer in Mammy's bed, as well as keeping him warm. Grandad was small and thin, so it wasn't too difficult to haul him up by his arms and legs and into Mammy's bedroom where, counting to three, we threw him on the bed and covered him up with Mammy's heavy coats. As well as locking the back door, we also made sure the brass window catch was firmly set in its locked position, then left by the front door. We made our way into town, where we bought a portion of chips and mushy peas to share amongst the four of us with my shilling, before going off to meet Shamie.

CHAPTER 33

Romeo, Romeo

—

We'd just turned the corner of Park Place when we stopped to watch four fire engines speed out from the station and head off up the street. In the silence that followed, we noticed the fire station seemed to have been left empty and so we decided, just out of curiosity, we would take a ganders inside.

There wasn't much to see downstairs and so we went upstairs, where we found the kitchen, homing in immediately on the long table with the half-empty plates of sausages, eggs and beans, buttered slices of bread and half-empty mugs of warm tea, left by the firemen as they hurried off to their emergency. It must have been ten minutes since we had polished off the bag of mushy peas and chips between us, yet there was still plenty of room for more in our hungry stomachs. And so, without ceremony, we snatched up handfuls of the food and greedily stuffed the lot down our throats, swilling it down with mouthfuls of the warm tea.

"Listen!" whispered Martin. "Did yah hear that?"

"Hear what?" I only just begged the question when we heard the flush of a toilet and then a door opening, followed by the sound of squeaky boots heading up along the corridor in our direction.

"We've been corrupt!" said Martin. He dashed behind the kitchen door with the rest of us following him, squeezing ourselves tightly together in an attempt to make ourselves as invisible as possible. The footsteps squeaked past us and across the kitchen floor, where they moved constantly around, backwards and forwards, backwards and forwards. It was so nerve-wracking I found myself wishing the poxty fireman would just walk over and find us.

Hearing the whistle of a boiling kettle and then the noise of a spoon stirring in a cup, I dared a peek around the door to see a giant of a black fireman standing sideways on, supping from a mug, which I could barely see in his huge hand!

"Aaaaah!" I just couldn't contain the scream of fear as I remembered the big black man at the prison, who plucked out children's eyes and sucked them like gobstoppers. The huge fireman almost jumped out of his skin. Spilling his steaming hot drink all down himself, he howled in pain and rushed over to the sink, where he stood throwing mugs of cold water all over himself. This was our opportunity to rush out of our hiding place and out the door, before he'd even had the chance to get a look at us.

We laughed all the way to Park Street, where we saw Shamie's cranky old van parked up near the corner of

Clarendon Street, and we sneaked up on our brother to give him a scare.

"Gotcha!" shouted Martin, as we had all banged our fists down on the back of the old heap and watched as the passenger side door was suddenly flung wide open. Out fell Shamie onto his knees, coughing, spluttering and spitting out bits of tobacco, while Jaffa got out from the driver's side, roaring with laughter.

"Yah bastards yah!" coughed Shamie.

"What's wrong with Shamie, Jaffa?' asked Martin. We had never seen him act in that way before.

"We thought you were the coppers!" laughed Jaffa. "Shamie only tried to swallow the joint he was smoking! That's the best laugh I've had in ages!"

"I nearly burnt me tonsils ta ashes, yah gimpy-eyed gormless bastards yah!" Shamie raged.

We said nothing, having learnt the hard way that it was better to say nothing as it only antagonised whoever it was doing all the bawling at us. Daddy was the worst to answer back to. Usually his reply would be a punch in the gob or, if you were too far away for him to reach you with his fist, the first thing that came to hand,.

Thankfully, Shamie seemed to get over the initial shock quickly. He leaned into the van and brought out a small polythene bag half full with dried peas.

"Here," he said, handing the bag to Martin. "Take these with yah ta number sixteen. Yea'll have to go down the back way an' throw a handful at a time up at the top window to the left-hand side of the house when y'er looking straight at it. An' when Maureen answers, tell her I'm waitin' up at the top of the street for her, if she's still interested."

"Interested in what?" I asked.

"Never mind!"

"What if she doesn't want ta come out?" asked Martin.

"She'll want ta come," said Shamie, all cocksure of himself, "An' if she doesn't, that'll be her loss! An' watch out for her mam or the game's up! Sly hen that one - got a face like a cow chewing grass. An' keep yer voices down, cos her half-dead, bed-bound granny kips in the bedroom off to your right."

"And how are we supposed ta know which house is sixteen?" asked Martin.

"Look for the puke-yellow painted back gate. It's the only one along there. Yea'd have ta be colour blind to miss it!"

Leaving Bernie and Nabby with Shamie and Jaffa, Martin and I set off towards the back alleyway between the houses. We walked in pitch darkness, save for the odd lights from the houses. The air along there had stunk to high heaven of dog shite and if you'd wanted to sneak down here without anyone knowing, it would have been a miracle. Once the first dog heard us and started barking and jumping up against the other side of the back gate, the rest followed suit, growling and barking and letting the whole of Park Street and adjoining

Welcome Street know we were on our way.

It had not taken us more than a couple of minutes to come across the puke-yellow gate and the pair of us quietly snook into the dark back yard, not that there wasn't enough noise going on around us with the barking dogs to have drowned out any noise we might have made. The only light on at the back of the house was downstairs in the backroom. We could see the dim light through the curtains but were unable to see inside. Martin tipped a handful of the hard peas into his hand and threw them up at the bedroom window on the left hand side as Shamie had instructed. Almost immediately, the window squeaked upwards and a soft female voice purred down from the dark. "Is that you Shamie?"

"No!" said Martin, keeping his voice to a whisper.

"Who is it then?"

"It's Martin an' Tommy."

"Shamie's brothers," I whispered.

"Shamie sent you, did he?"

"Yeh." I kept the conversation flowing as we both looked skywards trying to get a glimpse of the "beautiful tart", our big brother had forever gone on about. We were having difficulty in making out any of her features, though she did have the soft voice of an angel.

"Why did he send you?"

"Are yea Maureen? Only Shamie says we've to be careful not to let the auld witch catch us," I said;

"The auld witch?"

"Aye, yer mammy."

Martin seemed impressed by the way I'd been handling things and had kept silent for a change, letting me do all the talking, which I'd always thought I was good at despite some people thinking I went on just a little too long. Daddy once told me, "You'll talk yer way into prison one day" though to be honest, I would have preferred to be a fireman or a policeman instead. Failing that, I liked the idea of working in Woolworths, just so I'd be able to walk behind any of the counters without having to worry about arousing suspicion. Giving me all the time in the world to nick whatever I wanted.

"Yes, I'm Maureen. What else did my Shamie say about me mam?"

"Only that she has a face like a cow chewin' grass," I'd said, "Anyway. Shamie wants ta know if you're comin' out with him tonight?"

"Just give me a tick while I get some things together." Maureen went away from the window.

"That was an easy two bob!" I said.

"Do yah think yah should have told her what Shamie said about her mammy?"

"She's getting her things isn't she?"

"Here! Cop this!" Maureen had come back to the window.

Squinting upwards into the dim light, I could just make out what had appeared to be a medium sized handbag."

"Just a small makeup bag and things," explained Maureen.

"Let me catch it!" said Martin, "Since yea did all the talking."

He reached into the air with his hands high at the ready. "I'm ready! Yea can drop it!"

"At the count of three then," whispered Maureen. "One. Two. Here it comes!"

"Aaah, Jaysus!" gargled Martin, as the contents of the pisspot hit him full in the face. "Yah dirty auld scrubber! I curse yah ta sunder!"

"Tell that disgusting sex maniac brother of yours," said the disembodied voice, no longer angelic but vicious and angry, "if I so much as catch him standing on the corner of this street, I'll cut his bollocks off! Now get away from the house before I get the police on to you!"

The curtain on the ground floor window had suddenly swung across and we came face to face with a young girl of around fourteen, staring wide-eyed back at us. She opened the window gentlly and popped her head out. "Tell Shamie me mam is going out in about half hour and I'll come just after then."

"Who are yah?" asked Martin.

"Maureen."

"We'd better get going or her mammy might get the coppers onta us," I warned my pissy-smelling brother. And so we hurried up the alleyway with Martin cursing

everyone who had lived in the house and on the whole
street, including all the barking dogs.

CHAPTER 34

The Walking Dead

"Jaysus! What's happened ta yea Martin?" asked Shamie with a smirk.

"She threw a pot of piss down on him," I volunteered.

"Maureen!"

"Her mother - we think."

"It must have been the old Grandmother's pisspot she tipped over yah," said Shamie. He and Jaffa were sniggering.

"It's not feckin funny!" snapped Martin.

"Ah, we're only joking with yah Martin. Here, let me pour this over yah." Shamie had pulled a big bottle of cherryade out of the van. "It'll at least help get rid of the stench." He slowly poured the whole bottle over Martin's head, with Martin rubbing it into his hair and face, managing to catch some in his cupped hands and drinking it, before drying himself with the dirty rag Jaffa handed to him. "Did ya get to speak ta Maureen?"

"I was me that spoke to her," I said.

"I'll tell Shamie what Maureen said ta tell him!" cut in Martin, who refused to give Shamie the message unless he gave him four shillings for his troubles.

Shamie's attempt to barter Martin down to three shillings fell on deaf ears and Shamie handed over the money with a scowl.

"Well? Is she or isn't she coming out?"

"She said - are yah sure yah want to hear this, Shamie?"

"Just tell me what her answer was!"

"She said, yah have big fat blubbery lips like lumps of bacon. An' the only humpin' yer up ta, is humping things on yer back. She also said, yeh have a mickey no bigger than a little maggot!"

"Shullup!" shouted Shamie.

"An' she also said yah can hump as many tarts as yah like because she never wants ta see yer ugly mug again," I added for good measure. Jaffa lent up against the side of the van holding his sides, in fits of hysterical laughter.

"How did she know about humping other tarts?" our furious brother asked me. "That's it Jaffa! She can kiss me arse, that one. Anyway she's so frigid, she'd even started to cry when I'd gone to get me mickey out. So she couldn't have seen how little it was. Let's go and find some tarts in the city."

We tried cadging a lift home in the van, which Shamie agreed to - if we paid four shillings. As we walked off, we heard the van brake sharply and turned to look, thinking Shamie, out of the goodness of his heart, had changed his mind about the lift. But instead, we watched him get out of the van holding a small lump of lead piping, hurry back the few yards to Maureen's house, then he threw the pipe straight through their front window before running back to the van.

Thanks to Martin's cherryade rinse, his short hair was standing on end like the spikes on a hedgehog. We bestowed him with a new name, Dennis the Menace, which I felt sure he would have preferred to his usual nickname, Crying Face, as he was lovingly known to us on account of him crying a lot, even when he was happy.

As we'd turned the corner of Stamford Street, we noticed the police car parked under the dim light of the lamp-post outside our house. Mammy and Uncle Christie were standing outside talking with a policeman, which was all too reminiscent of the many times they come along to arrest one of the family, but mainly Daddy, even though this time we knew he was already in jail.

We took our time walking up along the street, attempting to hear what the nosey neighbours were whispering, but they suddenly became dumb as we approached, finding their voices again once we had passed by. Auntie Mary came outside to join Mammy and Uncle Christie and we could only think there must have been another big row which wouldn't have been out of the ordinary at one of our gatherings. Weddings, christenings, midnight Mass, St Patrick's Day - all would have a big-fight finish to end the day on a high note. "Here they are now," said Mammy and all eyes suddenly fixed on the four of us.

When a group of people stood staring at me, I would come over all guilty, even when I knew I'd done nothing wrong. If anyone should take the blame for this, it would have to have been our Daddy. He'd beaten us and had accused us of doing things we had not done, to the point where we would admit to having done it just to stop the beatings. "I can see by the look in yer eyes, it was yea that did it!" Daddy would stare directly into the eyes of which ever one of us he was accusing and would hold our gaze until our eyes watered and stung so much we would have to concede defeat.

"Have yah been back ta the house since yah left?" asked Mammy, slipping another fag into her mouth and lighting it with the dimp of the one she had just finished.

"No Mammy," said Martin.

"The doors were locked," said Bernie, digging us into a hole - again!

"I thought Martin just said yah hadn't been back ta the house?" said Mammy suspiciously.

"I said we've not been in the house, Mammy," said Martin.

"Did yah see anyone while yah were here?"

"How d'ya mean Mammy." said Martin.

"Only Grandad," said Bernie.

"Yea'd hang the feckin' lot of us, so yah would!" said Nabby under his breath.

"How d'ya mean yah saw yer Grandad! Where?"

"Ah - Well he was -"

"Peering out the window at us." I said, helping out my tongue-tied brother.

"What da'ya mean! He was peering out the window at yah! What window?"

"Yer bedroom window, Mammy."

"He waved to us," added Nabby.

"Are yah sure it was yer Grandad yah saw Tommy?" questioned Uncle Christie, as Mammy and Auntie Mary scurried back into the house.

All those questions made me feel nervous, bringing on that awful guilty look. There was something not right and no one was telling us. And where was Grandad? He obviously hadn't woken up yet - unless - oh God forgive us! I was on the point of blurting out, "It was an accident! We banged him on the head with the big box and put him in Mammy's bed!", when an almighty scream shocked everyone into silence.

"He's in the bed!"

"It was us!" confessed Nabby. "We did it!"

"Yea did what, Nabby?"

"We killed Grandad - well, Martin, Tommy and Bernie, did all the killin'!" said the little snitcher. "I just stood and watched them pushing the big box out of the way. It must have fell on his head! Martin said Grandad was drunk, that's all. 'An' so we put him in Mammy's bed to keep him warm." He pretended to cry and after we finished snarling at him, the three of us followed suit.

"What the feck are they carryin' on about?" snapped

Mammy as she came back outside and lit another cigarette. "I've enough on me plate with yer dead grandfather!"

"What's goin' on in the house?" asked Uncle Christie.

"The auld man's lying in me bed! An' unless he's one of them feckin' walking dead people, somebody's been up ta no good! Mary's in there on bended knees swearing blind it's a miracle. The police have called the doctor, though I can't see what the feck for. He's as dead as he's ever goin' ta be for sure."

"Here Martin," Uncle Christie had taken us to one side and placed a half-crown into Martin's hand, telling us to go to the sweet shop, "Don't worry about a thing, I'll sort it out," he assured us in a low voice. "And say nothin' ta yer Mammy or anyone else."

Then he turned to Mammy and, with the hint of a wry smile on his face, asked her "D'ya think he wasn't dead after all?"

"He's been laying in his coffin for five feckin' days doing nothing Christie! What d'ya think he was doin'? Havin' a long kip?"

CHAPTER 35

Battle of the Boyds

Standing alongside Martin, Bernie and Nabby, we watched the flames soar high towards the sky and wrap themselves around the Guy Fawkes sitting at the top of the bonfire. The frenzied cheers and shouts from the crowd, "Burn yah bastard! Yah fucking traitor!", echoed around the croft and mingled with the acrid smell of gunpowder and smoke as the fireworks whizzed in all directions across the dark Tuesday sky.

Earlier that morning, we'd gone to the church to see our Grandad off to heaven, though Uncle Bernard, along with a few of the others, was minded to believe, "the Devil would have been hard-pressed to have him". Mammy and Granny were still none the wiser as to how Grandad could have managed to climb out of his box and walk through the house and make himself comfortable in Mammy's bed, when he hadn't budged an inch all the time he'd laid in the morgue for the previous five days. As for us, we had not known what a 'wake' was, until we saw Grandad standing in his coffin, which was leaning up against the far wall by the window, giving him a good view of the drunken mourners gathered around him. To be honest, he hadn't looked much different to some of the others in the room - small, gaunt, skinny and pale - only his eyes were closed and he was dead sober.

At the church, Father Murphy seemed to have had a lot of nice things to say about Grandad, which must have been all lies, considering what some of the family had been saying about him. The old priest even said how lovely it had been to see all his family coming together from as far afield as Ireland and Scotland to pay their last respects to a dear family member. He must have then cursed the lot of us when our Grandad Jim, Daddy's daddy, boxed Uncle Bernard in the gob for no other reason than our uncle had a coughing fit when Grandad was singing his solo song, "Kevin Barry".

"He did it on feckin' purpose ta drown out me singing, so he did!" said our drunken Grandad.

"Drown out yer singing by feck! It's yea that needs drowning, so we don't have ta put up with the noise anymore!" snapped Uncle Bernard.

"Will yah keep the peace!" pleaded Auntie Brenda. "Bernard's had a bad cold all the week! Just look at the state of that nose of his, all red and sore like it is."

"Ah shallup, yah feckin who-ere!" Mammy took a swing at Auntie Brenda, completely missing her target and falling in a heap on the church floor. As small as she was, our auntie could put up a good fight and she had given Mammy a good kick up the backside, warning her, she

wouldn't be responsible for what would happen next if
Mammy carried on giving out to her. But there wasn't
much she was able to do when Mammy staggered to her
feet and suddenly grabbed a handful of Auntie Brenda's
hair, before dragging the poor woman off up the church
aisle. Mammy would probably have dragged her all the
way back to Stamford Street, if it hadn't been for the big
clump of hair that had suddenly separated from her head.

Having already decided between us that we didn't
want to see our Grandad put down into a hole in the
ground, Martin and me had managed to sneak off
around the corner of the church to the old unused
graveyard, where we had hid ourselves from view
behind the gravestones, until we were sure everyone had
gone. Then we headed into Longsight where we would
often spend hours on end scavenging amongst the empty
streets of derelict houses.

We met up with Paul Ryan, Kevin Taylor and a
few other kids we knew. We drifted onto each other's
territories without many problems as long as none
of us took the piss by refusing to let each other join
in searching the same derelict houses. We had this
unspoken understanding that nothing belonged to
anyone until they had found it, as in Finder's Keepers.
Not long afterwards, we were joined by two of our older
cousins, Michael and Sonny O'Connor, who would
normally hang out with Shamie and his gang. They
lived in Gorton with their mammy and daddy and seven

sisters. Their daddy was also in prison for stabbing their uncle for humping their mammy and eldest sister Nancy. Daddy had warned us to keep away from the whole family: "Especially cousin Sonny! That fella's a feckin' screw loose in his head!"

Sean Docherty, a tall skinny lad with a long beanpole neck and a tiny head balanced on the top of it, invited us to play a game of six-a-side football. There were six of them up against four of us, but we agreed anyhow because we were Manchester United, the greatest team to have ever lived, up against Manchester City who went four-nil up within the first two minutes of the game. They were a much better class of footballer than we were ever going to be and it seemed we were on a hiding to nothing. Yet, five minutes later, City had suddenly conceded defeat to United, because of too many injuries. I like to think it was more to do with the fact that they realised they had met their match and we were just too good for them.

The later part of the afternoon took the four of us across to Hulme Lock to explore some of the derelict warehouses there. This is where Shamie had once taken Martin and me rat hunting. The place to catch them was in the once-busy loading bay tunnels of the derelict Merchant Warehouse, where the barges used to float in every day to offload their goods. Lots of kids would go up there with their toy catapults and shoot at the rats with small pieces of brick or mortar or anything else small and hard enough to do some damage.

Shamie made his own catapults and they were powerful. But unlike my big brother, who was a deadeye shot, me and Martin were hopeless. The nearest I had ever come to shooting a rat was on that very first occasion Shamie had taken us along with him. He'd spotted a cat-sized rat sitting on a windowsill of the Irwell Rubber Company. There it had sat with its back to us, minding its own business and washing itself clean. Shamie indicated in sign language so the rat wouldn't hear, that he had wanted me to have the kill. Martin, who had been standing close to me, had stopped still while I had slowly inched my way nearer, until I was no further than about five yards away from it. Closing the one eye, I had taken careful aim and had let the stone fly. I'd heard a squeal as the rat had dived off the windowsill back into the water.

"Feckin' hell Tommy!" Shamie had not been too pleased about my useless shot. Holding his hand to the tip of his bleeding nose, he bellowed at me. "It was there! A huge feckin' rat, the size of an Alsatian dog. Right there in front of yer gimpy eyes! I'm standin' a mile away from yah, an' yah still manage to feckin' hit me!" And that was the last time and only time he'd taken me rat hunting with him.

By the late afternoon, our two cousins decided to call it a day and we made arrangements to come over into Gorton the following day and hang around with them. We watched from the top windows of the derelict warehouse as they made their way back along the edge of the canal bank, until they eventually disappeared from our view. And that was when we suddenly noticed the two fellas, one carrying a smaller kid on his shoulders, heading from the other direction straight towards the warehouses.

It would have been impossible not to have recognised the Boyd brothers, Pat and Jimmy, with their youngest brother Billy sitting on his brother's shoulders. The fact that Jimmy Boyd was pointing a finger straight up in our direction was a good enough indication they'd seen us.

"Sonny! Michael!" We shouted at the top of our voices, in the hope our two cousins might still have been close enough to have heard us as the Boyd brothers reached the derelict warehouse and were gawking upwards.

"Yeas can come down!" Paddy Boyd shouted up to us. "I only want ta have a word with yeas," said Paddy, though he was pointing the barrel of the air rifle straight up at us. With the light fading quickly, we thought there may have been a slight chance we would be able to get out of the warehouse and slip away unnoticed. Parts of the back walls and roof were already missing, with large areas of flooring ripped out for firewood or other useful purposes, leaving wide areas of empty space where, in the dim light, we were just able to see all the way down to the ground floor.

"Yea'll have to come up here, if yea want ta talk to us!"

Martin called down. But there was no response from the Boyd brothers, who had moved out of our sight.

Accepting the only possible escape route out of the top room was to make our way across the thick wide wooden beams, spanning about fifteen feet of empty space with a twenty-foot drop to the ground floor on both sides and then making our way down the demolished parts of the outer wall, we committed ourselves and made our move. My fear of looking downwards would have been a problem in the daylight, but I felt relatively safe making my way across the bean with the darkness below me and Martin leading the way, staying close to me.

We eventually reached ground level without any mishaps, before quietly sneaking out through a small hole in the wall at the side of the building, relieved not to have come across the Boyd brothers and minded to believe the cowardly bastards had decided not to risk coming all the way up to the top of the building in the ever-decreasing light. But unfortunately for us, we had let our guard down.

"Thought we'd gone did yah!" Pat Boyd appeared from out of the thick undergrowth along the edge of the water. He was pointing the barrel of the air rifle straight at Martin, who instinctively threw his arms up into the air, like the cowboys did in the films when John Wayne pointed a gun at them. His brothers Jimmy and Billy stood behind us, blocking off any escape route.

"You. Ugly fucker. In the water. Now!" Pat Boyd

snapped at Martin.

"He can't swim," I said.

"Boo-fuckin' hoo for him! Then you can jump in! Know-all! Or I'll shoot yah dead!" he snarled, pointing the barrel of the rifle at me. But unlike my brother Martin and for no particular reason that I could explain, I did not throw up my arms. Instead, I had defiantly glared up at him just like John Wayne would have done.

"He can't swim either," said Martin.

"Well yah can both fuckin' learn! Yah pair of Irish bastards!"

"Can't yah leave them alone?" said Billy Boyd. "They've done nowt to us."

"Haven't we seen yer ugly mug before?' said Pat Boyd, ignoring his little brother and pointing the rifle back at Martin, who was shaking so much I could have sworn I'd been able to hear every bone in his body rattling. Of course, my brother denied having ever set eyes on the two bastards.

"We're not gettin' in the water," I heard myself say, before swallowing the lump of fear down my throat. And though my bones had joined Martin in a duet, it seemed I'd lost all sense of reality and I carried on, "An' if yah want us to get in there, then yea'll have ta put us in there yerself! An' if yah try to put us in there yerself, I'll bite yer feckin' nose off yer face, so I will!"

"Oh yah will, will yah!" raged Pat Boyd, once again aiming the barrel of the air rifle straight at me. "Gobby

little fucker aren't yah! Well let's see how gobby yah are!"
He handed the air rifle to his brother Jimmy, before
suddenly grabbing hold of me and throwing me to the
ground and undoing the buttons of his trousers. 'Yah can
give me a gobble for yer lip. An' shoot that little fucker's
eyes out and throw him in the canal if he doesn't!" he
told Jimmy Boyd, referring to Martin.

"Leave him alone!" shouted Billy Boyd, rushing away
from his brother Jimmy to stand between me and Pat
Boyd, giving me time to get back on my feet.

"Ouch, what the fuck!" Jimmy Boyd yelped, his hand
automatically shooting up to the side of his bleeding
head.

"Prepare ta die yah Boydy bastards yah!"
My heart had jumped up into my mouth as Shamie
and Jaffa had appeared from nowhere brandishing their
catapults. They were followed closely by our two cousins
Michael and Sonny, charging in from the opposite
direction like a pair of demented cavemen wielding
lumps of wood high in the air.

The battle, if you could have called it a battle, lasted
all of a minute, with Jimmy Boyd, after getting a couple
of clubs around the head, jumping into the canal and
heading off across to the far side. Pat, the tougher of the
two, held his ground and shoved the barrel of the gun
straight up Sonny's left nostril. "It might be just a lead
pellet but it can still do a lot of damage to what's left of
your brain!" threatened Paddy. But the threat had no

impact on Sonny, who brought the lump of wood down with a heavy blow on Pat Boyd's shoulder, causing him to drop to his knees and let go of the air rifle in the process.

"Ahh! Yah broke me fuckin' shoulder!"

"That's what I meant ta do." Sonny whacked Paddy across the side of the head. "An' I'm goin' ta break every other bone in yer body!" he said, raising the lump of wood for another swing.

"Hang on Sonny!" said Shamie, who had suddenly appeared along with Jaffa and stood looking down at Billy Boyd. 'Who've yah got there with yah?"

"Billy," said Billy, "I'm their brother."

"An' our friend," Martin added quickly, stepping closer to the little kid. "He's nothin' to do with any of this. An' how'd yah know we was here?"

"Yah can recognise Tommy's big gob, anywhere,' said Shamie. 'It's like a foghorn! Lucky for you, me an' Jaffa were further along breaking windows when Sonny and Michael came along and we heard yah! Anyway the three of yea can go now, while we have a chat with this fecker."

"Yea won't be hurting him? I mean, not too much, will yah not," asked Billy.

"Nah. We only want to show him the errors of his ways, especially why he shouldn't be asking little kids to gobble him, that's all," lied Shamie.

"Just yea wait!' Jimmy Boyd shouted across from the other side of the canal, where he'd managed to pull himself up out of the dirty water and on to the towpath. "Y'er already fuckin' dead an' buried the lot of yah," he threatened while holding the side of his head. "Git over here, Billy. They won't dare hurt yah!"

"I'm not comin' with yah!"

"Just wait till Mammy an' Daddy hear yer hanging about with them dirty Irish bastards! There'll be murders in the house!"

"There'll be more murders if Mammy an' Daddy find out yea were showing your mickey to Cathleen when they were off down the pub last week!" shouted Billy.

"Don't be feckin' showin' me up with them lies now, Billy!"

"Sure they're not lies! Me and Connor were peeping in at the pair of yah through the keyhole! We saw her kissin' yer mickey! We've seen her doing it before as well!"

"Me mickey got caught in me zip an' she was only helpin', that was all! So don't be makin' up these things as yah go along!"

"Yah weren't wearin' any trousers when we were doing all the peepin' an' she was sucking it like a lollypop! We could see everything goin' on!"

"Just wait till I get me fuckin' hands on yah, Jimmy! Yah dirty bastard yah!' screamed Pat Boyd.

"He's a liar Pat! He's makin' it all up! I swear!" pleaded Jimmy.

"I wouldn't mind this Cathleen helping me with me

zip and kissing me mickey better," laughed Jaffa. "Whose girlfriend is it anyway?'

"Cathleen's our sister." said Billy.

CHAPTER 36

Wrong Side of the Tracks

I was over in Gorton scavenging amongst some derelict houses with Nabby and Martin. They had already been stripped to the bone, with hardly any upstairs floorboards left to walk on. But, as we had not searched them, we did so on the off-chance we might find something of value that someone else might have missed.

The kids around the surrounding towns lived dangerously throughout their childhood, though I don't suppose as kids we'd had any thoughts of the dangers we had risked day after day. Until of course something had happened to serve as a reminder. It seemed we had become so blinded by the opportunity of finding something worthwhile to take home, that we had never heeded the warning signs of danger. We had walls and roofs crashing down on the houses we'd been searching through just moments earlier. We'd fallen through floors and burnt ourselves, as we burned off the rubber casing from the electrical flex. We'd grazed, bruised and badly cut ourselves. And yet, we still came back again and again for no other reason than we had to. It was in our blood, our way of life. For the poorest families of Manchester, this was our means to survival. And if Manchester hadn't been ripped asunder by the demolition gangs, then God only knows how the poor children of Hulme, Moss Side, Gorton, Longsight and the surrounding towns could have survived.

In the early part of the afternoon we were playing in the car park up by the Speedway Stadium near Belle Vue Zoo. This was the place where lots of kids came to race their handmade bogeys around the cindered surface, pretending to be one of their heroes from the Aces Speedway team. It was great fun, if you'd had a bogey to ride, which we hadn't this time, because a few days previously some thieving bastards had stolen the one we had stolen some weeks earlier. So we had to ride the two ladies' bikes we'd stolen from the graveyard of St John's Church.

We had great fun racing across the cinder surface before hitting the front brakes, causing the back of the bikes to go in a different direction from the front. The idea being to try and get the bike to skid a full circle, as well as kicking up as much dust as possible. It seemed easy, if you were just a bystander watching, but it wasn't easy. You had to get the pressure of the braking just right and if you didn't, then there was every chance the back of the bike would rear up in the air, as Martin had found out to his detriment at his first attempt, which had everyone watching in stitches.

It was one of the funniest things I had ever seen in my

whole life! There was Martin, madly peddling down the gravel slope before suddenly slamming on his front brake, with the front of the bike coming to a sudden stop, as expected, only for the back of it to keep going, causing the bike to complete a full somersault, with Martin hitting the deck and the bike landing on top of him!

We sold the bikes on to a rag-and-bone man for two shillings before heading off back in the direction of Longsight, where we were chased up along the railway sidings by one of the rail workers after he'd spotted us searching around in one of the engineering sheds. Where we'd found ourselves a small metal sandwich box sticking up from one of the engineer's lunch bags. Martin opened the lid for us to see the four doorstep Spam and pickle sandwiches and the three shelled boiled eggs staring up at us.

"Hoy! What are yah doin' in here?" cried the rail worker.

Like greyhounds out of their traps and taking the lunch box with us, we set off at speed out of the side door of the works shed and up along the track sidings, making our way across the rail lines toward the coal depot on the opposite side. Martin told Nabby, who was a stride behind us, to hop over the rails and not to touch them as they might be alive. But moments later we heard him scream out loud, much louder than any of the screams our older sisters had screamed when Daddy was beating them. We hurried back to find Nabby desperately wriggling his skinny right leg as he tried to pull his foot out from between the two rails that were gripping it. "They just snapped at me foot and grabbed me!" cried Nabby. "Is it 'cos we stole that fella's food? Martin, get me out! I don't want to be eaten!"

"Yah won't be eaten, so shallup or yea'll have everyone on top of us!" I snapped.

"Yah said they were alive!"

"I didn't mean alive as in feckin' them breathin' alive!"

"Anyway, these ones are dead. Otherwise you'd be dead by now!" I said, trying to to pacify him.

"There's a train coming!" Martin pointed up along the track in the direction of Longsight station, where we could see one of the coal trains slowly moving in our direction, causing Nabby to scream even louder.

"Run to the train and make it stop!" said Martin. And so I took off along the track in the direction of the oncoming coal train, waving my arms and screaming at the top of my voice for it to stop. I could see the driver as the train came alongside me and then just glided past, separating me from my brothers.

"Martin! Nabby!" I screamed, but my voice had been drowned out by the noise of the train's brakes suddenly grinding against the wheels. They squealed and slid along on the shiny metal surface of the rail lines, before the giant metal monster shuddered to a sudden halt.

I ran back along the side of the train, fearful for my brothers, until I suddenly heard Martin's voice, calmly talking above the other voices. "His foot got stuck!" and then I heard my little brother asking, "Has anyone any sweets?"

"Hey! You!" The two rail workers had ran round from the back of the train and hurried down the track towards me. But they were never going to be quicker than me and I scarpered off like a frightened fox, across the rest of the rail lines and back into Longsight, while they could only stop and look on breathlessly.

The fact that Martin and Nabby had not been hurt had filled me with so much joy, I almost skipped along the street heading up to the recreation ground, known to us as Sand Park. It was here we had picked as our meeting place in the event of us becoming separated, which was a common event for us, considering we were always being chased. The Policeman, the Shopkeeper, the Bus Conductor, the Milkman, the Truant Man, the park Pervert, the Priest, the Drunk! It seemed the whole world had wanted to chase us down.

Once, Sergeant Turner had shown Martin and me some old documents while we were sitting in the police station waiting to be charged with grand larceny. It was our impressive one hundred and eighty fifth charge to date. Mainly for petty thieving, but mostly for stealing bicycles. This time we'd been caught by the police as we ran up the road on a Sunday afternoon carrying a chewing gun machine, which we had managed to force off the wall of a corner shop. We told them we'd found it and were bringing it to the police station, but our protestations of innocence had fallen on deaf ears. The fact we had been hurrying off in the opposite direction from the police station hadn't helped our argument.

"Look at this!" Sergeant Turner, had stabbed his stumpy finger down on a tatty page of the old document. "Ten years! That's how old this child was when he was hanged by the neck until he was dead. And what for, hmm? Stealing a silk hanky! That's what for! And another here!" He had gone down the list of children's names, those hanged for the most minor of crimes. "Hanged by the neck for stealing a goat! Children the same age as you pair of little toe-rags! Doesn't it even bother you?"

"We don't steal dirty hankies - or goats, for that matter." said Martin.

"Where yea a young lad in them days?" I asked sincerely, but instead of answering me, the Sergeant had turned on his heels shaking his head with despair and walked off muttering something about us being, "Born too late!"

I had not known how long I waited in the park for Martin and Nabby to show up. Time was always a hard thing to judge, especially when the days grew darker early. So I had no real idea as to how long I had sat on the swing in the light drizzle, waiting for the pair of them to come along. But it did seem an age since the three of us had become separated by the train. For a while, I joined in a game of football up inside the large, open-sided shelter. But as the grey light of day had slowly faded towards darkness, everyone drifted off to their homes in small groups until eventually I was on my own. Not that being alone in the dark had bothered me too much. But even so, I had taken some comfort from the fact there had been some working street lights dotted about the area.

I toyed with the idea that perhaps my two brothers had already been taken home by the police and I wondered whether I should make my own way home. But thinking that the pair of them could suddenly show up any minute, I decided to hang about for just a little while longer. It was the flare of a light that had first grabbed my attention before noticing the young couple standing together in the gloom.

CHAPTER 37

The Strangers

I could see the top half of them standing on the opposite side of the small boundary wall of the park as the man lit a cigarette and had then held the flame to the woman's cigarette before he took a long look across in my direction. Then the pair continued on their way along Ducie Street, seemingly paying no more attention to me. I began to swing myself high into the air and noticed that the man and woman had stopped a short distance from the shelter at the top of the park and seemed to be having a conversation with each other. Then they headed back down the path in my direction, with the woman stopping a short distance away from the swings.

I slowed myself down with my foot and watched her approach, while the man remained some fifteen yards or so away, the fag dangling from his mouth and both his hands pushed deep into his dark raincoat, which had the collar of it turned up around his ears. He seemed uninterested in me and stood looking about his surroundings while the woman threw me the sweetest of smiles. I anticipated her saying something to me, but when she just stood looking at me and saying nothing, I threw her back a brief smile to let her know, at the very least, I was approachable. Then I returned my face to its usual scowl, reserved for those people I didn't know, as well as serving its purpose to keep my emotions unreadable.

Standing sideways on to me, the woman lent her head coyly to one side. "Hello," she said, speaking in a soft reassuring voice, "are you waiting for your friends?"

"No!" I said quickly, as if the question had been an accusation. In some way, she reminded me of my eldest sister Rosemary, though my sister would have been a little younger, around seventeen years of age. This woman was taller and much heavier in build, but her features, especially her eyes, seemed to soften when she smiled, just as my sister's always did. Their hair, too, matched in style, though my sister's hair was naturally fair, while the woman's, from what I could see underneath her pink nylon headscarf, looked to be a dull white.

"You're a bit too young to be out in the dark by yourself aren't you?"

"I'm seven and a bit." I said proudly. "An' I'm not scared of the dark."

"You don't have to be," she said, moving a little closer to the swings, while I used my foot to keep it gently moving backwards and forwards. "I'm not either."

There was a brief lull in the conversation before she continued, "Haven't seen you round these parts before. What street are you from?"

"24 Stamford Street, Hulme, Manchester, 15." My

address rolled off my tongue off by heart, just as my sister Helen had taught all of us to remember it, until it had been ingrained on our brains. This had served its purpose on the odd occasion we had travelled much further than we ought to have done, such as the time me and Martin ended up in Newcastle after sneaking into the back of a removal truck while the removal men had taken a break.

"Hulme!" The woman seemed quite surprised and looked back over her shoulder in the direction of the man. "The lad's from Hulme!"

"Hurry up!" The man spoke impatiently.

"You hungry?" she asked. "You look hungry."

Bringing the swing to a halt, I nodded. She walked the few yards to me and placed her hand on the swing's chain. "What's the little lad's name then?"

In the cool breeze, I could smell a heavy mixture of her perfume and hairspray, reminding me of the nice lady who had cuddled me when she thought the dead old lady who had fallen down the concrete steps was my granny.

"Tommy." She didn't tell me her name. It would be months later, as I watched a TV news programme about the arrest of two suspected child killers that I discovered she was called Myra Hindley and her male companion was Ian Brady. "How about a jam buttie? Then we'll get you straight home?" She raised her dark eyebrows enticingly and I nodded my agreement.

"Come on then Tommy!' She shook the swing chain

playfully and I slid off, offering my hand out for her to take, but she ignored the offer and instead threw her hands deep into her coat pockets. "You mustn't be seen walking with me, or you'll get in to trouble," she warned. "I'll call you when to come." Hindley then walked off around the swings away from both myself and Brady and headed in the direction of Ducie Street.

I had taken her warning to mean, I mustn't get caught talking to her, as we were strangers to one another. We had been told of the potential dangers of talking to strangers on so many occasions by Sister Joseph, Mr Coleman, our Headmaster and Father Murphy. But we had to make use of every opportunity that came our way; it was an important part of our survival. Life would have been much harsher without the many kind strangers who gave us their pennies, some even allowing us into their homes where they washed and fed us before sending us on our way.

I had always considered myself to be more streetwise than the average kid, because I knew the streets better than most having begged off them and almost lived off them. And as well as being aware of those places not to venture near, I had a gift of being able to read every given situation that I had found myself in.

We would often deliberately go to the parks where the perverts hung out. Sometimes one of them would peek out of a bush, asking one of us to come over and see something. And as I'd been the fastest runner, I would be the one to go to the bush and ask for a shilling, promising to come into the bushes once they'd handed over the dosh. And when they did, I'd flick the coin to Martin and we'd both make off in a hurry.

Streetwise as I was, I would never have gone off with a man if he had been on his own. But a woman on her own, or a woman with a man was an exception to the rule. I always felt safe being in the company of a woman - unless she was a nun - and Myra Hindley seemed no different to the many other women we had met on our adventures through the streets.

"Come on then Tommy," said Hindley, who had stopped a short distance away. She glanced over at Brady who took a last deep drag of his cigarette, before throwing the dimp to the ground and digging his hand back into his coat pocket.

"Come on then!" Hindley said again and I had immediately followed her out onto the street and we set off towards Gorton. There was no urgency in Hindley's pace as she walked ahead of me, allowing me to be able to keep the same distance between us. At one stage of my journey I felt a sudden pang of guilt as I thought of Martin and Nabby. I wished the pair of them could have been walking with me, so we could have all shared in the treat. But the guilt had quickly subsided, as I had reminded myself that they had the railway man's lunch box and would probably have already scoffed the lot down them.

The roads along the way were relatively quiet, with only the odd car passing us by. Above me, the sky grew darker, the chimney stacks already at work spewing out their plumes of thick black smoke, which rose up into the darkening grey sky.

Gorton, like Hulme, had its fair share of dilapidated housing hiding away in the shadows of the better streets with their tarmacked roads, nice Edwardian houses and front gardens all lit up by bright electric streetlights. And yet, just a stone's throw away in any one direction, you could walk into a street of back-to-back Victorian slums, some still with their cobbled streets and lit by the depressive aura of the gas lamps, which was made even bleaker by the fine wispy smog hanging in the air.

Looking back, I saw that Ian Brady was following some way behind us. His hands were still deep inside his coat pockets and his head still bowed low, half-hidden inside the collar of his coat, though it had not been a particularly cold or wet evening.

Hindley suddenly turned off the main road into a side street, forcing me to quicken my pace so I wouldn't lose sight of her. And as I followed her around the corner, I noticed she slowed her own pace and was looking over her shoulder in my direction, I assumed to make sure I still had her in my sights, before she upped her pace again, crossing over the road and walking in through the gate leading into Gorton Park.

As I followed Hindley into the park, I suddenly had

a flashback of the summer just passed, when Martin, Bernie, me and Nabby had walked through the same gates and joined lots of other people sitting in the warm sun on the freshly cut grass where a brass band was giving an impromptu performance in preparation for an upcoming tournament. Another of Daddy's old sayings was, "Where there is lots of people gathered, there are lots of opportunities to be had." There might be the odd coin that slipped from someone's pocket, or the odd shopping bag to dip a hand into. And so we had settled ourselves down on the grass with our vulture-like eyes scouring the area for potential opportunities.

When the band had finished their practising, we circled the people who had gathered around to wish the band well for the tournament. I had my eye on an open shopping bag and the box of Ritz biscuits resting inside when I saw Martin from the corner of my eye, hurrying backwards away from the crowd, dragging a huge brass tuba with him. We always had an unspoken understanding about stealing only the smallest of objects, especially when there were lots of people around. So it was beyond my understanding to know what had possessed my brother to grab the biggest feckin' thing he could lay his thieving hands on and drag it across the grass in full view of everyone. The three of us had instinctively dashed off to help Martin, managing between the four of us, to lift the heavy instrument off the ground and run across the park with it.

"What are yah goin' ta do with it?" asked Nabby.

"Play the feckin' thing, what d'ya think!" said Martin.

"Yea can't play one of them things - can yah?"

"He's only coddin' yah Nabby," I said.

"We'll hide it in the bushes and come back for it when it gets dark," said Martin.

How had he thought no-one would have noticed four children running across a park with a huge brass tuba? The whole of Manchester must have seen us unless they'd either been fast asleep or blind! So it had hardly come as a surprise to see what appeared to be the whole of Manchester, led by the band's conductor, hot on our heels.

Accepting we had no chance of getting away, we'd stopped on the footpath and faced down the conductor, who held back the crowd with his baton held high in the air, as if readying himself for the next tune.

"Ten bob or we'll drop it an' dance all over it!" threatened Martin. We'd settled for three-and-six, sending Bernie to get the money from the conductor first. When she'd returned to us, we'd gently placed the tuba down on the grass before fleeing out of the park and back in the direction of Longsight.

CHAPTER 38

A Sense of Evil

Following Myra Hindley across to the other side of Gorton park and out along the streets. I could see to the right the silhouette of the huge red-bricked building of St Francis' Friary standing off in the distance, its tall tower lost somewhere in the mist. I had often stood on the wide open wasteland looking across at the huge red-bricked building and wondered what I would be able to see if I could have climbed right to the top. But as well as suspecting the Fire Brigade would not have had a long enough ladder to be able to bring me back down again, I think all I would have seen was a panoramic view of what I could already see from ground level: the derelict houses, the slums, the smoking chimneys, the empty mills.

Walking under the bright light shining at the entrance of a pub on a corner of Taylor Street, Hindley peered back over her shoulder at me and smiled briefly, as she had done on a number of occasions throughout our journey. Nearby, I heard the faint sound of a train and then a group of young Teddy Boys, five in all, suddenly appeared from around the corner.

Smartly dressed in collars and ties, one of them stood

playfully in Hindley's way and shimmied from side to side, like a footballer ready to make a tackle, as a few wolf whistles echoed along the street. But Hindley completely ignored their antics, walking straight on without deviating from her path and forcing the fella to step to one side, to his friends' amusement. As they disappeared into the pub, I noticed they couldn't have been much older than sixteen or seventeen. A quick glance over my own shoulder told me Ian Brady was no longer behind us and I wondered if he had gone off into the pub for a pint. But other than that fleeting thought, I thought no more of his sudden disappearance.

Throughout our journey we walked along streets that were familiar to me from my scavenging expeditions. And despite the mix-match of gas and electric streetlights, this part of Gorton had seemed slighter better in some parts than those parts of Hulme where I roamed, though it still radiated the same dismal, dank atmosphere along its endless dark and relatively silent corridors of streets and alleyways.

Turning off the main street, Hindley paused for a moment, allowing me to get closer to her, before she walked out into Bannock Street. By the time I had hurried the short distance to reach her, she'd already opened the front door of her house, beckoning to me with her gloved hand to come quickly. And I upped my pace to her.

To my surprise, Ian Brady suddenly appeared from

nowhere and was beside me, his hand on my shoulder, guiding me gently through the open doorway and into the house. I looked straight up at him and our eyes had met briefly. His distant unsmiling eyes reminded me of my brother Paddy. With his baby face and deep blue eyes, Paddy was always serious looking, as if he'd forever had something playing on his mind. Like Brady, he had a thick mop of sweptback hair, but there the similarities ended. For Paddy's hair was jet-black and greasy and swept back with an added twist, teddy-boy style, while Ian Brady's hair was browner, wavier, and not as greasy as my brother liked to have his. Turning his gaze away from mine, Brady closed the front door behind us.

Following Hindley through the house in to a back room, with Brady following close behind me, I stood watching her as she took off her black leather gloves and dropped them on to the table top, which had only the one leaf up. Undoing her coat, she then took off her pink scarf and a long black silk neck scarf she'd had tucked inside her coat. She hung the black scarf over the back of one of three old chairs around the table, which stood beneath the sash window overlooking the back of the house.

Hindley invited me over to sit down, and I sat on the frayed seat of the chair opposite the one over which she had hung her scarves. My back was to the fireplace and I was facing a small alcove with an open doorway that led off into what I assumed to be the kitchen. Despite the house feeling much warmer, dryer and devoid of that distinctive damp smell that lingered inside 24 Stamford Street, I was surprised at how dreary the place looked and felt, considering both Hindley and Brady, by appearance, were smartly dressed people with a self-assured confidence about them. Myra Hindley, especially oozed what I could only describe as a childlike charm, despite her age.

It was here in the back room that I could smell a mixture of stale tobacco and alcohol mingled with whiffs of Hindley's hairspray, which had smelled much stronger inside the house. On the table were some empty glass tumblers alongside a small saucer that had been used as an ashtray and was full with tipped and untipped cigarette ends. Over to my right stood an old wooden cabinet with a couple of small framed photographs plus other odds and sods on the top. Brady walked into the kitchen without saying a word. I smiled at Myra Hindley. She lit a cigarette and blew a plume of fresh smoke across the room, before dropping the Ten Park Drive cigarette packet down onto the table top and returning my smile. I liked her, especially her smile, which made her blue eyes light up.

"Do you have brothers and sisters? Won't your mam be going up the wall? What are you doing so far away from home?" Jaysus! She was as bad as the coppers!

"Me Mammy's gone off and left us on our own and she wouldn't give a shite if she never set eyes on the lot of us again. And me Daddy's in prison and I hate him and wouldn't care if I never saw him again!" was the answer I wanted to give. But none of us ever spoke about the goings-on within our family because to us that would have been worse than committing an original sin. And so Yes or No was about the best Hindley was going to get out of me. Not that she seemed all that interested, as she let her fag dangle from her mouth and slipped off her coat to reveal her knee-length black boots, black skirt and black top. She walked away from the table just as Brady came out and hung his coat on a hook screwed onto a smaller door under the stairs, leading either to a cellar or a cupboard. Hindley hung her coat over his, before the pair of them walked off into the kitchen together. I could hear their low muffled voices but not what they were saying. Not that I was particularly interested in their conversation. As usual, my only reason for being in the house was on the promise of a bite to eat.

Taking in the rest of my surroundings, I saw behind me an open fireplace with a dirty brass coloured mesh fireguard across it. Mammy had always kept our fireplace clean and ready to light again. But this fire hadn't been cleaned and was filled with the ashes from a previous fire. I heard the ticking of the wooden clock sitting on the mantelpiece, its face hidden by the envelopes resting up against it. Over in the corner of the room next to the fireplace, the door of a cupboard stood slightly ajar, wide enough for me to to spot an assortment of bottles on a shelf, easily recognising the large Bell's Whisky bottle, because it had been one of Daddy's favourite drinks even though he was Irish.

I heard Myra Hindley suddenly speak sharply before lowering her voice. And for some unknown reason, this unsettled me. I wasn't able to understand why I felt this way. It wasn't fear. There was nothing in my thoughts that had made me feel afraid of anything in particular. Indeed, it was nothing new for me to be sitting in a stranger's house, sometimes much later than this. But the nagging feeling inside my head was telling me, "Something isn't right!". But what that something was, I just couldn't put my finger on. The thought had earlier passed through my mind, that Brady and Hindley somehow didn't seem to fit the house, in the sense that everything around me had given me a feeling of much older people. The furniture, the décor, everything about the room had seemed too old for such a smartly dressed young couple and it didn't fit that they would have bought such a mishmash of old bits and pieces of furniture.

Hindley walked back out of the kitchen and plonked the plate down on the table. She'd a glass in the other hand with a dark red liquid drink inside, which she took a swig of as I looked down, wide-eyed and my mouth watering, at the large inviting knocker of bread thickly coated in red jam.

"Hurry up and get that down you and we'll get you off home," she said. And I immediately smelled the alcohol from her breath, which was a little like the pungent smell of the sherry Mammy always drank. Hindley then left the room, leaving her glass on the sideboard and I heard her footsteps walking up the stairs.

Alone in the backroom with just the tick-tock-ticking of the mantle clock for company, I pulled the plate over to me and noticed straight away, perhaps somewhat disappointed, that the thick slice of bread had not been buttered. "What is wrong with me?" Usually I would have been tucking into this kind offering by now, but instead, I had been throwing questions at myself. Had I just imagined that the young woman seemed slightly apprehensive, almost nervous? And certainly not as talkative or as cocksure of herself as she had been before. Had I noticed her hand tremble slightly as she'd dropped the plate onto the table instead of placing it there? Had I imagined that the warmth in her piercing blue eyes had diminished, leaving them slightly cold looking and distant as she had spoken those words to me? Had I imagined that her childlike charm had been replaced by a harsher tone in her voice? Why, unlike every other house I had been into, had this man and woman been the only people to have left me to eat on my own? Oh God! Speak to me! What is it? What are you trying to tell me?

I couldn't help, but feel how the atmosphere had changed since first walking into the house. Perhaps on account of me worrying over nothing? I started to feel cold, which was unlike me, because even in the winter I didn't really feel the cold that much. But here in this house, I had begun to feel a different kind of coldness, the kind that seemed to creep slowly inside my skin, gripping me tight and not wanting to let me go.

It is hard to put into words the awful feelings swirling around inside me. I became very unsure of my surroundings and I began questioning why I was sitting in this house in the first place. Although I had sat in the houses of many kind people unknown to me, I had always made the first approach to them.

"What is it? What is different? Why am I even worried?" With my mind asking questions to which I had no answer and my senses on red alert, I had an overwhelming sense of panic all the way down in the pit of my stomach, so I almost felt like vomiting. These two people had shown me only kindness and yet I knew I could not accept their kindness. I had a frantic urge to leave the house - and quickly!

CHAPTER 39

A Narrow Escape

I was on the point of calling out, "I want to go home!" when I heard footsteps coming back down the stairs and then Hindley walked back into the room. "Are you ok?" she asked.

"Can I have a drink of water, please?"

"Course you can." She picked up her glass from the sideboard and headed into the kitchen, where I was able to hear a muffled conversation again but just as before, not able to hear what they were saying. A moment later, she brought me back a glass of water and placed it in front of me. "Come on. You need to get all that down you so we can get you home!" she said with a smile and I couldn't help but notice that the sparkle was no longer there.

Back in the kitchen, I heard Hindley raise her voice again, although the pair were talking in whispers, and then Brady snapped at her, "Fucking wait!" Then they continued speaking in very low, whispery tones. Taking one last look at the huge slice of bread and jam, I swallowed my hunger, deciding it was my time to leave. Why had I not just eaten the bread and jam and then told them, "I'm off!" Why had I not just picked the slice of bread and jam up off the plate and walked out with it through the front door? I am unsure of the answers to those questions. But I let my instincts take over and got to my feet quietly and quickly.

Slipping the brass catch open on the sash window, I gently lifted the bottom half of the sash upwards, but the window had suddenly jammed and the bottom half of the sash wouldn't move further than a couple of inches. I began to feel physically sick and thought I might faint in panic when I remembered that our own back window had wooden blocks fixed onto the inside runners to prevent it from opening all the way up. Fortunately for me, this wasn't the case here and with every ounce of my strength I pulled the window until the weights on each side suddenly dropped and the bottom half of the sash shot upwards with the loudest of noises.

"Little shit's out the window!" cried Hindley. I heard someone running through from the kitchen into the room and I felt a hand grab at my right foot, which had become tangled around the curtain. As my momentum kept me going forwards, the curtain untangled and I dropped the few feet to the ground on the other side, just as I heard the distinct sound of the bolt from the back door drawing back and hitting its stopper.

"Basta -' was all I had heard Ian Brady say before I hopped on top of the covered motorbike resting against the back wall and, with the extra height, was able to climb over the wall and drop to the other side. Then

I ran. I had no clue as to where I was running to, or which way I should go, or even why I was running. But my instincts took me through alleyways and along some wasteland until I came to a row of three bombed houses. I caught sight of an old dark green toilet door which had been resting up against a large mound of debris in what was once someone's backyard and it was here, beneath the door, that I had hidden myself away from the world for what had seemed like an eternity. Now and again, I would hear voices of passing people. And at one time, I listened as the approaching footsteps came to a sudden halt right next to me. I could clearly see a pair of men's black polished shoes, with the toes pointing directly at me, and as I held my breath, my mind was conjuring up all sorts of scenarios leading to my demise. The owner of the shoes had dropped the lit cigarette dimp on the ground and it came to rest just a few inches away from the edge of the door and my face. I was in two minds whether to scream and make a run for it, or just lay still and keep quiet, when a line of steaming piss had suddenly extinguished the dimp, pushing it further under the upturned door while splashing me in the face. Then the shoes walked off.

It was then that I finally ventured out from the safety of the green door and made my way home, managing to beg eight pennies on the way.

It didn't surprise me to find Mammy wasn't there when I'd arrived back home. Maggie was sitting by the fireside,

warming her hands on the last remnants of the embers.
I noticed the slight flicker of relief across her drawn face,
before she had gone up the wall at me.

"Where the feck have yah been Tommy! It's half ten!
We've been out all the hours searching for yah. Well
Helen an' Bernie have! Yah could have been dead or
murdered or something else for all we knew! And we
don't have the money ta be burryin' yah!"

"I've eight pence." I pulled the handful of coppers
out of my trouser pocket and offered them to Maggie.
She took them out of my hand and placed them on the
mantelpiece before continuing to give out at me, "Where
have yah been all these hours?"

"Nowhere."

"There's no such place as nowhere."

"I meant, nowhere ta write home about. It's only half-
ten!"

"Yah know yah should never be out on yer own in the
pitch dark at these hours, Tommy. Yah had us all worried
ta death." She walked into the kitchen.

"I wasn't out on me own all these hours."

"Who were yah with then?" I wasn't going to tell her
I'd been sitting in front of a huge lump of bread with
half a jar of jam spread on the top and I'd run away
from it for no reason other than I wasn't sure of the
people that had given it to me. She'd have probably
killed me, after wanting to know every single detail as
to why I hadn't eaten it, why I hadn't brought it home

with me, why I'd been in a stranger's house on my own. She had not mentioned Martin or Nabby and as I wasn't sure whether she was trying to catch me out on a lie, I changed the subject.

"Is Mammy home?"

"Mammy got arrested in the pub for hittin' Patsy McGuire after she'd asked after Daddy. Mammy accused her of having an eye on him, but when Patsy said she wouldn't have been seen dead with the likes of him, Mammy boxed her one in the gob, knocking out two of her front teeth."

"What about Martin and Nabby?"

"What about them?" Maggie came back from the kitchen with two slices of bread and dripping on a plate, which she handed to me.

"They must be home. Aren't they?"

"The police brought the pair of them home a few hours back. Poor Nabby! He's lucky to be alive or standing up with both his legs still attached to his skinny little body."

"He's not been hurt has he?"

"He's okay, the pair of them are. He got his foot stuck in the rail tracks up by Longsight station, when him and Martin were being chased by a pack of wild dogs! The train driver only saw the pair of them at the very last second and slammed his brakes on, managing to stop the train no more than half an inch away from their faces!" Wild dogs? Jaysus! Those two could spin a good yarn!

My sister never made mention as to the fate of the imaginary pack of wild dogs and as there'd been no mention of me being with the pair of them, I blagged my way through a few more of her questions before telling her I'd been out with our two cousins Paddy and Martin Ward, which seemed to satisfy her curiosity. Devouring the last slice of bread and dripping, I went off to bed and left Maggie to wait for Helen and Bernie to come back from searching for me and give them the good news.

The following Saturday there was tragic news. It seemed as if the whole of Hulme had suddenly gone into mourning, especially amongst the Irish community, when the news spread of the assassination of the American president John. F. Kennedy. With the streets empty and the pubs full, with the whiskey and the beer flowing along with the crocodile tears, there were outpourings of grief, for "one of our own"- an American none of them had ever met or knew a thing about.

CHAPTER 40

The Phantom Door Rattler

Christmas day was one week away and lots of things had gone on in the weeks leading up to it. Just after the American President had been shot dead, twelve-year old John Kilbride had vanished from the market in Ashton-Under-Lyne, where he'd been helping stallholders in exchange for pocket money. Despite extensive enquiries by the police, and help from the people of the surrounding communities, there had been no sign of the kid.

Mammy had come home. The charges against her for assault had been dropped because Patsy McGuire was too afraid of losing the rest of her teeth, which is what Mammy promised her would happen if she gave evidence against her. Mammy walked back in the house as if nothing had happened. No explanation as to where she'd been or why she'd left us on our own. But if she didn't talk to us, she'd had plenty to say to the neighbours about Auntie Rose's new baby.

"It's not possible that child can be Mike's baby," said Mrs Kinsella, who'd no children of her own.

"There's nothing that surprises me any more," said

Mrs Spencer. "They're all at it. Well, except for Mrs Kinsella!" she whispered behind her back.

"If that's Mike's baby," said Mammy, "it'd be the biggest Christmas miracle since the Virgin Mary gave birth to the Baby Jesus."

Mammy was humpy with Martin and me and had gone on at us: "Because of yea two half-wit eejits, yer father has ta stay in prison for longer. What the pair of yea poxty bastards told the two detectives would have hung him twice over. An' because of it, he had to plead guilty ta child cruelty, even though he was completely innocent. Another eighteen months! Because of yea two!" She cursed the day the both of us had been born.

I'd no idea how long eighteen months would last, but I had hoped it would be for a long while, so there would be no more beatings and drunken rows, with Mammy having to run off across the street to number nineteen, where Mrs Shaw and her young daughter Anne would take us in for hours on end until Daddy had either gone off or had fallen asleep.

In the last week leading up to Christmas, Martin, me, Nabby and Bernie were always busy carol singing. We knew lots of people were strapped for money, but it still pissed us off to see them skulking behind their net curtains, pretending they were not at home. We'd stick our fingers up at them, or drop our kecks and flash our backsides, which soon had them out the front doors, hollering all sorts of lewd names. It was such good fun and kept us warm!

This Christmas wasn't much to write home about either, with us earning even less money than usual, even though we sang like angels. Well, our Granny had told us we did one year when we'd called around her house and had given her an impromptu carol concert on her doorstep.

"Ah Jaysus will yah get a listen ta them! Yah sing like a choir of feckin' little angels in heaven, so yah do!" Standing on the doorstep, blind drunk, she cut into "Away in a Manger", with her own rendition of, "It's a Long Way to Tipperary" while attempting a knees-up, before staggering backwards into her house.

"Can we have a few coppers, or some biscuits Granny?" asked Martin.

"Lord Jaysus!" she slurred, almost toppling over with the shock of the asking. "Don't be beggin' off yer own kind! Git the feck off an' beg from them that can afford it!" Then she slammed the front door in our faces.

Deciding not to pay Granny a visit this Christmas, Martin came up with another of his ideas. "We should sing as lousy as we can and see what difference it makes."

Well, it certainly made a difference. We had cold water thrown down on us. We were told we were the worst carol singers in the whole world and that we sang like cats with strangulated hernias. We were even threatened with a potato gun if we didn't hop it. But at the end of the day, we made a little more money than the previous Christmas, with a lot of people giving us their spare coppers on the promise we'd shut up and never darken their doors ever again.

Two days to Christmas and Mammy was absent again. She had stayed with us for a whole week without the "Devil's drink". And for the short while she was there, life had seemed much easier for us. She had taken everything upon herself and promised us, "Things will be different", giving Helen and Maggie some breathing space for themselves. But then she left and Helen had to take on her duty of looking after us again. Mammy had often complained about us causing her nerves to give out on her and of how she hadn't long left on this earth. Sometimes, when I watched Mammy sitting by the fireside, chain-smoking her way through cigarette after cigarette, looking so melancholic and distant, I had felt so sad that none of us were able to be part of her world. I was unable to ask her, "What is wrong Mammy?" for fear of being told to "Feck off and mind yer business!" I was unable to put an arm around her to comfort her, for fear of being pushed away.

Helen warned us not to say a word to anyone about Mammy leaving us, "Otherwise we'll all be separated and will never see each other ever again".

For two nights running, someone had been at the back door attempting to get into the house. There had been no calling out to identify themselves, just the rattling of the door handle and the pushing of their foot at the bottom corner of the door to test the bolt. And by the time Helen had found enough courage to peer from behind the curtains of the backroom window, whoever had been there would be gone.

"Do you think it's Grandad, come back ta haunt us for hurting his head?" asked Bernie fearfully.

"Well, he wouldn't be after me!" said Nabby, hiding behind me and Martin. "I wasn't even pushing on the coffin!"

"Jaysus! How many times have I got ta tell yah, Grandad was already dead in the coffin!" said Helen. "What d'ya think he was doin' in it in the first place? Anyway yah can't hurt the dead!" Her attempts to reassure us were hindered somewhat by the almighty scream she let rip when the back door handle had suddenly rattled a couple of times before going silent again. Petrified, I was the first out of the back room and up the stairs, hiding under the pile of coats and bedcovers on the big double bed in the girl's room where I was soon joined by the others, barring Maggie and Helen. None of us emerged from our hiding place until the following morning.

In the very early hours of Christmas Day, while everyone else was fast asleep in bed, Martin and me were gawking out of our bedroom window waiting for the tight-fisted Santa Claus to fly past so we could open the window and call him every name under the sun! A day or so previously, we had found Shamie's old air pistol and some lead pellets under his bed and we planned to take a few pot shots at fatty Claus and Rudolph's big red conk.

Also, with the back door directly below our window, we decided to bring up the heavyweight fire companion, which held the poker, brush and shovel, as a Christmas surprise for the phantom door rattler if he should call while we were still awake.

It didn't take Martin too long to lose interest before falling into bed and drifting off to sleep, snoring like a pig. Not long afterwards, as I was contemplating calling off the watch for big belly and his reindeers, I had noticed the back gate creeping open silently.

"Martin! Martin!" I frantically shook my brother awake.

"What's wrong?"

I'm not too sure which noise came first, the soft thupp or the scream from Nabby, who suddenly leapt out of the bed as if his bum was on fire. Dancing around in the dim light he was holding one side of his bum cheeks and telling us, "I've been feckin' bitten!"

I'd forgotten Martin still had the loaded air pistol in his hand which, when I'd asked him to let me have it before he'd fallen off to sleep, he had refused. "It's too dangerous for little kids to hold," said Martin.

Ignoring Nabby, I opened the window silently and was able to make out the dim outline of a shadowy figure peering up in my direction. Whoever it was seemed to be very unsteady on their feet and was talking in a strange language.

"I think he's an Indian," whispered Martin.

"He's no feathers," I whispered back.

"I meant a Pakistani Indian! Not a feckin' Red Indian!"

"We've no chickens for sale!" I'd shouted down to the fella, but he continued to talk gibberish.

Picking up the hefty fire companion, I hung it out the window, taking careful aim at the face still peering up at us. "Bombs away!" I dropped it, knowing I'd scored a direct hit when we heard the loud howl of pain before the phantom door-rattler staggered across the yard and out the back gate.

"I've been bit by an animal or something!" moaned Nabby. "Light the lighter an' take a look will yea?"

"It's a bite," I told him, looking at the large welt the lead pellet had made.

"I know it's a poxty bite! I can feel it. I just want to know what kind of bite it is."

"It looks like a flea bite to me."

"A flea bite! I've been bitten by hundreds of fleas and never felt anythin' like this! It's drawn blood!"

"Can yah get vampire fleas?" I asked Martin.

"Feckin' vampire fleas!" cried Nabby, "Yer havin' a feckin' laugh aren't yah! If there was such a ting we'd all have bled ta death by now!"

"It must have been Gosson or Michael then," said Martin, closing the window with the one hand while hiding the pellet gun behind his back with the other. "They must have thought yer arse was a drippin' sandwich."

"Ah bollocks to this!" said Nabby, climbing back into the bed. "Anyways, Gosson and Michael haven't got any proper teeth yet, unless one of them's wearin' Mammy's falsies. It was worse than a flea bite, more like a mouse bite. Or even a snake bite."

"Ah, give over and go ta sleep!"

CHAPTER 41

Farewell My Family

It seemed I had not been asleep all that long when I was shaken awake by Helen. "We have to hurry out of the house! Now!" Helen spoke with such urgency we all hopped straight out of the bed immediately and without question. With no need to get dressed, as we always wore our clothes in bed in the colder months, we slipped on our shoes and had hurried down the stairs following Helen, who was carrying Michael, while Maggie carried Gosson.

Leading us along the narrow hallway, Helen opened the front door and led us onto the damp street. She handed Michael to Martin before hurrying back through the house, bringing out the big pram, into which she placed Michael, Gosson and Kathleen. Then, with us all grouped tightly together and holding firmly onto the pram's framework, we walked out of Stamford Street as a family for the very last time.

Down on the Stretford Road, we stood outside the Chinese restaurant and gawked through the window, tasting every mouthful of food the diners were enjoying. I was so hungry I was unable to stop myself from drooling from the corners of my mouth.

A Chinese man came out from the restaurant and handed out Crunchie bars to us. He was having a brief conversation with Helen as a police car and a big van pulled up. The two police women walked over to speak with Helen and she seemed happy enough to talk with them.

Cold, hungry, tired and fearful, we waited for Helen to return to us. She assured us that everything was going to be fine. She told us we had to get into the police van as we were going off to the police station to get a bite to eat. Obviously, we did not need a second invitation and had been only too happy to hop straight in to the van without a second's thought.

"How are they going ta fit the pram in?" asked Maggie, unwilling to just leave it there on the pavement. Besides the clothes we stood up in, the pram was the only other useful thing we possessed.

"Shall I run it back to the house and then come back?' I volunteered, worried that someone would steal it.

"There's no need," said Helen. And as the police van drove away from the kerb with all nine of us inside, I could only watch, incensed, as the Chinaman pushed our pram around the corner, left it there and walked back into his restaurant.

At the police station, we were taken straight to a waiting room away from the main counter and the two drunks giving out to the Sergeant as they were being booked in. One of the lady coppers said she would fetch us something to eat and drink, before closing the door and leaving us in relative silence.

Looking across at Helen, I wondered what she might have been thinking. Poor Helen. She'd seemed to have carried the whole world on her shoulders and though the thought must have played on her mind at times, she never did abandon us. As she looked down on Michael, asleep in her arms, I noticed how her frown, which had been a permanent feature for a long while, seemed to have softened. And when she caught my eyes, I could see her tears welling up, as she gave me a brief smile. But she never cried. "What is it Helen? What are you thinking right now? What are your hopes, your dreams? Will you stay with us forever and ever?" I had wanted to ask her all these questions and more. But the fear of the answer not being what I wanted to hear stopped me from doing so.

We heard a loud commotion going on outside the waiting room and when Martin, nosy as ever, opened the door slightly to take a peek out into the main foyer, I could have sworn the gibberish language and voice we could hear was the same voice of the phantom door rattler.

"It's our Shamie!" exclaimed Martin.

"Here, get a hold of Michael!" Helen handed baby Michael to Martin and went to the counter, where our big brother was giving out to the two coppers standing either side of him. One of them was telling the desk sergeant how they had found Shamie shadow boxing

in the middle of Stretford Road up near the Town
Hall, where they had arrested him for being drunk and
incapable of looking after himself. When Helen calmed
Shamie down, the Sergeant agreed to let our brother stay
in the room with us, provided he kept his big gob shut.
Jaysus! The state of his half-closed eyes and swollen conk!

"Yah feckin' see this, Tommy?" Shamie pointed a finger
to his swollen face as he glared at me through his swollen
eyes. "Yah ought ta see the state of the other two bastards!
I beat the shite out of all three of them all at once."

The police rustled up platefuls of corned beef
sandwiches, and a Victorian jam sponge, along with cups
of sweet hot tea, which we ate gratefully, tasting every
last morsel and licking our dirty hands clean. Shamie,
after being given some Disprins for his sore head,
declined any of the grub and lay himself across three
chairs where he went to sleep.

A while later, the policewoman who spoke with Helen
outside the Chinese restaurant sat with us to explain
what was happening. "We've been in contact with the
Social Services," she said. "But as there isn't anything
they can do until tomorrow, we are taking all of you to
Nazareth House. It's a nice children's home and you'll
be taken care of there until the Social Services decide
what's best for you. But rest assured you will all be kept
together." She looked reassuringly at Helen.

Not long afterwards, we were back in the big police
van and heading out of Hulme. Shamie was still drunk

and moaning about his head. While I had already made my mind up that I wasn't going into any children's home and I whispered my intentions to the others. "Once this van stops and my feet touch the ground, I'm off!" And true to my word, as the van had pulled into the driveway of Nazareth House and we all bailed out of the van. I was off like a greyhound.

A quick peek over my shoulder told me the footsteps following close behind were Martin's. All the others, except Shamie, who was leaning against the van and puking, were just standing in the glare of the van's headlamps, silently looking on. There were no shouts of "Stop!" or "Come back Tommy an' Martin!" And as we ran out of the main gates, we had no idea that this was the last image we were ever going to see of our family all together.

Making our way back to Stamford Street we found the front door was still slightly ajar, just as Helen had left it hours earlier. Making sure both front and back doors were securely locked, we hid under Mammy's bed, covering ourselves with the quilt and coats, waiting for the morning to hurry along.

We must have fallen into a deep sleep straight away and the next thing I knew was being suddenly woken by the sound of footsteps coming along the hallway. We'd listened in fear as they paused outside Mammy's bedroom before coming in. I held my breath as the black winklepickers walked across the uncarpeted bedroom

floor, before the owner of them began to rummage
through the cupboards and drawers.

Then we saw the points of his shoes facing in our
direction. 'Yea can come out from under the bed, I know
y'er there. I can smell yah from here," said our brother
Paddy.

We dragged ourselves out from under the bed. "Where
is everyone?" he asked.

"The coppers took them away to a home," said
Martin.

"We escaped!" I added proudly.

"Yea should have stayed with them," said Paddy.

"Have yah seen Mammy?" I asked.

"The auld woman's gone off ta Chatham last time I
heard. An' she won't be comin' back. An' it's no good
whingein' about it 'cos she doesn't give a shite about any
of you lot. I'm only back ta pick up anythin' worth takin'
and I'm out of it. And yea two should do yourselves a big
favour and give yerselves up ta the coppers. They'll look
after yah better than she ever will."

"Can't we come with yea?" asked Martin.

"Yah can't. Even if I wanted ta, which I don't, I can
barely look after meself. Anyway, the whole of Stamford
Street is comin' down in the next few weeks so there's no
point stayin' around this dump any longer. Here!" He
flicked a two-bob coin high into the air. "Catch!"

We both jumped to catch the florin flying over our
heads, but we missed it and we were soon down on our

knees chasing after it.

"Got it!" cried Martin.

When we got to our feet, our big brother was no longer in the bedroom. "Paddy! Paddy!" I called up the stairs to him, before running through the house and out into the back yard. "Paddy! Paddy!" I had called his name again and again, kidding myself he was still close by when I already knew he had left us for good. I so desperately wanted to cry, but I couldn't find any tears.

We spent the next three days in the house, only daring to venture out in the very early hours of the mornings to steal the odd bottle or two of sterilised milk from the milk float. Martin gave me the last morsel of stale bread we had left and I shoved it greedily into my gob before going out into the kitchen to swig some water from the tap. I found my brother in there, eating the old paper lining from the drawer. I felt so desperately upset to know he had done this for me, when I would have wanted to have shared the last morsel of food with him, like we had always shared things equally. And as we stood looking at one another, there was no need to say a word. I knew that he knew: we had to give ourselves up to the police. In that moment, we had finally accepted no one would ever be coming back for us.

Taking one last look around the house, we walked into Mammy and Daddy's bedroom. In the glass tray on the bedside table, I spotted two of Daddy's old lighters. I don't know what possessed me at the time, perhaps it was a symbolic gesture, I just don't know. There were no thoughts running through my head the moment I flicked one of the lighters into life and held it to the bed covers, setting them alight. And as I stared down into the flames, I began to hear the voices of my family calling out, crying, laughing, shouting, screaming and singing. In that moment, the memories came flooding back, reminding me of what had passed within the four walls of this house. I had no feelings of sadness or happiness or regret for what I had just done. In some way it was perhaps an instinct to protect my family's past and keep the secrets locked forever inside 24 Stamford Street.

As we had closed the front door for the very last time and went outside, the dull grey sky seemed to lift a little, letting a faint glimmer of the sun's rays burst through the clouds. And as we made our way down the street we were met by Auntie Rosie pushing a big pram in our direction.

"Where is everyone?" she asked. "I haven't seen any of you lot for days on end. Are you all okay?"

"Yeh, we're all okay, Auntie Rosie," lied Martin. "Can we get a peek at your baby can we?"

"Of course you can." Auntie Rosie gave us a big smile as she pulled back the covers proudly to let us take a peek. And there, before our very eyes, Martin and I had witnessed for ourselves the "Christmas Miracle" Mammy had spoken about, as the chocolate-skinned baby's beautiful big brown eyes stared out at us.

Sitting on the front doorstep of the last house on the corner of Stamford Street, six-year-old Georgie Taylor and his younger sister Lucy were tucking into a sandwich and hurriedly pushed the last remnants of food into their gobs as we approached. As we passed them by, I couldn't help but notice the remnants of jam around their mouths and I had a sudden urge to rush over and lick their faces clean. And in that instant, as Martin and I had walked out of Stamford Street forever, I couldn't help wondering, what wouldn't I give for a slice of bread and jam?

Epilogue

I know, for some of you who have come along with me on my brief journey through 1963, my story will have evoked memories of your own struggles as a kid growing up in the surrounding industrial towns of Manchester and beyond. When looking back on that era now, the realities of our lives may seem harsh, especially if you had been Irish and poor. But in truth, as children we had nothing to measure our lives against, and therefore what we endured had been nothing out of the ordinary, just our everyday lives. And which of us, in all honesty, wouldn't wish to be able to walk back to our past, if only to take a quick peek?

This story is based solely on my own personal memories of living in Hulme. There were so many things to write about, but I was aware that I didn't want to encroach upon the memories of my own family who have their own recollections to share or keep locked away. For me, growing up in an era of constant change, I can truly say that the three years I spent as a child living in Hulme were the happiest days of my childhood. Saturday matinees. Exploring the streets of bombed-out buildings.

Being chased by the police. Lighting fires to burn off electric flex for copper wiring. Breaking windows. Wagging off school. Stealing bikes. Belle Vue Zoo. Travelling freely around Manchester and going where I wanted to go and doing what I wanted to do. The challenges, the excitement, all of which can be summed up in just the one word - freedom!

I am also keenly aware of the grief, the deep heartache and sadness that the names of Myra Hindley and Ian Brady will evoke in those touched by their evil. Unfortunately, those names will forever be synonymous with the names of their victims and the people whose lives have been blighted by their cowardly, monstrous acts. But remembering those monsters and their dark legacy will also keep alive the memory of all their victims, in particular the undying devotion of one particular mother, Winnie Johnson, who went to her grave without ever laying to rest her lost boy Keith.

Whilst writing this book, I have had the privilege of chatting with a number of people who live or have lived in Hulme, Gorton, and other surrounding towns of Manchester. Some have told me about their own experiences with Ian Brady and Myra Hindley. For me, this strengthens my belief that there were most probably more unaccounted-for victims. I could have been one of them. Unknowingly at the time, I had been picked

out as a potential victim. I followed her, like a lamb
to the slaughter. I was there with them in the house. I
looked up into his eyes and I looked up into her eyes.
I witnessed for myself the confidence and charm of a
young woman whose beaming smile, together with the
promise of bread and jam, had enticed me within a
matter of minutes to go with her to her house. She oozed
charisma, as well as a somewhat nervous energy. And Ian
Brady seemed the complete opposite: isolated, unsmiling,
somewhat timid in his demeanour, with Hindley
seemingly the stronger willed of the two.

After my fleeting encounter with the pair, the next time
I saw their faces was on the TV news when their chilling
acts had been uncovered. At that point, I was living in
the children's home and, referring to Hindley, I said to a
staff member, "She took me to her house for bread and
jam!" The laughing reply came back: "And I expect she
sent you home with a Lucky Bag!" Well, I certainly had
been lucky. I don't think I really understood just what
a lucky escape I'd had until years later, when I was a
teenager and could truly comprehend the evil inflicted
by Brady and Hindley. It was a lucky escape that has
haunted me all my life.

There are, of course, those who sincerely believe they
knew the true, repented Myra Hindley. And there are
those who have written their books, based on whatever

information she either gave them or that they gleaned from her personal diary, in her feeble attempt to show she was in some way a victim of Ian Brady. But it seems those people may have been blinded by Hindley's calculating, murderous charm and lies, just as her victims were.

As one of her potential victims, I experienced her deadly power. Hindley was very much in control of the situation when she enticed me to follow her to her grandmother's house. She could easily have told me to run away at any given time during our journey, especially when Brady had walked out of sight for a short time, only appearing again when he'd guided me into the house which, when looking back, seemed a well-rehearsed plan. Do I believe there are unaccounted-for victims? Yes I certainly do. Though the only person who could give a definitive answer to this and many other questions, including the whereabouts of Keith Bennett's body, is Ian Brady himself. And those are secrets that he may well take with him to the grave. Unlike the innocent young souls whose lives he stole so cruelly, it is hard to imagine how Brady will ever rest in peace.

Acknowledgements

Writing this book has, inevitably, brought back many memories for me. At times, I have struggled emotionally to continue my journey as a free spirit, soaring through scenes from my childhood past, only compromising by taking a fleeting glance at dormant memories I have not fully awakened, while setting those I have, in stone.

Along the way, I've had many friends and, indeed, strangers offering me their kind words of encouragement (and threats) to finish the journey I had started.

Of course, my biggest fear is making the mistake of not mentioning a name and so to this end I would like to say a big thank you to all those members of the abundant Manchester Facebook Groups, including: Row Cardew, Manchester Memories, Dennis Heald, Gorton Manchester 18, Vix Row, Rocking Robins charity, The Reverend David Grey, Growing Faith in Community, Neil Docherty, Linda Fernhead and Ruth Schilling. With a special mention to Rose McGivern, my agony aunt and one of the kindest human beings I have never met!

I find myself fortunate, after hearing dismal stories of

literary agents and publishers, to have fallen into the hands of Mirror Books and their Publishing Director, Paula Scott and Executive Editor, Jo Sollis, whose professional as well as personal advice has been second to none.

Also by Mirror Books

Published April 2017

The Boy in 7 Billion
Callie Blackwell and Karen Hockney

If you had a chance to save your dying son… wouldn't you take it?

Deryn Blackwell is a walking, talking miracle. At the age of 10, he was diagnosed with Leukaemia. Then 18 months later he developed another rare form of cancer called Langerhan's cell syndrome. Only five other people in the world have it. He is the youngest of them all and the only person in the world known to be fighting it alongside another cancer, making him one in seven billion. Told there was no hope of survival, after four years of intensive treatment, exhausted by the fight and with just days to live, Deryn planned his own funeral.

But on the point of death – his condition suddenly and dramatically changed. His medical team had deemed this an impossibility, his recovery was nothing short of a miracle. Inexplicable. However, Deryn's desperate mother, Callie, was hiding a secret…

Callie has finally found the strength and courage to reveal the truth about Deryn's battle. The result is a book that everyone should read. It truly is a matter of life and death.

Mirror Books

Also by Mirror Books

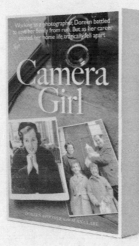

Camera Girl
Doreen Spooner with Alan Clark

The true story of a woman coping with a tragic end to the love of her life, alongside a daily fight to establish herself and support her children.

A moving and inspiring memoir of Doreen Spooner – a woman ahead of her time. Struggling to hold her head high through the disintegration of the family she loves through alcoholism, she began a career as Fleet Street's first female photographer.

While the passionate affair and family life she'd always dreamed of fell apart, Doreen walked into the frantic world of a national newspaper. Determined to save her family from crippling debt, her work captured the Swinging Sixties through political scandals, glamorous stars and cultural icons, while her homelife spiralled further out of control.

The two sides of this book take you through a touching and emotional love story, coupled with a hugely enjoyable portrait of post-war Britain.

Also by Mirror Books

Eating the Elephant
Alice Wells

A shocking but inspiring true story that tackles the dark, modern crisis of internet pornography in a frank and groundbreaking way.

Alice, a dedicated doctor and mother of two children, bravely tells the story of her marriage to a man hiding a terrible secret – one into which he has drawn their 4-year-old daughter, Grace. As the shocking truth about their family life unfolds at a heartstopping pace, Alice struggles to learn how to survive the impact and piece together her shattered world.

The devastation of what she is forced to face when her life is hit by catastrophic pain, and the horror of wondering if she overlooked the signs, is laid bare in a moving and honest way that will stay with you for a long time to come.

How do you eat an elephant?
One piece at a time

Alice Wells* is a UK doctor. She has two children. This is her first book. *pseudonym*

Mirror Books

Also by Mirror Books

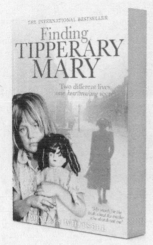

THE INTERNATIONAL BESTSELLER

Finding Tipperary Mary
Phyllis Whitsell

The astonishing real story of a daughter's search for her own past and the desperate mother who gave her up for adoption.

Phyllis Whitsell began looking for her birth mother as a young woman and although it was many years before she finally met her, their lives had crossed on the journey without their knowledge. When they both eventually sat together in the same room, the circumstances were extraordinary, moving and ultimately life-changing.

This is a daughter's personal account of the remarkable relationship that grew from abandonment into love, understanding and selfless care.